Expert Data Visualization

Breathe life into your data by learning how to use D3.js V4 to visualize information

Jos Dirksen

BIRMINGHAM - MUMBAI

Expert Data Visualization

First published: April 2017

Production reference: 1170417

Published by Packt Publishing Ltd.
Livery Place
35 Livery Street
Birmingham
B3 2PB, UK.
ISBN 978-1-78646-349-4

www.packtpub.com

Credits

Author
Jos Dirksen

Reviewer
Nikita Rokotyan

Acquisition Editor
Smeet Thakkar

Content Development Editor
Aditi Gour

Technical Editor
Pranav Kukreti

Copy Editor
Dhanya Baburaj

Project Coordinator
Ritika Manoj

Proofreader
Safis Editing

Indexer
Mariammal Chettiyar

Graphics
Jason Monteiro

Production Coordinator
Shantanu Zagade

Cover Work
Shantanu Zagade

About the Author

Jos Dirksen has worked as a software developer and architect for more than a decade. He has a lot of experience in a large range of technologies, ranging from backend technologies, such as Java and Scala, to frontend development using HTML5, CSS, and JavaScript. Besides working with these technologies, Jos also regularly speaks at conferences and likes to write about new and interesting technologies on his blog. He also likes to experiment with new technologies and see how they can best be used to create beautiful data visualizations, the results of which you can see on his blog at `http://www.smartjava.org/`.

Jos is currently working as a fullstack engineer for Philips Lighting working, on a large IoT and Scala project. Previously, Jos has worked in many different roles in the private and public sectors, ranging from private companies such as ING, ASML, Malmberg, and ASML to organizations in the public sector, such as the Department of Defence.

Jos has also written three books on Three.js: Learning Three.js, which provides a complete overview of all the features of Three.js; Three.js Essentials, which uses an example-based approach to explore the most important feature of Three.js; and Three.js Cookbook, which provides a recipe-based approach to cover important use cases of Three.js. Jos has also written a book on Scala called *Restful Web Services with Scala*, and two books on SOA and software integration.

Besides his interest in Javascript, Data Visualization, and HTML5, he is also interested in backend technologies related to Scala, Go, and DevOps.

Writing a book isn't something you do yourself. A lot of people have helped and supported me when I was writing this book. A special thanks to the following people: all the guys from Packt who have helped me during the writing, reviewing, and laying out part of the process. Great work, guys! Of course, Mike Bostock, for creating the great D3.js framework. Many thanks go to the reviewers, who gave me great feedback and comments that really helped improve the book. Their positive remarks really helped shape the book! Also, I'd like to thank my family. I would like to thank my wife, Brigitte, for supporting me every time I start a new book, and of course my two girls, Sophie and Amber, who continuously make me realize what is really important.

About the Reviewer

Nikita Rokotyan is a data-visualization engineer with a background in physics and creative technologies. He specializes in creating enriched, data-driven experiences with strong dynamic and interactive components.

Focusing on aesthetics and information content, Nikita has worked on a number of applied and artistic data visualizations for various startups as well as large organizations such as University of Tokyo, Proctor & Gamble, and the Paul Mellon Centre for Studies in British Art.

Currently he's co-running a company in NYC - CultivateMe - that explores how data visualization can help with a better understanding and cultivating human talent.

www.PacktPub.com

For support files and downloads related to your book, please visit www.PacktPub.com.

Did you know that Packt offers eBook versions of every book published, with PDF and ePub files available? You can upgrade to the eBook version at www.PacktPub.com and as a print book customer, you are entitled to a discount on the eBook copy. Get in touch with us at service@packtpub.com for more details.

At www.PacktPub.com, you can also read a collection of free technical articles, sign up for a range of free newsletters and receive exclusive discounts and offers on Packt books and eBooks.

https://www.packtpub.com/mapt

Get the most in-demand software skills with Mapt. Mapt gives you full access to all Packt books and video courses, as well as industry-leading tools to help you plan your personal development and advance your career.

Why subscribe?

- Fully searchable across every book published by Packt
- Copy and paste, print, and bookmark content
- On demand and accessible via a web browser

Customer Feedback

Thanks for purchasing this Packt book. At Packt, quality is at the heart of our editorial process. To help us improve, please leave us an honest review on this book's Amazon page at https://www.amazon.com/dp/1786463490.

If you'd like to join our team of regular reviewers, you can e-mail us at customerreviews@packtpub.com. We award our regular reviewers with free eBooks and videos in exchange for their valuable feedback. Help us be relentless in improving our products!

Table of Contents

Preface

Data is everywhere around us, and each day more of it is made available freely as open data or is published as a result of big data analytics. Although the data in itself is already really valuable, it is usually very difficult to present this data in a clear and concise way to a larger audience. D3.js gives us a way to easily represent this data and create standard-based, interactive data-driven visualizations, which can run on all devices, from phone to desktop. In this book, we'll explore all the different visualizations options provided by the D3.js APIs and show how you can use common patterns to create beautiful interactive visualizations using a minimal amount of coding. We'll also explore how you can prepare the data so that it can be easily visualized.

What this book covers

Chapter 1, *Getting Started with D3*, shows you how to get the code for this book and set up your development environment. We'll also explain the basic concepts behind D3.js and create our very first visualizations.

Chapter 2, *Basic Charts and Shapes*, explains how you can use the D3.js APIs to create basic shapes and charts. We'll show you how to create interactive line charts and animate pie charts.

Chapter 3, *Working with Hierarchical Data*, shows which APIs D3.js provides to work with hierarchical data. We'll use D3.js to created different kinds of trees, and also show treemap and pack visualizations.

Chapter 4, *Visualizing Graphs*, uses the force layout to visualize graphs of data. We'll use this D3.js API to visualize relations between Simpson characters in different and interactive ways. We'll also show a custom matrix visualization, which can be used to visualize a large matrix of interconnected relations.

Chapter 5, *Working with Geo Data*, shows one of the most interesting features of D3.js, that is, how to work with geographical data. We'll show you all the various map projections provided by D3.js and also how easy it is to manipulate and enrich maps through D3.js.

Chapter 6, *Visualizing Streaming Data*, explores different options on how you can use D3.js to visualize real-time streaming data. We'll show you how to receive information through websockets and visualize that information in different ways.

Chapter 7, *Voronoi Diagrams and Heatmaps*, shows two final ways of visualizing data. We'll show various Voronoi-based visualizations and approach, which you can use to generate art, using these Voronoi diagrams. In this chapter, we'll also show you a way to create heatmaps, which show a way to visualize occurrence data during a specific period of time.

Chapter 8, *Custom Shapes and Paths and Using a Brush Selection*, goes deeper into the tools provided by D3.js to create custom shapes and paths. We'll also explore the brush API provided by D3.js, which can be used to easily select elements from a visualization.

Chapter 9, *ES6, TypeScript, and External D3.js Libraries*, concludes this book by looking at how you can use D3.js together with ES6 and TypeScript, and we'll explore a couple of libraries build on top of D3.js that provide a number of standard charts out of the box.

What you need for this book

To work with the examples in this book, you don't need any special software requirements besides having Node installed and having an editor that you can use to explore and append the examples. The first chapter explains how to install and use these tools to run and extend the examples.

Who this book is for

This book is great for you if you are a JavaScript developer and want to start creating data visualizations. This book will explain all the steps you need to take to create beautiful interactive visualizations using D3.js and show you examples, which you can reuse and extend for your own purposes. This book will also explain how to prepare the data to be visualized.

Conventions

In this book, you will find a number of text styles that distinguish between different kinds of information. Here are some examples of these styles and an explanation of their meaning.

Code words in text, database table names, folder names, filenames, file extensions, pathnames, dummy URLs, user input, and Twitter handles are shown as follows: "In this page, we also define a single `div` tag that has an `id` with a value `output`."

A block of code is set as follows:

```
<script>
    (function() {
        show();
    })();
</script>
```

Any command-line input or output is written as follows:

```
$ geo2topo -V
  2.0.0
$ toposimplify -V
  2.0.0
```

New terms and **important words** are shown in bold. Words that you see on the screen, for example, in menus or dialog boxes, appear in the text surrounded by quotes, or like this: "Just hit the **Download** button and click **OK**."

Warnings or important notes appear in a box like this.

Tips and tricks appear like this.

Reader feedback

Feedback from our readers is always welcome. Let us know what you think about this book—what you liked or disliked. Reader feedback is important for us, as it helps us develop titles that you will really get the most out of.

To send us general feedback, simply e-mail `feedback@packtpub.com`, and mention the book's title in the subject of your message.

If there is a topic that you have expertise in and you are interested in either writing or contributing to a book, see our author guide at `www.packtpub.com/authors`.

Customer support

Now that you are the proud owner of a Packt book, we have a number of things to help you to get the most from your purchase.

Downloading the example code

You can download the example code files for this book from your account at `http://www.packtpub.com`. If you purchased this book elsewhere, you can visit `http://www.packtpub.com/support` and register to have the files e-mailed directly to you.

You can download the code files by following these steps:

1. Log in or register to our website using your e-mail address and password.
2. Hover the mouse pointer on the **SUPPORT** tab at the top.
3. Click on **Code Downloads & Errata**.
4. Enter the name of the book in the **Search** box.
5. Select the book for which you're looking to download the code files.
6. Choose from the drop-down menu where you purchased this book from.
7. Click on **Code Download**.

You can also download the code files by clicking on the **Code Files** button on the book's webpage at the Packt Publishing website. This page can be accessed by entering the book's name in the **Search** box. Please note that you need to be logged in to your Packt account.

Once the file is downloaded, please make sure that you unzip or extract the folder using the latest version of:

- WinRAR / 7-Zip for Windows
- Zipeg / iZip / UnRarX for Mac
- 7-Zip / PeaZip for Linux

The code bundle for the book is also hosted on GitHub at `https://github.com/PacktPublishing/Expert-Data-Visualization`. We also have other code bundles from our rich catalog of books and videos available at `https://github.com/PacktPublishing/`. Check them out!

Downloading the color images of this book

We also provide you with a PDF file that has color images of the screenshots/diagrams used in this book. The color images will help you better understand the changes in the output. You can download this file from `https://www.packtpub.com/sites/default/files/downloads/ExpertDataVisualization_ColorImages.pdf`.

Errata

Although we have taken every care to ensure the accuracy of our content, mistakes do happen. If you find a mistake in one of our books—maybe a mistake in the text or the code—we would be grateful if you could report this to us. By doing so, you can save other readers from frustration and help us improve subsequent versions of this book. If you find any errata, please report them by visiting `http://www.packtpub.com/submit-errata`, selecting your book, clicking on the **Errata Submission Form** link, and entering the details of your errata. Once your errata are verified, your submission will be accepted and the errata will be uploaded to our website or added to any list of existing errata under the Errata section of that title.

To view the previously submitted errata, go to `https://www.packtpub.com/books/content/support` and enter the name of the book in the search field. The required information will appear under the **Errata** section.

Piracy

Piracy of copyrighted material on the Internet is an ongoing problem across all media. At Packt, we take the protection of our copyright and licenses very seriously. If you come across any illegal copies of our works in any form on the Internet, please provide us with the location address or website name immediately so that we can pursue a remedy.

Please contact us at copyright@packtpub.com with a link to the suspected pirated material.

We appreciate your help in protecting our authors and our ability to bring you valuable content.

Questions

If you have a problem with any aspect of this book, you can contact us at questions@packtpub.com, and we will do our best to address the problem.

1
Getting Started with D3

Welcome to this first chapter of *Expert Data Visualization* with D3 (also sometimes called D3.js or data-driven documents, in this book we'll use **D3** to refer to this library). In this book, we'll walk you through most of the features and APIs D3 provides and show you how you can use this functionality to create great looking, interactive, and animated data visualizations. In this first chapter, we'll slowly introduce you to D3 and create our first simple visualization. We'll do this by exploring the following subjects:

- We start by giving a short overview of what D3 is, and what it can be used for.
- After that, we'll show you how to get the sources for this book. All the sources are stored on GitHub or can be downloaded from the Packt Publishing website.
- Once you've got the sources, the next thing we'll do is set up a local development environment. This environment will allow you to quickly and easily run the provided examples, and provide a simple way to experiment and write visualizations yourself.
- When we've got a working environment, we'll start by exploring how D3 works by looking at the basic flow of selecting, adding, and removing elements that make up your visualization.
- Then we'll move on to creating our first simple data visualization, using real data (various countries' population sizes).

At the end of this chapter, you should have a good understanding of the core concepts of how D3 works, how to load data, and the details of the D3 selection API.

If you've picked up this book, you probably already know what D3 is. However, let's do a very quick overview of what D3 is, and what you can do with it.

What is D3?

The best description of what D3 is can be found by looking at the website: `https://d3js.org/`. You can find a very nice quote there that sums up pretty well what D3 does.

> "D3.js is a JavaScript library for manipulating documents based on data. D3 helps you bring data to life using HTML, SVG, and CSS. D3's emphasis on Web standards gives you the full capabilities of modern browsers without tying yourself to a proprietary framework, combining powerful visualization components and a data-driven approach to DOM manipulation."

Looking at this quote, it is pretty clear what D3 provides. With D3 you get a set of libraries which can be used to easily create visualizations using web standards (especially SVG). This means that the visualizations created with D3 will run on all modern browsers and most of the mobile browsers.

SVG is an abbreviation of **Scalable Vector Graphics**. This is an XML-based format that is used to define 2D vector images. The advantage of vector images is that they can be easily scaled and transformed without losing detail (in comparison with bitmap images such as `.PNG` and `.GIF`). SVG is a W3C standard and is supported by almost all browsers on all platforms and also supports interactivity and animations. You can load SVG images directly as an image file, but also create them programmatically by manipulating the browser DOM (which is what D3 can do for us).

A big added advantage of using D3 instead of other frameworks is that it allows you to easily bind data to the elements you see on the screen (more on that later in this chapter). This allows you to create visualizations that respond to changes in the data. This approach makes creating animations, interactive elements much easier than alternative approaches. A very nice example is shown in the following figure (from `http://bl.ocks.org/mbostock/4060606`), which shows the unemployment rate in 2008 in the US:

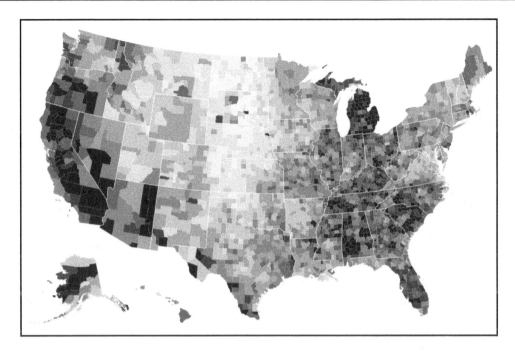

You can also make more basic visualizations, such as the baby name trends in the UK:

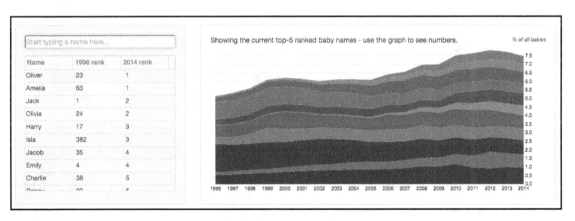

You can make a large range of different visualizations with D3. To get a good idea of what D3 is capable of, check out the D3 gallery (`https://github.com/d3/d3/wiki/Gallery`), which has a large number of impressive examples.

Before we start working with D3, first some information on how this book is set up.

Setup of this book

Learning D3 can be a bit overwhelming. There are a large number of APIs to learn, you need to think about styling, animations, and formatting your data in the correct way. To help you with these subjects, this book will use an example-driven approach to show you the various features of D3. Each chapter will have a number of examples in the sources accompanying this book, and in each of the chapters we'll walk through these examples and explain what is happening, and in this way show you what can be done by D3.

Installing an editor

The easiest way for you to learn D3 is by playing around with the examples, and see what happens when you change part of the code. So when you're reading through this book, looking at the examples it is probably best to do this while sitting at your computer, and running and modifying the examples while you read. Since D3 is just plain old JavaScript and CSS (or SCSS, as we'll explain in a later chapter), all you need to edit the examples from this book is a text editor. However, it is easier to use a text editor that understands JavaScript. If you haven't got a preferred one installed, the following text editors are good for working with JavaScript:

- **Sublime**: This is one of the most popular editors for editing JavaScript (and other languages for that matter) and it provides builds for all major platforms. Sublime is a commercial product, but provides an evaluation copy you can use for free. You can download Sublime from here: `https://www.sublimetext.com`.
- **Notepad ++**: This is a Windows-only editor and a great choice when you're running a MS Windows environment. Notepad++ is an open source editor and can be easily extended with a number of plugins. While Notepad++ doesn't support JavaScript out of the box, it can be easily extended through the use of plugins. Notepad++ can be downloaded from here: `https://notepad-plus-plus.org/`. A good JavaScript plugin for Notepad++ can be found here: `http://www.sunjw.us/jstoolnpp/`.
- **Atom**: A final great cross-platform editor is Atom (from the guys behind GitHub). Atom is an editor that can be easily extended with plugins to provide a very good development environment. Atom is open source, and you can use it without any costs. Atom can be downloaded from here: `https://atom.io/`. A good plugin that provides additional JavaScript support can be added by installing the `language-JavaScript` package.

The aforementioned editors have great JavaScript support (or it can be added by using a couple of plugins). The following figure shows how Atom highlights and provides JavaScript support:

Besides editors that support JavaScript, there are also a number of **Integrated Development Environments** (**IDEs**) you can use to edit JavaScript. These provide a lot of additional functionality for testing, running, and debugging your code (which we won't touch upon in this book), and also provide a somewhat better JavaScript editing experience. A couple of good IDEs, which have a free or community edition that you can use, are listed as follows:

- **WebStorm**: This is a great JavaScript IDE (and anything else web related) from IntelliJ. WebStorm is provided in a community edition and a commercial one. For developing JavaScript, the community edition provides all the features that you need. You can get the community edition from here: `https://www.jetbrains.com/webstorm/`.
- **Visual Studio**: If you're on a MS Windows system, you might also have a look at the Visual Studio Community edition. It provides JavaScript support out of the box. The Visual Studio Community edition is free to use and can be found here: `https://beta.visualstudio.com/vs/community/`.

My personal opinion is that if you want to use a simple text editor, you should go for either Sublime or Atom, and if you want to go the IDE way, I'd pick WebStorm.

The following screenshot, for example. shows how WebStorm provides code completion for JavaScript:

But, once again, every text editor can be used, since we're just editing standard text files. If you haven't installed an editor yet, now is a good time, since in the next section we'll explain how to get the sources for this book and set up a local web server so you can run the samples.

Getting the sources and setting up a web server

In this section, we'll show you how you can access the sources that are provided together with this book. There are a couple of different ways you can get the sources.

We've got two locations where you can download a zip file with the sources:

- You can download them directly from the Packt Publishing website here: `https://www.packtpub.com/books/content/support`
- You can alternatively download them from GitHub here: `http://github.com/josdirksen/d3dv/archive/master.zip`

Once you've downloaded these, just unzip them to a location of your choice. This should result in a directory structure which looks something like this:

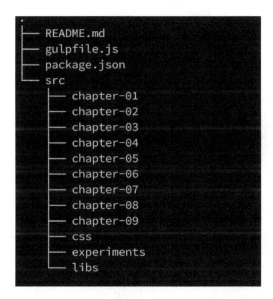

For the rest of this book, we'll reference the directory where you extracted the sources to `<DVD3>`. We can then use it to point to specific examples or files like this: `<DVD3>/src/chapter-01/D01-D01.js`.

All the sources of this book can be found on GitHub in the `http://github.com/josdirksen/d3dv.git` repository. If you've already got Git installed on your machine, you can of course just clone the repository to get access to all the latest sources:

```
> git clone https://github.com/josdirksen/d3dv.git
Cloning into 'd3dv'...
remote: Counting objects: 3, done.
remote: Total 3 (delta 0), reused 3 (delta 0), pack-reused 0
Unpacking objects: 100% (3/3), done.
Checking connectivity... done.
```

If you do it this way, you can be sure you'll always have the latest bug fixes and the latest samples. Once you've cloned the repository, the rest of the book can be followed in the same manner. When we mention <DVD3> in this book, in this case it'll point to the cloned repository.

Once you've got the sources extracted to the <DVD3> directory, we could already run some examples by just opening the corresponding HTML file directly. For instance, if you open the <DVD3>/src/chapter-01/D01-01.html file in your browser, you'll see the following results:

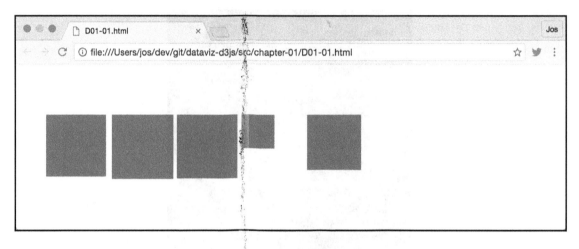

While this will work for the basic examples, this won't work when we're loading external data, due to the restriction that you can't use JavaScript to asynchronously load resources from the local filesystem. To get the examples in this book working, which use external data (most of them), we need to set up a local web server. In the following section, we'll explain how to do this.

Setting up the local web server

There are many options for setting up a local web server. For this book, we've created a simple **gulp** build file which starts a local web server. The advantage of this web server is that it will automatically reload the browser when any of the sources change, which makes developing D3 visualizations a lot more convenient.

To start this web server, we need to first install **node.js**, which is required to run our build file. Node.js can be downloaded from here: `https://nodejs.org/en/download/`. Once you've installed node.js, you need to run the following command once (`npm install`) in the `<DVD3>` directory:

```
$ npm install
├──┬ gulp@3.9.1
│  ├── archy@1.0.0
...
<removed dependencies for clarity>
...
│     └──┬ websocket-driver@0.6.5
│        └── websocket-extensions@0.1.1
├── livereload-js@2.2.2
└── qs@5.1.0
```

You will see a large number of dependencies being downloaded, but once it is done, you can simply start the web server by running the `npm start` command (also in the `<DVD3>` directory):

```
$ npm start

> dataviz-d3js@1.0.0 start /Users/jos/dev/git/dataviz-d3js
> gulp

[11:20:18] Using gulpfile ~/dev/git/dataviz-d3js/gulpfile.js
[11:20:18] Starting 'connect'...
[11:20:18] Finished 'connect' after 30 ms
[11:20:18] Starting 'watch'...
[11:20:18] Finished 'watch' after 34 ms
[11:20:18] Starting 'default'...
[11:20:18] Finished 'default' after 12 µs
[11:20:18] Server started http://localhost:8080
[11:20:18] LiveReload started on port 35729
```

At this point, you've got a web server running at `http://localhost:8080`. If you now point your browser to this URL, you can access all the examples from your browser:

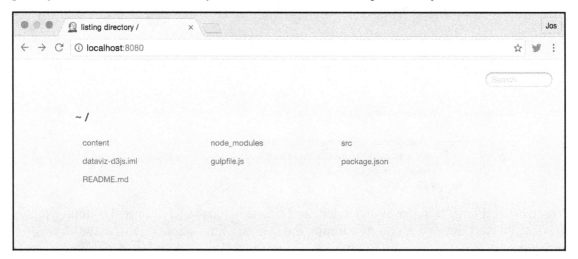

Note that I use Chrome in all the screenshots. While everyone has their own preference for a browser, I feel that the Chrome browser, currently, has the best developer tools. In the rest of this book, I'll show some examples of how you can use Chrome's developer tools to get more insight into your visualization.

Basic HTML template

When we create our visualizations, we need to first load the D3 library and the CSS styles that we want to apply. For each of the samples, we'll use the following basic HTML skeleton:

```html
<html>
<head>
    <!-- generic stuff -->
    <script src="../libs/d3.js"></script>
    <script src="../libs/lodash.js"></script>
    <link rel="stylesheet" href="../css/default.css">

    <!-- specific stuff -->
    <script src="./js/D01-01.js"></script>
    <link rel="stylesheet" href="./css/D01-01.css" type="text/css">
</head>
<body>
```

```
<div id="output">
    <svg class="chart"></svg>
</div>

<script>
    (function() {
        show();
    })();
</script>

</body>
</html>
```

This is a standard HTML page, where we first load the complete D3 sources (`./libs/d3/js`), the `lodash` JavaScript library, and CSS styles (`../css/default.css`) that we want to apply to all the examples in this book. We also load the example specific JavaScript (in this example, `./js/D01-01.js`) and the example specific CSS (`./css/D01-01.css`). In this page, we also define a single `div` tag that has an `id` with a value `output`. This is the location in the page where we add our visualizations. A quick note on **lodash**. Lodash provides a large set of useful collection-related functions, which makes creating and working with JavaScript arrays a lot more convenient. You can see when we use a `lodash` function when the function call starts with an underscore: for example, `_.range(2010, 2016)`.

There are different ways to load the D3 libraries. In our examples, we load the complete D3 library as a single JavaScript file (the `<script src="../libs/d3.js"></script>` import). This will load all the APIs provided by D3. D3, however, also comes in a set of micro-libraries, where each library provides a standalone piece of functionality. You can use this to limit the size of the required JavaScript by only including the APIs you need.

 A complete overview of the modules that are available can be found by looking at the D3 API reference (`https://github.com/d3/d3/blob/master/API.md`). In this book, we'll explore most of the APIs provided by D3 and explain which D3 module provides the specific piece of functionality.

Once the page is loaded, the following code block runs, which calls the `show` function which we'll implement in the example specific JavaScript (`./js/D01-01.js` in this case):

```
<script>
    (function() {
        show();
    })();
</script>
```

The `show` function implementation will differ for each example, but this way we can keep the basic skeleton the same, and we can focus on JavaScript and the D3 APIs. Note that in this book, we won't explain in detail the JavaScript concepts we use. If you need a reminder on how anonymous functions, closures, variable scope, and so on, work in JavaScript, a great resource is the **Mozilla Developer Network** (**MDN**) page on JavaScript: `https://developer.mozilla.org/en-US/docs/Web/JavaScript`.

How does D3 work?

At this point, you should have a working environment, so let's start by looking at some code and see if we can get D3 up and running. As we've mentioned at the beginning of this chapter, D3 is most often used to create and manipulate SVG elements using a data-driven approach. SVG elements can represent shapes, lines, and also allow for grouping. If you need a reference to check what attributes are available for a specific SVG element, the Mozilla Developer Network also has an excellent page on that: `https://developer.mozilla.org/en-US/docs/Web/SVG`.

In this section, we'll perform the following steps:

1. Create and add an empty SVG group (g) element, to which we'll add our data elements.
2. Use a JavaScript array that contains some sample data to add rectangles to the SVG element created in the previous step.
3. Show how changes in the data can be used to update the drawn rectangles.
4. Explain how to handle added and removed data elements using D3.

At the end of these steps, you should have a decent idea of how D3 binds data to elements, and how you can update the bound data.

Creating a group element

The first thing we need to do is create a g element to which we can add our own elements. Since we're visualizing data using SVG, we need to create this element inside the root SVG element we defined in our HTML skeleton in the previous section. We do this in the following manner:

```
function show() {

    var margin = { top: 20, bottom: 20, right: 40, left: 40 },
        width = 400 - margin.left - margin.right,
```

```
      height = 400 - margin.top - margin.bottom;

  var chart = d3.select(".chart")
      .attr("width", width + margin.left + margin.right)
      .attr("height", height + margin.top + margin.bottom)
      .append("g")
      .attr("transform", "translate(" + margin.left + "," + margin.top +
")");
  }
```

In this code fragment, we see the first usage of the D3 API. We use `d3.select` to search for the first element with the class `chart`. This will find the SVG element we defined in our HTML template (`<svg class="chart"></svg>`), and this will allow us to modify that element. D3 uses a **W3C Selectors API** string to select elements (more information here: `https://www.w3.org/TR/selectors-api/`). Summarizing this means that you can use the same kind of selector strings that are also used in CSS to select specific elements:

- `.className`: selects the elements that have a class with the name `className`.
- `.elemName`: selects the elements of type `elemName`
- `#id`: selects the element that has an attribute `id` with a value `id`.
- `.className1 .className2`: selects all elements with the class name `.className2` which are descendants from the element with class name `.className2`

A lot more options are available: a good overview can be found here: `https://www.w3.org/TR/CSS21/selector.html`

Now that we have the SVG element, we use the `attr` function to set its width and height, leaving a bit of margin at all sides. Finally, we add the `g` element using the `append` function and position that element by taking into account the margins we defined by setting the `transform` attribute. D3 has a *fluent* API which means we can just chain commands and functions together (as you can see in the previous code fragment). This also means that the result of the `final` operation is assigned to the `chart` variable. So in this case, the `chart` variable is the `g` element we appended to the svg element.

A `g` element isn't rendered when you add it to a SVG element. The `g` element is just a container in which you can add other elements. The most useful part of the `g` element is that all of the transformations applied to this element are also applied to the children. So if you move the `g` element, the children will move as well. Additionally, all the attributes defined on this element are inherited by its children.

This might seem like a lot of work to just get an empty group to add elements to, but it is good practice to use a setup like this. Using margins allows us to more easily add axes or legends later on, without having to reposition everything and having a clear and well defined height and weight allows us to use other D3 features (such as scales) to correctly position elements, as we'll see later in this chapter.

At this point, it's also a good point to explain the transform attribute we use to position the g element inside the svg element. The transform attribute allows a couple of operations we can use to change the position and rotation of any SVG elements (such as g, text, rect). You'll see it used throughout this book, since it is the standard way to position SVG elements. The following table shows what can be done with the transform attribute:

Operation	Description
translate(x [y])	With the translate attribute, we can move the specified element along its X or Y axis. For example, with translate(40 60), we move the specified element 40 pixels to the right and 60 down. If you just want to move an element along the X axis, you can omit the second parameter.
scale(x [y])	The scale operator, as the name implies, allows you to scale an element along the x and y axes. To double the width of an element, you can use scale(1 2), to half the size you use scale(0.5 0.5). Once again, the first parameter is mandatory, and the second one is optional.
rotate(a [x] [y])	The rotate operation allows rotation of the element around a given point (x and y) for a degrees. If the x and y parameters aren't provided, the element is rotated around its center. You can specify a positive a to rotate clockwise (for example, rotate(120)) and a negative value to rotate counter-clockwise (rotate(-10)).
skewX(a) / skewY(a)	The skewX and skewY functions allow you to skew (to slant) an element alongside an axis by the specified a degrees: skewX(20) or skewY(-30).
matrix(a b c d e f)	The final option you can use is the matrix function. With the matrix operator you can specify an arbitrary matrix operation to be applied to the element. All the previous operations could be written using the matrix operator, but this isn't really that convenient. For instance, we could rewrite translate(40 60) like matrix(1 0 0 1 40 60)

If you entered this code in your editor and looked at it in your browser you wouldn't really see anything yet. The reason is that we didn't specify a background color (using the `fill` attribute) for the `svg` or `g` element, so the default background color is used. We can, however, check what has happened. We mentioned that besides a good editor to create code, we'll also do a lot of debugging inside the browser, and Chrome has some of the best support. If you open the previous code in your browser, you can already see what is happening when you inspect the elements:

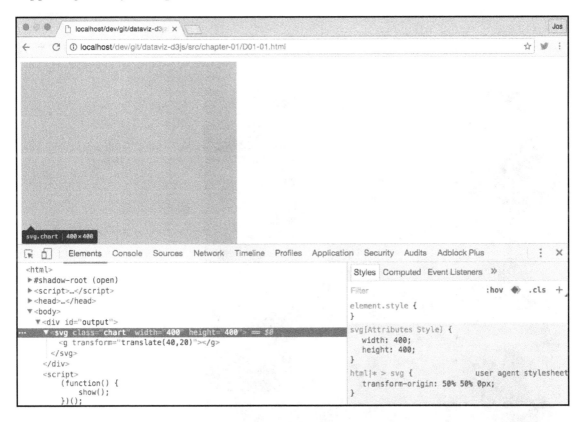

As you can see in this screenshot, the correct attributes have been set on the `svg` element, a `g` element is added, and the `g` element is transformed to position it correctly. If we want to style the `svg` element, we can use standard CSS for this. For instance, the following code (if added to the `css` file for this example) will set the `background-color` attribute of the `svg` element to black.

```
svg {
    background-color: black;
}
```

It is good to understand that CSS styles and element attributes have different priorities. Styles set using the `style` property have the highest priority, next the styles applied through the CSS classes, and the element properties set directly on the element have the lowest priority.

When we now open the example in the browser, you'll see the `svg` element as a black rectangle:

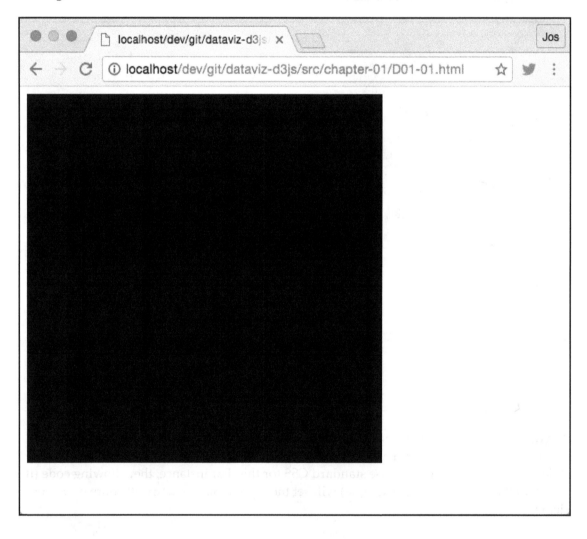

At this point, we've got an `svg` element with a specific size, and one `g` element to which we'll add other elements in the rest of this example.

Adding rectangles to the group element

In this step, we'll look at the core functionality of D3 which shows how to bind data to elements. We'll create an example that shows a number of rectangles based on some random data. We'll update the data every couple of seconds, and see how we can use D3 to respond to these changes. If you want to look at this example in action, open the example `D01-01.html` from the `chapter 01` folder in your browser. The result looks something like this:

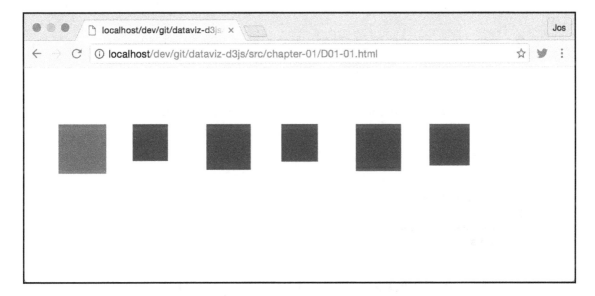

The size and number of rectangles in the screen is randomly determined and the colors indicate whether a rectangle is added or an existing one is updated. If the rectangle is blue, an existing rectangle was selected and updated; if a rectangle is green, it was added to the rectangles already available. It works something like this:

1. The first time the rectangles are shown, no rectangles are on screen, so all the rectangles are newly added and colored green. So, for this example, assume we add three rectangles, which, since no rectangles are present, they rendered green.

2. After a couple of seconds, the data is updated. Now assume five rectangles need to be rendered. For this, we'll update the three rectangles which are already there with the new data. These are rendered blue since we're updating them. And we add two new rectangles, which are rendered green, just like in the first step.
3. After another couple of seconds, the data is updated again. This time we need to render four rectangles. This means updating the first four rectangles, which will turn them blue, and we'll remove the last one, since that one isn't needed anymore.

To accomplish this, we'll first show you the complete code and then step through the different parts:

```
function show() {
    'use strict';

    var margin = { top: 20, bottom: 20, right: 40, left: 40 },
        width = 800 - margin.left - margin.right,
        height = 400 - margin.top - margin.bottom;

    var chart = d3.select(".chart")
        .attr("width", width + margin.left + margin.right)
        .attr("height", height + margin.top + margin.bottom)
        .append("g")
        .attr("transform", "translate(" + margin.left + ","
                                         + margin.top + ")");

    function update() {

        var rectangleWidth = 100,
        data = [],
            numberOfRectangles = Math.ceil(Math.random() * 7);

        for (var i = 0 ; i < numberOfRectangles ; i++) {
            data.push((Math.random() * rectangleWidth / 2)
                                    + rectangleWidth / 2);
        }

        // Assign the data to the rectangles (should there be any)
        var rectangles = chart.selectAll("rect").data(data);

        // Set a style on the existing rectangles so we can see them
        rectangles.attr("class", "update")
            .attr("width", function(d) {return d})
            .attr("height", function(d) {return d});

        rectangles.enter()
```

```
            .append("rect")
            .attr("class", "enter")
            .attr("x", function(d, i) { return i * (rectangleWidth + 5) })
            .attr("y", 50)
            .attr("width", function(d) {return d})
            .attr("height", function(d) {return d});

        // Handle rectangles which are left over
        rectangles.exit().remove();

        // we could also change the ones to be remove
        // rectangles
        //     .exit()
        //     .attr("class", "remove");
    }

    // set initial value
    update();
    // and update every 3 seconds
    d3.interval(function() { update(); }, 3000);
}
```

In the beginning of this function, you once again see the code we use to create and set up our SVG and main g elements. Let's ignore that and move on to the update() function. When this function is called it will take a couple of steps:

Creating dummy data

The first thing it does is that it creates some dummy data. This is the data that determines how many rectangles to render, and how large the rectangles will be:

```
var rectangleWidth = 100,
    data = [],
    numberOfRectangles = Math.ceil(Math.random() * 7);

for (var i = 0 ; i < numberOfRectangles ; i++) {
    data.push((Math.random() * rectangleWidth / 2)
                        + rectangleWidth / 2);
}
```

This is just plain JavaScript, and this will result in the data array being filled with one to seven numeric values ranging from 50 to 100. It could look something like this:

```
[52.653238934888726, 88.52709144102309, 81.70794256804369,
58.10611357491862]
```

Binding the data and updating existing rectangles

The next step is assigning this data to a D3 selection. We do this by using the `selectAll` function on the `chart` variable we defined earlier (remember this is the main `g` element, we added initially):

```
var rectangles = chart.selectAll("rect").data(data);
```

This call will select all the rectangles which are already appended as children to the `chart` variable. The first time this is called, rectangles will have no children, but on subsequent calls this will select any rectangles that have been added in the previous call to the `update()` function. To differentiate between newly added rectangles and rectangles which we'll reuse, we add a specific CSS class. Besides just adding the CSS class, we also need to make sure they have the correct `width` and `height` properties set, since the bound data has changed.

In the case of rectangles which we reuse, we do that like this:

```
rectangles.attr("class", "update")
        .attr("width", function(d) {return d})
        .attr("height", function(d) {return d});
```

To set the CSS we use the `attr` function to set the `class` property, which points to a style defined in our CSS file. The `width` and `height` properties are set in the same manner, but their value is based on the value of the passed data. You can do this by setting the value of that attribute to a `function(d) {...}`. The `d` which is passed in to this function is the value of the corresponding element from the bound `data` array. So the first rectangle which is found is bound to `data[0]`, the second to `data[1]`, and so on. In this case, we set both the width and the height of the rectangle to the same value.

The CSS for this class is very simple, and just makes sure that the newly added rectangles are filled with a nice blue color:

```
.update {
    fill: steelblue;
}
```

Adding new rectangles if needed

At this point, we've only updated the style and dimensions of the rectangles which are updated. We repeat pretty much the same process for the rectangles that need to be created. This happens when our data array is larger than the number of rectangles we can find:

```
rectangles.enter()
    .append("rect")
    .attr("class", "enter")
    .attr("x", function(d, i) { return i * (rectangleWidth + 5) })
    .attr("y", 50)
    .attr("width", function(d) {return d})
    .attr("height", function(d) {return d});
```

Not that different from the update call, but this time we first call the enter() function and then create the SVG element we want to add like this: .append("rect"). After the append call, we configure the rectangle and set its class, width, and height properties, just like we did in the previous section (this time the CSS will render the newly added rectangle in green). If you look at the code, you can see that we also set the position of this element by setting the x and y attributes of the added rectangle. This is needed since this is the first time this rectangle is added, and we need to determine where to position it. We fix the y position to 50, but need to make the x position dependent on the position of the element from the data array to which it is bound. We once again bind the attribute to a function. This time we specify a function with two arguments: function(d, i) {...}. The first one is the element from the data array, and the second argument (i), is the position in the data array. So the first element has i = 0, the second i = 1, and so on. Now, when we add a new rectangle we calculate its x position by just multiplying its array position with the maximum rectangleWidth and add a couple of pixels margin. This way none of our rectangles will overlap.

If you look at the code for adding new elements, and updating existing ones, you might notice some duplicate code. In both instances, we use `.attr` to set the `width` and the `height` properties. If we'd wanted to, we could remove this duplication by using the `.merge` function. The code to set the new width and height for the new elements and the updated ones would then look like this:

```
rectangles.attr("class", "update");

rectangles.enter()
    .append("rect")
    .attr("class", "enter")
    .attr("x", function(d, i) { return i * (rectangleWidth + 5) })
    .attr("y", 50)
    .merge(rectangles)
    .attr("width", function(d) {return d})
    .attr("height", function(d) {return d});
```

This means that after merging the new and updated elements together, on that combined set, we use the `.attr` function to set the `width` and the `height` property. Personally, I'd like to keep these steps separate, since it is more clear what happens in each of the steps.

Removing elements which aren't needed anymore

The final step we need to take is to remove rectangles that aren't needed anymore. If in the first call to update we add five rectangles, and in the next call only three are needed, we're stuck with two leftover ones. D3 also has an elegant mechanism to deal with that:

```
rectangles.exit().remove();
```

The call to `exit()` will select the elements for which no data is available. We can then do anything we want with those rectangles. In this case, we just remove them by calling `remove()`, but we could also change their opacity to make them look transparent, or animate them to slowly disappear.

For instance, if we replace the previous line of code with this:

```
rectangles.exit().attr("class", "remove");
```

Then set the CSS for the `remove` class to this:

```
.remove {
    fill: red;
    opacity: 0.2;
}
```

In that case, we'd see the following:

In the preceding screenshot, we've reused two existing rectangles, and instead of removing the five we don't need, we change their style to the `remove` class, which renders them semi-transparent red.

Visualizing our first data

So far we've seen the basics of how D3 works. In this last section of this first chapter, we'll create a simple visualization of some real data. We're going to visualize the popularity of baby names in the USA. The final result will look this:

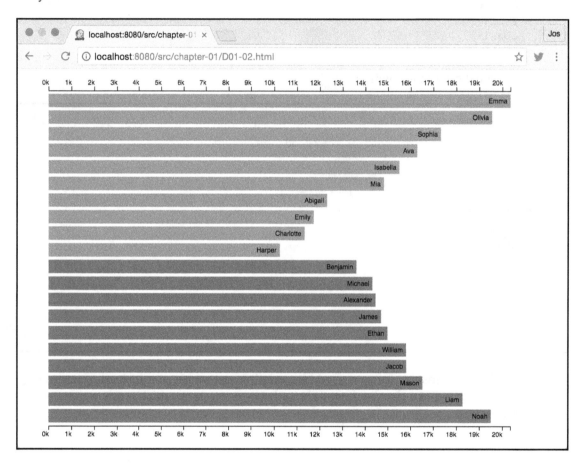

As you can see in this figure, we create pink bars for the girl names, blue bars for the boy names, and add an axis at the top and the bottom, which shows the number of times that name was chosen. The first thing, though, is take a look at the data.

Sanitizing and getting the data

For this example, we'll download data from
`https://www.ssa.gov/oact/babynames/limits.html`. This site provides data for all the
baby names in the US since 1880. On this page, you can find national data and state-specific
data. For this example, download the national data dataset. Once you've downloaded it,
you can extract it, and you'll see data for a lot of different years:

```
$ ls -1
NationalReadMe.pdf
yob1880.txt
yob1881.txt
yob1882.txt
yob1883.txt
yob1884.txt
yob1885.txt
...
yob2013.txt
yob2014.txt
yob2015.txt
```

As you can see, we have data from 1880 until 2015. For this example, I've used the data from
2015, but you can use pretty much anything you want. Now let's look a bit closer at the
data:

```
$ cat yob2015.txt
Emma,F,20355
Olivia,F,19553
Sophia,F,17327
Ava,F,16286
Isabella,F,15504
Mia,F,14820
Abigail,F,12311
Emily,F,11727
Charlotte,F,11332
Harper,F,10241
...
Zynique,F,5
Zyrielle,F,5
Noah,M,19511
Liam,M,18281
Mason,M,16535
Jacob,M,15816
William,M,15809
Ethan,M,14991
James,M,14705
Alexander,M,14460
```

```
Michael,M,14321
Benjamin,M,13608
Elijah,M,13511
Daniel,M,13408
```

In this data, we've got a large number of rows where each row shows the name and the sex (M or F). First, all the girls' names are shown, and after that all the boys' names are shown. The data in itself already looks pretty usable, so we don't need to do much processing before we can use it. The only thing, though, we do is add a header to this file, so that it looks like this:

```
name,sex,amount
Emma,F,20355
Olivia,F,19553
Sophia,F,17327
Ava,F,16286
```

This will make parsing this data into D3 a little bit easier, since the default way of parsing CSV data with D3 assumes the first line is a header. The sanitized data we use in this example can be found here: `<DVD3>/src/chapter-01/data/yob2015.txt`.

Creating the visualization

Now that we've got the data we want to work with, we can start creating the example. The files used in this example are the following:

- `<DVD3>/src/chapter-01/D01-02.html`: The HTML template that loads the correct CSS and JavaScript files for this example
- `<DVD3>/src/chapter-01/js/D01-02.js`: The JavaScript which uses the D3 APIs to draw the chart
- `<DVD3>/src/chapter-01/css/D01-02.css`: Custom CSS to color the bars and format the text elements
- `<DVD3>/src/chapter-01/data/yob2015.txt`: The data that is visualized

Let's start with the complete JavaScript file first. It might seem complex, and it introduces a couple of new concepts, but the general idea should be clear from the code (if you open the source file in your editor, you can also see inline comments for additional explanation):

```javascript
function show() {
    'use strict';

    var margin = { top: 30, bottom: 20, right: 40, left: 40 },
```

```
        width = 800 - margin.left - margin.right,
        height = 600 - margin.top - margin.bottom;

    var chart = d3.select('.chart')
        .attr('width', width + margin.left + margin.right)
        .attr('height', height + margin.top + margin.bottom)
        .append('g')
        .attr('transform', 'translate(' + margin.left + ','
                                    + margin.top + ')');

    var namesToShow = 10;
    var barWidth = 20;
    var barMargin = 5;

    d3.csv('data/yob2015.txt', function (d) { return { name: d.name, sex:
d.sex, amount: +d.amount }; }, function (data) {
        var grouped = _.groupBy(data, 'sex');
        var top10F = grouped['F'].slice(0, namesToShow);
        var top10M = grouped['M'].slice(0, namesToShow);

        var both = top10F.concat(top10M.reverse());

        var bars = chart.selectAll("g").data(both)
            .enter()
            .append('g')
            .attr('transform', function (d, i) {
                var yPos = ((barWidth + barMargin) * i);
                return 'translate( 0 ' + yPos +  ')';
            });

        var yScale = d3.scaleLinear()
            .domain([0, d3.max(both, function (d) { return d.amount; })])
            .range([0, width]);

        bars.append('rect')
            .attr("height", barWidth)
            .attr("width", function (d) { return yScale(d.amount); })
            .attr("class", function (d) { return d.sex === 'F' ? 'female' :
'male'; });

        bars.append("text")
            .attr("x", function (d) { return yScale(d.amount) - 5 ; })
            .attr("y", barWidth / 2)
            .attr("dy", ".35em")
            .text(function(d) { return d.name; });

        var bottomAxis = d3.axisBottom().scale(yScale).ticks(20, "s");
        var topAxis = d3.axisTop().scale(yScale).ticks(20, "s");
```

```
        chart.append("g")
            .attr('transform', 'translate( 0 ' + both.length * (barWidth +
    barMargin) + ')')
            .call(bottomAxis);

        chart.append("g")
            .attr('transform', 'translate( 0 ' + -barMargin + ' )')
            .call(topAxis);
    });
}
```

In this JavaScript file, we perform the following steps:

1. Set up the main `chart` element, like we did in the previous example.
2. Load the data from the CSV file using `d3.csv`.
3. Group the loaded data so we only have the top 10 names for both sexes. Note that we use the `groupBy` function from the `lodash` library (https://lodash.com/) for this. This library provides a lot of additional functions to deal with common array operations. Throughout this book, we'll use this library in places where the standard JavaScript APIs don't provide enough functionality.
4. Add g elements that will hold the `rect` and `text` elements for each name.
5. Create the `rect` elements with the correct width corresponding to the number of times the name was used.
6. Create the `text` elements to show the name at the end of the `rect` elements.
7. Add some CSS styles for the `rect` and `text` elements.
8. Add an axis to the top and the bottom for easy referencing.

We'll skip the first step since we've already explained that before, and move on to the usage of the `d3.csv` API call. Before we do that, there are a couple of variables in the JavaScript that determine how the bars look, and how many we show:

```
var namesToShow = 10;
var barWidth = 20;
var barMargin = 5;
```

These variables will be used throughout the explanation in the following sections. What this means is that we're going to show 10 (`namesToShow`) names, a bar is 20 (`barWidth`) pixels wide, and between each bar we put a five pixel margin.

Loading CSV data with D3

To load data asynchronously, D3 provides a number of helper functions. In this case, we've used the d3.csv function:

```
d3.csv('data/yob2015.txt',
        function (d) { return { name: d.name, sex: d.sex, amount: +d.amount
}; },
        function (data) {
        ...
        }
```

The d3.csv function we use takes three parameters. The first one, data/yob2015.txt, is a URL which points to the data we want to load. The second argument is a function that is applied to each row read by D3. The object that's passed into this function is based on the header row of the CSV file. In our case, this data looks like this:

```
{
    name: 'Sophie',
    sex: 'F',
    amount: '1234'
}
```

This (optional) function allows you to modify the data in the row, before it is passed on as an array (data) to the last argument of the d3.csv function. In this example, we use this second argument to convert the string value d.amount to a numeric value. Once the data is loaded and in this case converted, the function provided as the third argument is called with an array of all the read and converted values, ready for us to visualize the data.

D3 provides a number of functions like d3.csv to load data and resources. These are listed in the following table:

Function	Description
d3.csv(url, [row], callback)	Retrieve a CSV file, optionally pass each row through the row function. When done the callback function is called with all the read data.
d3.tsv(url, [row], callback)	Retrieve a TSV (same as a CSV file but separated by tabs) file, optionally pass each row through the row function. When done the callback function is called with all the read data.
d3.html(url, callback)	Get a HTML file, and pass it into the callback function when loaded.

d3.json(url, callback)	Get a JSON file, and pass it into the callback function when loaded.
d3.text(url, callback)	Get a basic test file, and pass it into the callback function when loaded.
d3.xml(url, [row], callback)	Get an XML file, and pass it into the callback function when loaded.

You can also manually process CSV files if they happen to use a different format. You should load those using the d3.text function, and use any of the functions from the d3-dsv module to parse the data. You can find more information on the d3-dsv module here: https://github.com/d3/d3-dsv.

Grouping the loaded data so we only have the top 10 names for both sexes

At this point, we've only loaded the data. If you look back at the figure, you can see that we create a chart using the top 10 female and male names. With the following lines of code, we convert the big incoming data array to an array that contains just the top 10 female and male names:

```
var grouped = _.groupBy(data, 'sex');
var top10F = grouped['F'].slice(0, namesToShow);
var top10M = grouped['M'].slice(0, namesToShow);

var both = top10F.concat(top10M.reverse());
```

Here we use the lodash's groupBy function,to sort our data based on the sex property of each row. Next we take the first 10 (namesToShow) elements from the grouped data, and create a single array from them using the concat function. We also reverse the top10M array to make the highest boy's name appear at the bottom of the chart (as you can see when you look at the example).

Adding group elements

At this point, we've got the data into a form that we can use. The next step is to create a number of containers, to which we can add the `rect` that represents the number of times the name was used, and we'll also add a `text` element there that displays the name:

```
var bars = chart.selectAll("g").data(both)
    .enter()
    .append('g')
    .attr('transform', function (d, i) {
        var yPos = ((barWidth + barMargin) * i);
        return 'translate( 0 ' + yPos + ')';
    });
```

Here, we bind the `both` array to a number of `g` elements. We only need to use the `enter` function here, since we know that there aren't any `g` elements that can be reused. We position each `g` element using the `translate` operation of the `transform` attribute. We translate the `g` element along its y-axis based on the `barWidth`, the `barMargin`, and the position of the data element (`d`) in our data (`both`) array. If you use the Chrome developer tools, you'll see something like this, which nicely shows the calculated `translate` values:

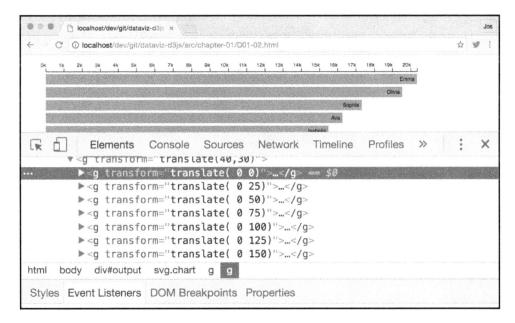

All that is left to do now, is draw the rectangles and add the names.

Adding the bar chart and baby name

In the previous section, we added the g elements and assigned those to the bars variable. In this section, we're going to calculate the width of the individual rectangles and add those and some text to the g:

```
var yScale = d3.scaleLinear()
    .domain([0, d3.max(both, function (d) { return d.amount; })])
    .range([0, width]);

bars.append('rect')
    .attr("height", barWidth)
    .attr("width", function (d) { return yScale(d.amount); })
    .attr("class", function (d) { return d.sex === 'F' ? 'female' : 'male';
});

bars.append("text")
    .attr("x", function (d) { return yScale(d.amount) - 5 ; })
    .attr("y", barWidth / 2)
    .attr("dy", ".35em")
    .text(function(d) { return d.name; });
```

Here we see something new: the d3.scaleLinear function. With a d3.scaleLinear, we can let D3 calculate how the number of times a name was given (the amount property) maps to a specific width. We want to use the full width (width property, which has a value of 720) of the chart for our bars, so that would mean that the highest value in our input data should map to that value:

- The name Emma, which occurred 20355 times, should map to a value of 720
- The name Olivia, which occurred 19553 times, should map to a value of 720 * (19553/20355)
- The name Mia, which occurred 14820 times, should map to a value of 720 * (14820/20355)
- And so on...

Now, we could calculate this ourselves and set the size of the rect accordingly, but using the d3.scaleLinear is much easier, and provides additional functionality. Let's look at the definition a bit closer:

```
var yScale = d3.scaleLinear()
    .domain([0, d3.max(both, function (d) { return d.amount; })])
    .range([0, width]);
```

What we do here, is we define a **linear** scale, whose input domain is set from 0 to the maximum amount in our data. This input domain is mapped to an output range starting at 0 and ending at `width`. The result, `yScale`, is a function which we can now use to map the input domain to the output range: for example, `yScale(1234)` returns `43.64922623434046`.

Once you've got a scale, you can use a couple of functions to change its behavior:

Function	Description
`invert(val)`	This function expects a value of the output domain, and returns the corresponding value from the input domain.
`rangeRound()`	You can use this instead of the `range` option we saw earlier. With this function, the scale only returns rounded values.
`clamp(bool)`	With the `clamp` function, you define the behavior of what happens when a value is passed in which is outside the input domain. In the case where `clamp` is `true`, the minimal or maximum output value is returned. In the case where `clamp` is `false`, an output value is calculated normally, which will result in a value outside the output domain.
`ticks([count])`	This function returns a number of `ticks` (10 is the default), which can be used to create an axis, or reference lines.
`nice([ticks])`	This function rounds the first and last value of the input domain. You can optionally specify a number of `ticks` you want to return, and the `rounding` function will take those into account.

This is just a small part of the scales support provided by D3. In the rest of the book, we'll explore more of the scales options that are available.

With the scale defined, we can use that to create our `rect` and `text` elements in the same way we did in our previous example:

```
bars.append('rect')
    .attr("height", barWidth)
    .attr("width", function (d) { return yScale(d.amount); })
    .attr("class", function (d) { return d.sex === 'F' ? 'female' : 'male';
});
```

Here we create a `rect` with a fixed height, and a width which is defined by the `yScale` and the number of times the name was used. We also add a class to the `rect` so that we can set its colors (and other styling attributes) through CSS. In the case where `sex` is `F`, we set the class `female` and in the other case we set the class `male`.

To position the `text` element, we do pretty much the same:

```
bars.append("text")
    .attr("class", "label")
    .attr("x", function (d) { return yScale(d.amount) - 5 ; })
    .attr("y", barWidth / 2)
    .attr("dy", ".35em")
    .text(function(d) { return d.name; });
```

We create a new `text` element, position it at the end of the bar, set a custom CSS class, and finally set its value to `d.name`. The `dy` attribute might seem a bit strange, but this allows us to position the text nicely in the middle of the bar chart. If we opened the example at this point, we'd see something like this:

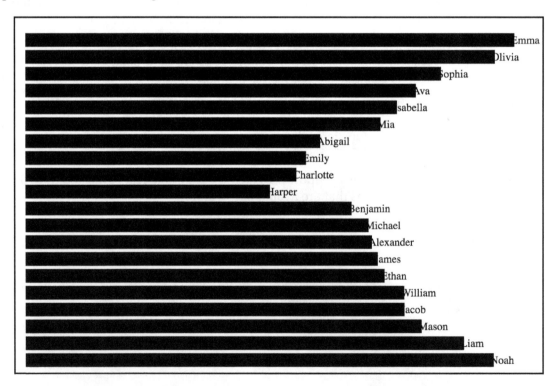

We can see that all the information is in there, but it still looks kind of ugly. In the following section, we add some CSS to improve what the chart looks like.

Adding some CSS classes to style the bars and text elements

When we added the `rect` elements, we added a `female` class attribute for the girls' names, and a `male` one for the boys' names and we've also set the style of our text elements to `label`. In our CSS file, we can now define colors and other styles based on these classes:

```
.male {
    fill: steelblue;
}

.female {
    fill: hotpink;
}

.label {
    fill: black;
    font: 10px sans-serif;
    text-anchor: end;
}
```

With these CSS properties, we set the `fill` color of our rectangles. The elements with the `male` class will be filled `steelblue` and the elements with the `female` class will be filled `hotpink`. We also change how the elements with the `.label` class are rendered. For these elements, we change the `font` and the `text-anchor`. The `text-anchor`, especially, is important here, since it makes sure that the `text` element's right side is positioned at the x and y value, instead of the left side. The effect is that the `text` element is nicely aligned at the end of our bars.

Adding the axis on the top and bottom

The final step we need to take to get the figure from the beginning of this section is to add the top and bottom axes. D3 provides you with a `d3.axis<orientation>` function, which allows you to create an axis at the bottom, top, left, or right side. When creating an axis, we pass in a scale (which we also used for the width of the rectangles), and tell D3 how the axis should be formatted. In this case, we want 20 ticks, and use the s formatting, which tells D3 to use the international system of units (SI).

This means that D3 will use metric prefixes to format the tick values (more info can be found here: https://en.wikipedia.org/wiki/Metric_prefix).

```
var bottomAxis = d3.axisBottom().scale(yScale).ticks(20, "s");
var topAxis = d3.axisTop().scale(yScale).ticks(20, "s");

chart.append("g")
    .attr('transform', 'translate( 0 ' + both.length * (barWidth +
barMargin) + ')')
    .call(bottomAxis);

chart.append("g")
    .attr('transform', 'translate( 0 ' + -barMargin + ' )')
    .call(topAxis);
```

And with that, we've recreated the example we saw at the beginning of this section:

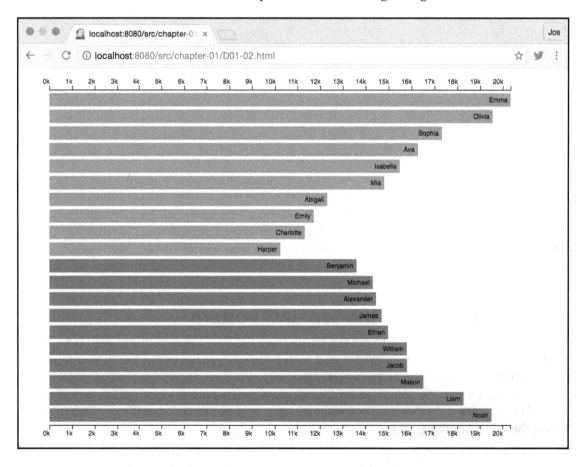

If you look back at the code we showed at the beginning of this section, you can see that we only need a small number of lines of code to create a nice visualization.

Summary

In this chapter, we've set up our working environment and introduced the first couple of concepts of D3. We've showed that there is a standard pattern for binding data to elements, and how we can use D3 to handle new elements, update existing elements, and how to remove obsolete elements. We've also created our first visualization in this chapter. We've used a standard CSV file, and converted that to a bar chart, complete with custom colors, text elements, and a set of axes. Throughout this chapter, we've touched upon a couple of D3 APIs and concepts, such as `d3.selectAll`, `d3.axisBottom`, and even explored a part of how D3 handles scales (`d3.linearScale`).

In the next chapter, we'll continue with the subjects we've seen so far, and look more closely at how you can use D3 to create different kinds of charts.

2
Basic Charts and Shapes

In the previous chapter, we created a simple bar chart using the SVG `rect` element. While this works for simple charts, using the standard SVG elements for more complex charts can be difficult. Luckily, D3 provides an extensive set of helper functions that we can use to easily create more complex visualizations, without having to manipulate basic SVG elements ourselves. In this chapter, we're going to create visualizations based on data from the US Census Bureau (`http://www.census.gov`). To be more precise, we're going to create the following data visualizations:

- **How long have American firms been in business visualized with pies and donuts**: The US census releases an overview that shows how long firms have been in business. This provides a nice data set to show how D3 allows you to create pie and donut charts.
- **Real Median Household income in the US visualized with a line chart**: In the US Census data, there is information present on how the average household income has changed during the last thirty years. This is information that can be very nicely visualized using a line chart.
- **Population growth estimates using a stacked graph**: The US Census Bureau provides information on how the population of the US is expected to change from 2014 to 2060. We'll use this data to show how this can be visualized using a stacked graph.

To make the visualizations more interesting, we'll also add interactivity and animations to them. Let's get started with the first visualization: the donut and pie charts.

How long have American firms been in business visualized with pies and donuts

In September 2016, the US Census Bureau released data that showed how long American firms have been in business. The US Census Bureau even created a nice-looking visualization themselves (`http://www.census.gov/newsroom/press-releases/2016/cb16-148.html`) showing the results from that data:

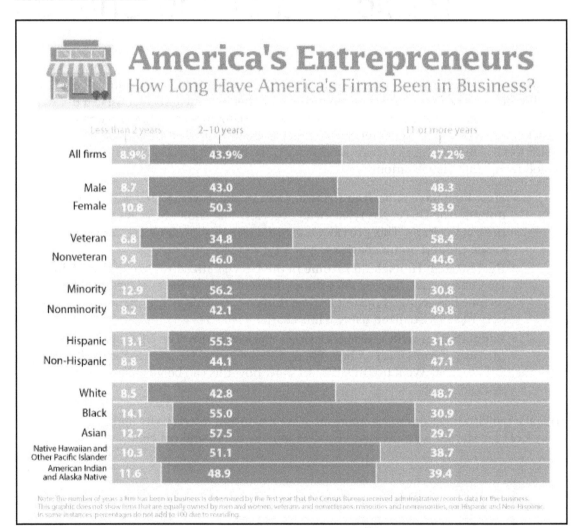

In this section, we'll create an alternative visualization using an animated donut chart. While making this, we'll explore the following subjects:

- Learning how to use animations to occur when data is loaded
- Using the various path generators from D3 to generate SVG paths
- Using color interpolators to color each individual part of the donut

You can see this sample for yourself by opening example: `<DVD3>/src/chapter-02/D02-01.html`. The results look like this:

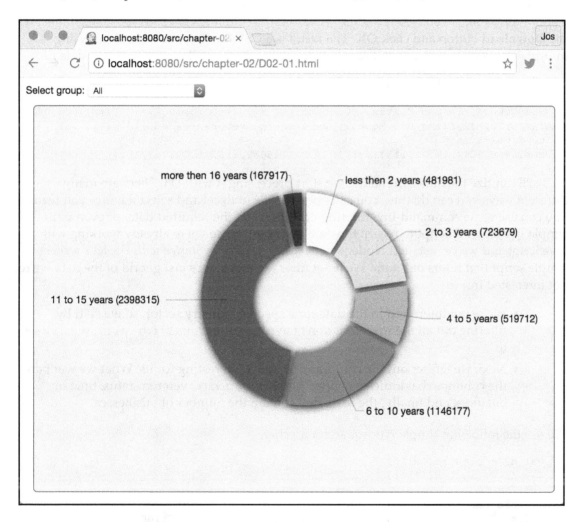

By selecting a different group of firm owners in the top left you can see the donut transition to its new state, and if you hover with the mouse over a donut segment, it'll grow a bit, and show its percentage in the middle of the donut.

First off, let's see what the data looks like in its raw form.

Get and cleanup the data

You can get a CSV file of the data from `https://factfinder.census.gov/faces/tableser vices/jsf/pages/productview.xhtml?pid=ASE_2014_00CSA01&prodType=table`. Just hit the **Download** button and click **OK**. The result is a CSV file that has lots of interesting information in it. If you open it, though, it doesn't really look like an easy-to-use data file.

A single data row looks like this:

```
00100000US,,United States,,00,Total for all sectors,,001,All firms,001,All
firms,00,All firms,003,Equally veteran-/nonveteran-owned,319,Firms with 4
to 5 years in
business,2014,12174,11571648,107722,2746052,6.3,15.3,17.8,16.4
```

So, we'll sanitize the data a bit before we start processing it with D3. There are many different ways you can do this. You can open the file in Excel and select the files you want, you can use some command-line filtering utilities to get the required data, or even write a simple Python or R script to return the data you want. Since we're already working with JavaScript and we've installed **Node.js** in Chapter 1, *Getting Started with D3*, let's write a simple script that filters our data. We'll not filter too much, let's just get rid of the data we're not interested in:

- We're not interested in the data for a specific industry sector, so we start by filtering out all the rows that don't have the value `Total for all sectors` set to `Y`.
- Next, we'll filter out the columns that aren't interesting for us. What we want are the columns that indicate gender, ethnic group, race, veteran status, time in business, and finally, the rows that contain the number of businesses.

We use the following simple Node.js script for that:

```
var d3 = require('d3');
var fs = require('fs');

// read the data
fs.readFile('./ASE_2014_00CSA02.csv', function (err, fileData) {
    var rows = d3.csvParse(fileData.toString());
```

```
// filter out the sector specific stuff
var allSectors = rows.filter(function (row) {
    return row['NAICS.id'] === '00'
});

// remove unused columns, and make nice headers
var mapped = allSectors.map( function(el) {
    return {
        sex: el['SEX.id'],
        sexLabel: el['SEX.display-label'],
        ethnicGroup: el['ETH_GROUP.id'],
        ethnicGroupLabel: el['ETH_GROUP.display-label'],
        raceGroup: el['RACE_GROUP.id'],
        raceGroupLabel: el['RACE_GROUP.display-label'],
        vetGroup: el['VET_GROUP.id'],
        vetGroupLabel: el['VET_GROUP.display-label'],
        yearsInBusiness:  el['YIBSZFI.id'],
        yearsInBusinessLabel:  el['YIBSZFI.display-label'],
        count: el['FIRMPDEMP']
    }
});

    fs.writeFile('./businessFiltered.csv',d3.csvFormat(mapped));
});
```

What happens in this script is that we use the `fs.readFile` API of Node.js to read the file we downloaded from the filesystem, and then use D3 to parse the CSV file. After parsing, we filter out the elements we don't want, and use `map` to convert each element to a simple one. Finally, we use the `fs.writeFile` API call to output the converted data as a CSV again using the `d3.csvFormat` function. To run this script yourself, navigate to the `<DVD3>/src/chapter-02/data/` directory and run the `./cleanBusinesses.js` node. The result of this is that now we have a very clean and easy-to-understand CSV to process in our visualization:

```
sex,sexLabel,ethnicGroup,ethnicGroupLabel,raceGroup,raceGroupLabel, ...
001,All firms,001,All firms,00,All firms, ...
001,All firms,001,All firms,00,All firms, ...
```

With this data, we can now very easily select specific groups to visualize by just filtering on the `sex`, `ethnicGroup`, `raceGroup`, and `vetGroup` properties.

Creating the donut

The complete source file for this sample is a bit long, so we won't show it completely. You can, of course, look at the complete annotated sources here: `<DVD3>/src/chapter-02/D02-01.html`. In the following sections, we'll explore the steps you need to take to create this visualization:

1. First, we need to load our sanitized data so that we can use it to create the donut.
2. Next, we're going to add the dropdown you can see at the top. With this dropdown, we can select which group we want to show in the donut.
3. Before we look at the D3 code needed to create the donut, we set up some helper objects for handling colors and determining the arc segments dimensions.
4. When you open the page for the first time, we see an empty gray donut. This one we'll add next.
5. Then we add the individual donut segments-based on the selected group from the dropdown and make sure that they are animated when a new group is selected.
6. Besides the arc segments, we also have labels that describe what a specific segment means. We add and animate these separately.
7. We also add and animate the lines pointing from the center of a donut segment to the text label.
8. Use mouse events to show a percentage and pop out a donut segment.

Lots of steps to take, but as you'll see, most will follow the same principles we've already learned about in the previous chapter.

Loading the data

The first thing we do is load the data. In the previous section, we already showed what the data looks like, and how we sanitized it. The only change we make here is that we change the labels indicating how long a firm has been in business. We do this because the default labels are a bit long and shorter labels look better in the final visualization:

```
var loadedData;
d3.csv('./data/businessFiltered.csv',
    function(row) {
        switch (row.yearsInBusiness) {
            case "001" : row.yearsInBusinessLabel = "All"; break;
            case "311" : row.yearsInBusinessLabel = "less then 2 years";
break;
            case "318" : row.yearsInBusinessLabel = "2 to 3 years "; break;
```

```
            case "319" : row.yearsInBusinessLabel = "4 to 5 years"; break;
            case "321" : row.yearsInBusinessLabel = "6 to 10 years"; break;
            case "322" : row.yearsInBusinessLabel = "11 to 15 years";
break;
            case "323" : row.yearsInBusinessLabel = "more then 16 years";
break;
        }

        return row;
    },
    function (data) {
        loadedData = data;
        updateCircle();
    });
```

As you can see we use the standard `d3.csv` to load the data and change the `row.yearsInBusinessLabel` field of each row. Once the data is loaded, we call the `updateCircle()` function. We'll show you what happens in that function later in this chapter. We'll first look at the dropdown you can use to select a specific group to show.

Adding the dropdown

The dropdown is just a standard `select` HTML element, which is added to the HTML file:

```
<div>
    <span>
        Select group:
    </span>
    <select>
        <option value="All" selected>All</option>
        <option value="Female">Female Owners</option>
        <option value="Male">Male Owners</option>
        <option value="AfricanAmerican">African American Owners</option>
        <option value="White">White Owners</option>
    </select>
</div>
```

With just this code, nothing will happen when we select one of the entries in the dropdown. We still need to connect this dropdown to our JavaScript. We do this directly using D3:

```
var select = d3.select('select').on('change', update);

...

function update() {
    var show = select.property('selectedOptions')[0].value;
```

```
        updateCircle(show);
    }
```

We select the `select` element, and use the `on` function to add an event listener. Now, whenever the value of the dropdown changes, the `update` function will be called. In this `update` function we just call the `updateCircle` function with the value of the dropdown. As we'll see later on in the `updateCircle` function, this will cause the donut to be redrawn with a different set of data.

Standard setup, helper objects, and a gray donut

At this point we've loaded the data, and added the HTML `select` dropdown element. Now we'll set up the chart, some additional helper objects and draw the gray donut you see when the page initially loads. Like we did in the other samples, first set up the chart:

```
var margin = {top: 20, bottom: 20, right: 20, left: 45},
    width = 700 - margin.left - margin.right,
    height = 500 - margin.top - margin.bottom;

var chart = d3.select(".chart")
    .attr("width", width + margin.left + margin.right)
    .attr("height", height + margin.top + margin.bottom)
    .append("g")
    .attr("transform", "translate(" + margin.left + "," + margin.top +
")");

// container, which holds the pie
var pieContainer = chart.append('g')
    .attr("transform", "translate(" + width / 2 + " " + height / 2 + ")")

// use some standard colors
var colors = function(i) { return d3.interpolateReds(i/6); }
```

Nothing new here, except the last line where we set up the colors we want to assign to the segments of the donut. For this, we use another standard D3 API call: `d3.interpolateReds`. This function returns a red color based on the provided input. The `d3.interpolateReds(0)` function returns the value at the left, the `d3.interpolateReds(0.5)` function the value at the center, and `d3.interpolateReds(1)` function the value at the right.

Color interpolation and color schemes

Besides the `d3.interpolateReds` function, D3 provides a large number of other color scales and schemes. In this sample, we directly return a color based on the provided `i` argument (which corresponds to a segment of our donut). We could also use a D3 scale for this:

```
var scale = d3.scaleSequential(d3.interpolateReds).domain([0, 5]);
```

D3 provides a large number of color scales you can use. It comes with the following ranges out-of-the-box:

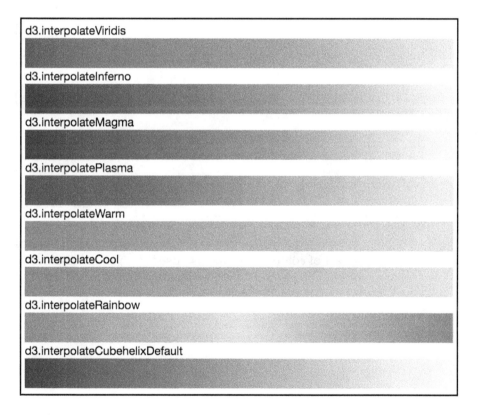

But if you include the `https://github.com/d3/d3-scale-chromatic` module, you get a large number of additional colors that you can use (the following image just shows a subset. If you want to see all the colors, open `<DVD3>/chapter-02/colors.html` in your browser):

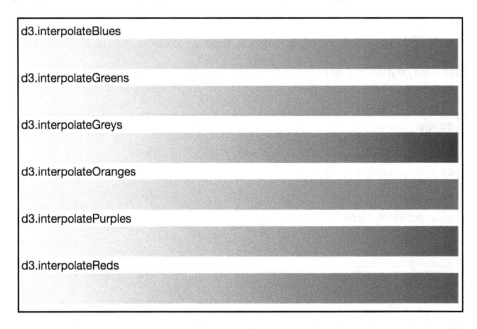

The previous two images show a sequential set of colors. If you want to use a specific color scheme (for example, a fixed set of colors), you can also use D3 for that. When you use the `d3-scala-chromatic` module you get the following standard color schemes:

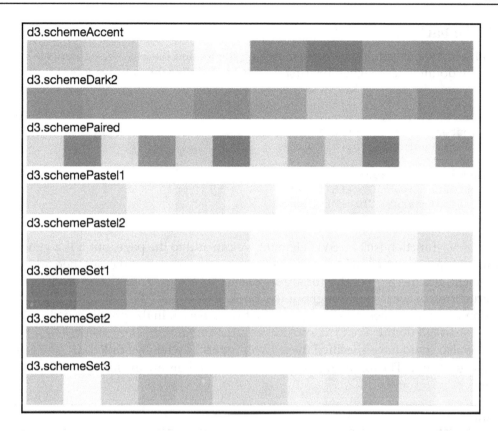

To use these color schemes, you need to create your scale in a slightly different way:

```
var scale = d3.scaleQuantize().domain([0, width]).range(d3.schemeAccent);
```

With a `scaleQuantize` function, the input range (zero to width) is mapped to an array of values (`d3.schemeAccent`). D3 will calculate which color is mapped to a specific input value. So, enough about the colors, let's go back to drawing the gray donut.

Create the background donut

The final setup we need to do before connecting the loaded data to arc segments is setting up the gray donut you see when the first data is loaded. For this, we use the d3.arc() function:

```
var arc = d3.arc()
    .outerRadius(height/2 * 0.6)
    .innerRadius(height/2 * 0.3);

// add a grey background arc
pieContainer.append('path')
    .attr("class", 'backgroundArc')
    .attr("d", arc({startAngle: 0, endAngle: 2 * Math.PI}));
```

The d3.arc() function isn't an SVG element we can add to the page, but it is a generator. A generator is a function that, when called, returns a path string that we can then add to a path element. Besides a generator for arc segments, D3 also provides generators for lots of other structures, as we'll see throughout this book. In this case, the generator allows us to create donut or pie segments as SVG paths that we can add. In the previous code, we used this to create a full donut: arc({startAngle: 0, endAngle: 2 * Math.PI}). Note that we've also could have specified these two properties when we called d3.arc() to create the generator. The following properties and functions are available on the d3.arc() function:

Operation	Description
centroid(arguments...)	Returns the [x, y-coordinates] of the center of the arc segment, which would be generated by the passed in arguments.
innerRadius(radius)	Sets the inner radius of the donut.
outerRadius(radius)	Sets the outer radius of the donut.
cornerRadius(radius)	Adds rounded corners to the individual donut segments.
startAngle(angle)	The angle where the donut segment should start from.
endAngle(angle)	The angle to where the donut segment should be drawn.
padAngle(angle)	Allows you to specify spacing between the individual donut segments.
padRadius(radius)	Sets the radius used to determine the padding between segments. If not specified, it is automatically computed.

Finally, let's add some CSS for this arc, and a nice border around the main container:

```
.backgroundArc {
    fill: #ddd;
}

.chart {
    margin: 10px;
    border-radius: 5px;
    border: solid #555555 thin;
    background-color: #eee;
}
```

We have our basic setup, which at this point looks like this:

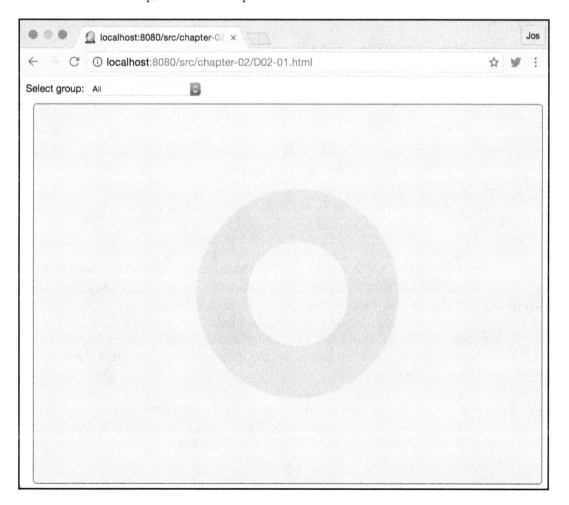

Not very exciting yet, so let's add the colored segments that make up the donut.

Individual donut segments

In the previous section, you've seen that we call the `updateCircle(show)` function when the data is loaded, or when we selected something else in our dropdown. In this part, we'll look how, based on the selected item, we update or add new donut segments, and animate the changes. Let's start by collecting the data we want to show:

```
function updateCircle(toShow) {
    // get the data for all the Firms
    var filtered = loadedData.filter(filterData(toShow));
    var totalFirms = filtered.reduce(function (total, el) {return total +
+el.count}, 0);

    // define the individual arc segments
    var pie = d3.pie()
        .sort(null)
        .padAngle(0.04)
        .value(function (d) {
            return +d.count;
        });

    // create the arcs segments, the data property of the arcs[i]
represents data.
    var arcs = pie(filtered);
    ...
}
```

In this section, we pass the data we loaded from the CSV file through a filter (`loadedData.filter(filterData(toShow))`), which filters out the data specified by the `toShow` argument. We won't show the implementation of the `filterData` function, since it is just plain JavaScript. If you're interested, look at the source code: `<DVD3/src/chapter-02/D02-01.js>`. We also calculate the total number of firms for this group that needs to be shown, which we'll use later on to calculate the percentage that we show in the center of the donut when you hover the mouse over a segment of the donut. The interesting part in the code is the `d3.pie()` function. Previously, we saw the `d3.arc()` function, which allows us to create a single donut segment. The `d3.pie()` function allows us to generate `startAngle`, `endAngle`, and `paddingAngle` based on the provided data, which we can then pass to a `d3.arc()` function. The `d3.pie()` function also can sort the data by passing in a function to sort (we use `null` for no sorting).

The d3.pie() function needs a numeric value to determine the angles. Since our data is in an object, we use the value function to return the count property of our data. This will help the d3.pie() function return the correct angles. After defining the pie, we use it by passing in our filtered data. The result from this (the arcs variable), is just a JavaScript array containing angles:

```
⊘  ▽  top                              ▼  ☐ Preserve log

  ▼ [Object, Object, Object, Object, Object, Object] 🔲
    ▼ 0: Object
      ▶ data: Object
        endAngle: 0.5756413760575728
        index: 0
        padAngle: 0.04
        startAngle: 0
        value: 481981
      ▶ __proto__: Object
    ▼ 1: Object
      ▶ data: Object
        endAngle: 1.4198897082199782
        index: 1
        padAngle: 0.04
```

The cool thing about the d3.pie() function is that we can now bind the arcs variable and use that to create our individual donut segments. Before we start animating them, we'll first just add them normally:

```
var arcElements = pieContainer.selectAll(".arc").data(arcs);

// handle the elements
arcElements.enter()
    .append("path")
    .attr("class", "arc")
    .style("fill", function (d, i) { return colors(i) })
    .merge(arcElements)
    .attr("d", arc)
```

Nothing new here. We just select all the elements with the class .arc and bind the configuration (arcs) generated by d3.pie() function using the data() function. To render a donut segment, we create a path element, set the fill based on the color interpolator we saw earlier, and generate the d attribute (which represents the SVG path), by calling the arc function (this is called with each of the elements from the generated arcs array). The result is a set of donut segments:

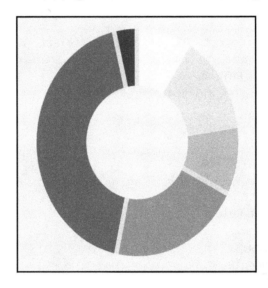

Now, let's see what we need to change to animate the donut segments instead of just specifying the d attribute directly. First, we'll show the code, and then explain the various parts:

```
// remove .attr("d", arc) and replace with
arcElements.enter()
    .append("path")
    .attr("class", "arc")
    .style("fill", function (d, i) { return colors(i) })
    .merge(arcElements)
    .transition()
    .ease(d3.easeCircle)
    .duration(2000)
    .attrTween("d", tweenArcs);

function tweenArcs(d) {
    var interpolator = getArcInterpolator(this, d);
    return function (t) {
        return arc(interpolator(t));
    };
```

```
    }

    function getArcInterpolator(el, d) {
        var oldValue = el._oldValue;
        var interpolator = d3.interpolate({
            startAngle: oldValue ? oldValue.startAngle : 0,
            endAngle: oldValue ? oldValue.endAngle : 0
        }, d);
        el._oldValue = interpolator(0);
        return interpolator;
    }
```

In this piece of code, you can see that we replaced the attr("d", arc) function call with a transition call. A transition manages the animation from one state to another. So, in our case, it allows us to transition the size of a donut segment. Transition in itself is a very big subject, so we'll show it in more detail in later chapters. The following table shows the most important transition-related API calls:

Operation	Description
<sel>.transition([name]])	Create a new transition on the selection <sel>. Optionally, you can specify a name that can be used to reference this transition later on. If no name is specified, null is used.
<sel>.interrupt([name])	Interrupt the transition on this selection with the specified name. If no name is specified, null is used.
<trans>.transition()	If you've created a transition, you can queue another transition using this call. This transition will be started when transition <trans> is finished. The new transition will use the same duration, name, and easing as the original transition.
<trans>.selection()	Returns the selection that belongs to the transition: <trans>.
<trans>.attr(name,value)	Transition the current value of name attribute to the specified value for the selection that belongs to the <trans> transition. Based on the type of value, an interpolator is selected. For a number, interpolateNumber is used; for a color, interpolateRgb; and for a string, interpolateString is used.

`<trans>.attr(name, value)`	See `attr`, but instead of changing the value of an attribute, this function changes a CSS style.
`<trans>.attrTween(name, value)`	If you need to change a type of value not supported by the `attr` function, you can use the `attrTween` function. This function allows you to specify an interpolator yourself.
`<trans>.styleTween(name, value)`	Same as the `attrTween` function, but allows you to change the value of a CSS style.
`<trans>.delay(value)`	Delay the start of the transition with the specified value in milliseconds.
`<trans>.duration(value)`	Set the total duration of the transition.
`<trans>.ease(value)`	Define the easing function to use when transitioning from the current value to the value specified by the `attr`, `attrTween`, `style`, or `styleTween` function. Below this table, we'll explain more about the different easing functions.

When you create a transition, you can also specify the `ease` function. An easing function defines how a value transitions from the start to the end value. If you specify `d3.linear`, the value will follow a linear path; with `d3.easeElasticInOut`, it will bounce at the beginning and the end of a transition; and D3 offers a large set of other transitions. A very easy way to see what is possible is by using the **easing explorer** (`http://bl.ocks.org/mbostock/248bac3b8e354a9103c4`):

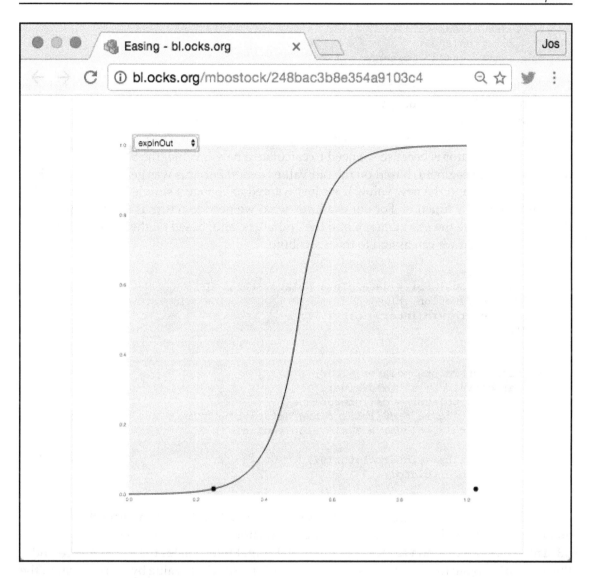

So, back to the code. Let's look a bit closer at the code that defines the transition for our donut segments:

```
arcElements.enter()
    .append("path")
    .attr("class", "arc")
    .style("fill", function (d, i) { return colors(i) })
    .merge(arcElements)
    .transition()
```

```
    .ease(d3.easeCircle)
    .duration(2000)
    .attrTween("d", tweenArcs);
```

Looking at the previous table and this code, we can see what is happening. We're creating a new transition that is executed whenever the arcElements are created or updated. In this transition, we use the d3.easeCircle easing function. It will take two seconds, and change the d attribute using a custom interpolator function (tweenArcs). The reason why we need a custom interpolator is because we need to calculate a new d value (the SVG path that draws our donut segment) based on the old value (remember, this was generated from the pie() function), and the new value. If we just wanted to change a simple value, we could have used the attr function. For our example, what we need to return is an interpolator that can interpolate the startAngle and the endAngle and, based on these values, return a new SVG path that we can assign to the d attribute:

```
function tweenArcs(d) {
    var interpolator = getArcInterpolator(this, d);
    return function (t) {
        return arc(interpolator(t));
    };
}

function getArcInterpolator(el, d) {
    var oldValue = el._oldValue;
    var interpolator = d3.interpolate({
        startAngle: oldValue ? oldValue.startAngle : 0,
        endAngle: oldValue ? oldValue.endAngle : 0
    }, d);
    el._oldValue = interpolator(0);
    return interpolator;
}
```

As you can see, our tweenArcs function takes the new data value (d) and uses that to create an interpolator with the getArcInterpolator function. This function uses the d3.interpolate function to create an interpolator that interpolates the startAngle and the endAngle. Note that we explicitly keep track of the previous value by storing that in the _oldValue property on the element itself (this). We don't directly return the interpolator created by the getArcInterpolator function, but convert the result from that interpolator to a SVG path by calling the arc(interpolator(t)) function. With this setup, we've got an interpolator that returns the correct SVG paths for our d attribute. If we add this and open the page, you can see that arcs grow to the correct sizes automatically:

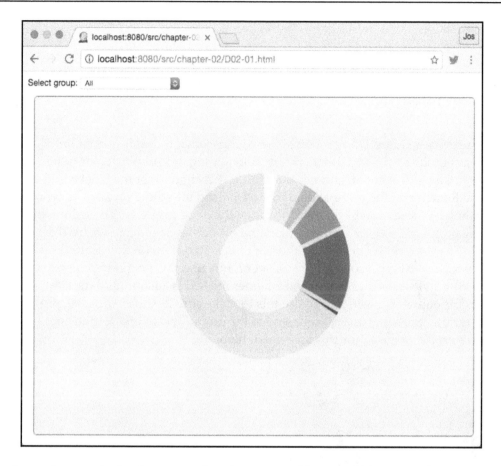

Now that we've got the basic arcs rendered, we can add some additional information that explains what this donut represents. In the next two sections, we'll use the same principles to add and animate text labels, and the lines pointing to these labels. First, we add the text labels.

Adding text legends

To add the text legends, we only need a couple of lines of JavaScript:

```
var textElements = pieContainer.selectAll(".labels").data(arcs);
textElements.enter()
    .append("text")
    .attr("class", "labels")
    .merge(textElements)
    .text( function(d) { return d.data.yearsInBusinessLabel + " (" +
```

```
d.data.count + ")" })
    .attr("dy", "0.35em" )
    .transition()
    .ease(d3.easeCircle)
    .duration(2000)
    .attrTween("transform", tweenLabels)
    .styleTween("text-anchor", tweenAnchor);
```

Here, we use the standard D3 approach of selecting elements, binding data (arcs, which are the result of the d3.pie() function call), and adding or updating elements. For the labels we add a text element, and use the text() function to set the label based on the input data. Remember, the original data that we passed into the d3.pie() function to generate the arcs array can be accessed through the data property. To position the labels, we once again use a transition with the same properties as the one we used for the donut segments. This time, however, we use the attrTween function on the transform attribute to position the labels. We also use a styleTween function for the text-anchor style. The text-anchor style is used to determine whether the text is anchored to the start, the middle, or the end of its position. We use this to make sure the text-anchor property is set to start for the text labels on the right side of the donut, and to end for the ones on the left side. The interpolators used for this are shown here:

```
var labelsArc = d3.arc()
    .outerRadius(height/2 * 0.7)
    .innerRadius(height/2 * 0.7);

function tweenLabels(d) {
    var interpolator = getArcInterpolator(this, d);
    return function (t) {
        var p = labelsArc.centroid(interpolator(t));
        var xy = p
        xy[0]= xy[0] * 1.2
        return "translate(" + xy + ")";
    };
}

function tweenAnchor(d) {
    var interpolator = getArcInterpolator(this, d);
    return function (t) {
        var x = labelsArc.centroid(interpolator(t))[0];
        return (x > 0) ? "start" : "end";
    };
}
```

As you can see, this looks very similar to the interpolator we used for the donut segments. The main change is that we use a different `arc` function. We use the `labelsArc` function to positon the text at the center of an invisible donut that is a bit larger than defined for the normal donut. We position the text at the center of each invisible donut segment using the `centroid` function to determine that position. For the `text-anchor` style, we just check whether we're on the right or left side of the donut, and either return `start` or `end`. With this code in place, we get animated text labels that move together with the donut segments:

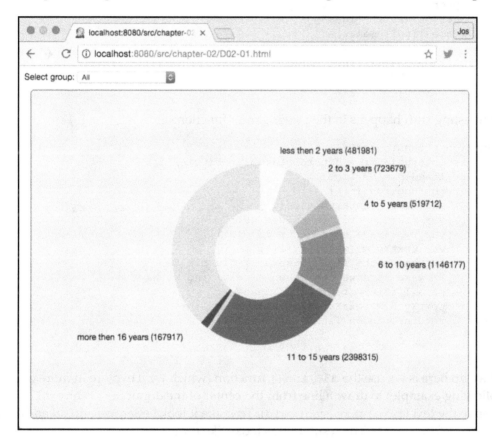

Now all that is left to do is add the lines pointing from the center of each donut segment to the start of the text elements.

Add the lines from the donut to the text

For the lines, we once again follow the same principle. We add the lines and use an `attrTween` function to determine how to draw the lines at each step of the animation:

```
// add the lines which point to the labels
var lineElements = pieContainer.selectAll(".lines").data(arcs);
lineElements.enter()
    .append("path")
    .attr("class", "lines")
    .merge(lineElements)
    .transition()
    .ease(d3.easeCircle)
    .duration(2000)
    .attrTween("d", tweenLines)
```

The interesting stuff happens in the `tweenLines` function:

```
function tweenLines(d) {
    var interpolator = getArcInterpolator(this, d);
    var lineGen = d3.line();
    return function (t) {
        var dInt = interpolator(t);
        var start = arc.centroid(dInt);
        var xy = labelsArc.centroid(dInt);
        var textXy = [xy[0],xy[1]];
        // Change the final line a little bit to
        // make sure we can tween nicely, and we have
        // a little bit of extra space
        textXy[0]= textXy[0] * 1.15
        return lineGen([start,xy,textXy]);
    }
}
```

What we do here is we use the `d3.line()` function (which we'll explore in more depth in the following example) to draw a line from the center of the donut (`arc.centroid`) to the position of the text (`labelsArc.centroid`). To make it look better, we add an additional corner just before the text. The result of this looks like this:

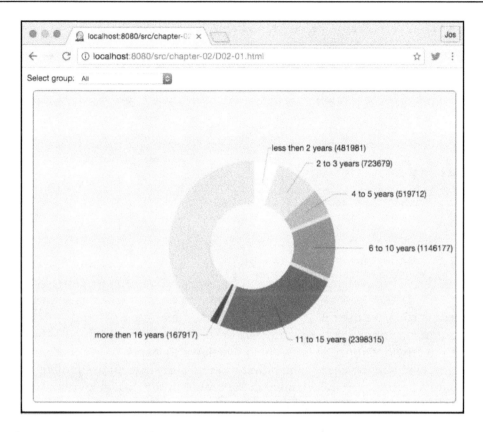

The final step we're going to take is add some interactivity to the donut.

Making the donut respond to mouse events

If you open the example in your browser, and hover your mouse over one of the donut segments, it pops out a little, and shows a percentage representing the donut segments share. Adding mouse events is very straightforward in D3:

```
var popupArc = d3.arc()
    .outerRadius(height/2 * 0.65)
    .innerRadius(height/2 * 0.3);

arcElements.enter()
    .append("path")
    .attr("class", "arc")
    .style("fill", function (d, i) { return colors(i) })
    .merge(arcElements)
    .on("mouseover", function(d) {
```

```
          d3.select(this).attr("d", function(d) {
              return popupArc(d);
          });
          var centerText = pieContainer.selectAll('.center').data([d]);
          centerText.enter()
              .append('text')
              .attr("class","center")
              .style("text-anchor","middle")
              .merge(centerText)
              .text( function(d) { return Math.round(+d.data.count /
  totalFirms * 100) + "%"});
      })
      .on("mouseout", function(d) {
          d3.select(this).attr("d", function(d) {
              return arc(d);
          });
          // remove the center text
          pieContainer.selectAll('.center').text("");
      })
```

In the preceding code, we use the `.on("mouseover", function(d)` and
`.on("mouseout", function(d)` parameters to add behavior to our donut. The code
specified in the provided function is executed whenever that specific event occurs. In the
`mouseover` case we slightly change the radius of the donut segment to simulate the pop-out
effect, and add a percentage `text` element in the center. In the `mouseout` case, we reset the
donut segment to its original size and remove the text.

> If you look at the donuts generated in the previous sections, you might
> notice that we're missing a shadow that was present in the donut shown at
> the beginning of this chapter. We've added the shadow to make it better
> looking, but this isn't standard D3 functionality. To add a shadow, we
> make use of a set of SVG filters that simulate this effect. If you want to add
> this to your own visualizations, just look at the relevant code in the source
> file for this example.

Now we've got our final donut, which animates, responds to changes in the menu, and can
respond to the mouse, we'll have a look at another standard often seen visualization: the
line chart.

Line charts that show income growth

A line chart is a very common way of visualizing linear data (for example, time-based data). For our discussion on line charts, we're going to create a chart that shows the increase in income in the US over the last 30 years. We'll show this data indexed to a specific year and the absolute growth. We'll use the following two datasets:

1. **Unadjusted dollars**: https://fred.stlouisfed.org/series/MEHOINUSA646N
2. **Adjusted dollars**: https://fred.stlouisfed.org/series/MEHOINUSA672N

These datasets are based on the US Census data, but have already been cleaned up. We can use the adjusted dollars to show the relative increase in income, and the unadjusted to show the absolute growth in income:

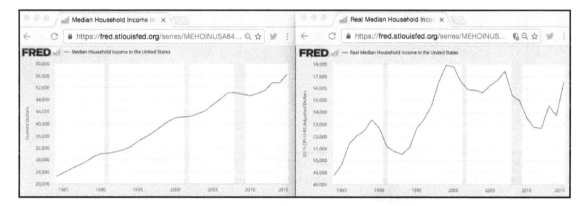

So, while it might seem that people are getting richer, at this point we're basically at the level of 1996, and in no way back before the 2008 crisis. At the top right, you can download the data in CSV format. When downloaded, we can use this data directly since it's in a very basic format:

```
DATE,MEHOINUSA672N
1984-01-01,48664
1985-01-01,49574
1986-01-01,51329
1987-01-01,51973
1988-01-01,52372
1989-01-01,53306
```

Now that we've got our data, let's look at the line graph that we'll create. The final chart that we'll create looks like this:

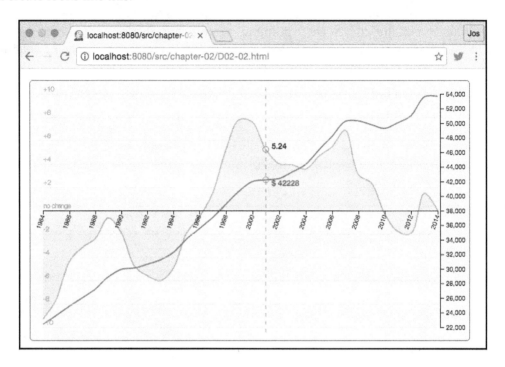

In this line chart (which you can see for yourself by opening `http://localhost:8080/src/chapter-02/D02-02.html`), you can see a line that shows the indexed income, and the absolute index. When you move your mouse over the chart, it will show the value of both graphs and highlight the exact value.

First, let's look at the different steps we need to take to accomplish this:

1. The first thing we need to do is load the data and set up the relevant D3 scales.
2. Next, we'll add the indexed line and the gradient area beneath it.
3. After that, we'll add the normal income line.
4. We've got multiple axes in this line chart. We add these next.
5. And finally, we add the mouse tracker, which highlights a specific data point.

For this chart, we'll skip the default setup of the margin and the basic chart, since we've already done that a couple of times. We'll start directly with how to load the data.

Loading the data and setting up D3 scales

For this example, we load the data slightly different than we did in the other examples. The main reason is that this time we've got two data sources we want to load instead of just one. For this, we'll use the functionality provided by the d3.queue library:

```
var yearMax = 2014;

// holds the loaded data
var adjustedData;
var unadjustedData;

// load data asynchronously, call update when done.
d3.queue()
    .defer(d3.csv, "./data/households.csv")
    .defer(d3.csv, "./data/householdsU.csv")
    .await(function (error, adjusted, unadjusted) {
        // set the data to the global variables
        adjustedData = adjusted;
        unadjustedData = unadjusted;
        // and call update
        update();
    });
```

In this code fragment you can see that we use the d3.queue() function call to load our two data sources. the households.csv file contains the indexed income, and the householdsU.csv file contains the unadjusted income. With the defer function, we queue the d3.csv function. The first defer function, when it is executed, will call d3.csv("./data/households.csv") function, and the second one will call the d3.csv("./data/householdsU.csv") function. Functions queued with the defer function will be executed (in parallel), when the await function is called. The await function takes a callback function as its argument, which is called when both resources have finished loading. In this callback, we just assign the incoming data to a global variable, and call the update() function.

This update() function looks like this:

```
function update(year) {

    year = year || yearMax;
```

```
    var yearIndex = (adjustedData.length - 1) - (yearMax - year);
    var adjustedIndexedData = adjustedData.map(function(d)
    {
        return mapToindexed(d, adjustedData[yearIndex])
    });
    var unadjustedCleaned = unadjustedData.map(mapToIncome);

    var maxAbove = Math.abs(100 - d3.max(adjustedIndexedData, function(d)
    {
        return d.indexed
    }));
    var maxBelow = Math.abs(100 - d3.min(adjustedIndexedData, function(d)
    {
        return d.indexed
    }));
    var xRangeAdjusted = Math.ceil(Math.max(maxAbove, maxBelow));

    var xScale = d3.scaleLinear().range([0, width]).domain([1984,2014]);

    var yIndexedScale = d3.scaleLinear()
        .range([height, 0]).domain([100-xRangeAdjusted,
100+xRangeAdjusted]);

    var incomeMin = d3.min(unadjustedCleaned, function (d)
    {
        return d.value
    });
    var incomeMax = d3.max(unadjustedCleaned, function (d)
    {
        return d.value
    });
    var yIncomeScale =  d3.scaleLinear()
        .range([height, 0])
        .domain([
            Math.floor(incomeMin/2000) * 2000,
            Math.ceil(incomeMax/2000) * 2000
        ]);

    addGradients(yIndexedScale);
    addArea(xScale, yIndexedScale, adjustedIndexedData);
    addIndexedLine(xScale, yIndexedScale, adjustedIndexedData);
    addIncomeLine(xScale, yIncomeScale, unadjustedCleaned)
    addAxis(yIncomeScale, yIndexedScale, xScale, xRangeAdjusted)
    addMouseTracker(xScale, yIndexedScale, yIncomeScale,
adjustedIndexedData, unadjustedCleaned);
}

  function mapToindexed(row, refRow) {
```

```
    var income = +row.MEHOINUSA672N;
    var reference = +refRow.MEHOINUSA672N;
    return { date: row.DATE.split('-')[0], indexed: (income/reference) *
100};
}

function mapToIncome(row) {
    var income = +row.MEHOINUSA646N;
    return { date: row.DATE.split('-')[0], value: income };
}
```

In this `update` function, we make some small changes to the two data arrays by calling the `map` function and changing the income column to an easier to understand name by passing it through the `mapToIndexed` and `mapToIncome` functions. Next, we set up a number of linear scales (`d3.scaleLinear`):

- `xScale`: Scales the years domain (from 1984 to 2014) to the width of the chart.
- `yIndexedScale`: Scales the `adjustedIndexedData` range (for example, 90 to 110) to the height of the chart.
- `yIncomeScale`: Scales the `unadjustedCleaned` range (for example, 22.123 to 53.453) to the `height` of the chart.

Nothing special happens here, except for one thing with the `yIncomeScale` parameter. What we do there is that we make sure the range is a multiple of 2000. We do this, so that the generated y-axis at the right side will always show the minimum and maximum value. The rest of the `update` function is divided into a number of function calls, which are explained in the following couple of sections.

Adding the index line and area gradients

We'll look at the first couple of functions we called in the `update` function: the `addGradients`, `addArea`, and `addGradients` function.

When you run the code with just these functions, you'll see the following:

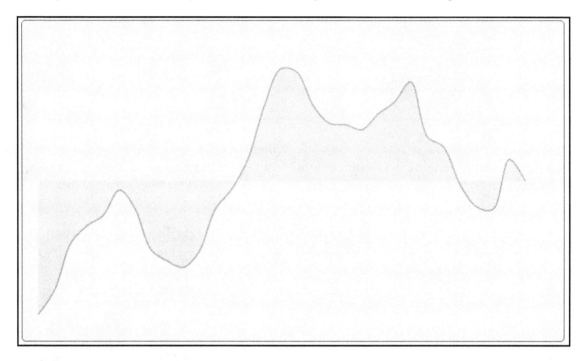

In this figure, you can see that we've got a colored gradient between the lines, and the lines themselves are also colored. To get these colors, we need to define two gradients, which we can later add as the `stroke` for the line and the `fill` for the area. These gradients are SVG gradients (a topic for a book in itself), on which you can find more information here: https://developer.mozilla.org/en-US/docs/Web/SVG/Tutorial/Gradients. What we do in the following code is create two linear gradients based on the `yIndexed` scale:

```
function addGradients(yIndexed) {

    var rangeMax = yIndexed.invert(0);
    var rangeMin = yIndexed.invert(height);

    chart.append("linearGradient")
        .attr("id", "area-gradient")
        .attr("gradientUnits", "userSpaceOnUse")
        .attr("x1", 0).attr("y1", yIndexed(100+xRangeAdjusted))
        .attr("x2", 0).attr("y2", yIndexed(100-xRangeAdjusted))
        .selectAll("stop")
        .data([
            {offset: "0%", color: "#E5F2D7"},
            {offset: "50%", color: "#eee"},
```

```
            {offset: "100%", color: "#EFDBE3"}
        ])
        .enter().append("stop")
        .attr("offset", function(d) { return d.offset; })
        .attr("stop-color", function(d) { return d.color; });

    // For the line gradient we do almost the same
    ...
        .data([
            {offset: "0", color: "#97D755"},
            {offset: "0.5", color: "#97D755"},
            {offset: "0.5", color: "#CD94AB"},
            {offset: "1", color: "#CD94AB"}
        ])
    ...
}
```

We'll skip over most of the code, since it's really SVG gradients internals. We use the x1, x2, y1, and y2 attributes the set the size of the gradient to the size of line we want to draw and use the data function to generate the stop points of the gradient. A stop point defines a color at a certain percentage in the gradient. SVG will calculate the required in-between colors. If we apply these gradients to a rectangle, you'd get something like this:

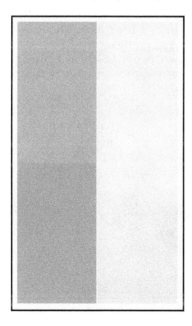

And as you can see, this lines up perfectly with the colors we want for the area beneath the indexed income line and maps to the color of the indexed line. With the colors managed, let's look at how we can draw the lines and the area. We do this in two steps. First, we add the area, and on top of the area we draw our indexed income line.

```
function addArea(xScale, yIndexedScale, adjustedIndexedData) {
    var area = d3.area()
        .x1(function(d) { return xScale(d.date); })
        .y1(function(d) { return yIndexedScale(d.indexed); })
        .x0(function(d) { return xScale(d.date); })
        .y0(function(d) { return yIndexedScale(100); })
        .curve(d3.curveCatmullRom.alpha(0.5));

    chart.append("path")
        .attr("d", area(adjustedIndexedData))
        .style("fill", "url(#area-gradient)");
}
```

To create the SVG string to assign to the d attribute of a path element, we use the d3.area function. To specify the area that needs to be filled, we define two lines. The area between these two lines is filled. So, in our case we draw an horizontal line in the center of the line graph (where the index is 100). In the preceding code that line is defined by the x0 and y0 functions. We also draw the curved line, which is drawn through our data points. This second line is defined by the x1 and y1 functions. The following figure shows what these lines would like when drawn as normal lines:

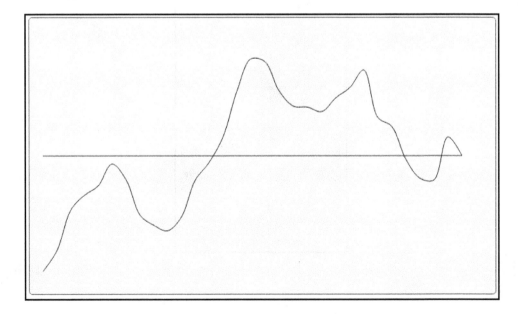

If we now call the `area()` function with our data, the area between the lines shown in the previous figure will be filled with the `fill` defined by the style function. In this case, we point to the gradient we defined earlier. The syntax to do that is `url(#name-of-gradient)`. If you look back at the code, you might see we skipped over the `curve` function. With this function, we define how the data points (generated by the `x0`, `y0`, `x1`, and `y1`) are combined into a line. D3 provides different interpolation functions to draw the curve. The following figure shows different approaches:

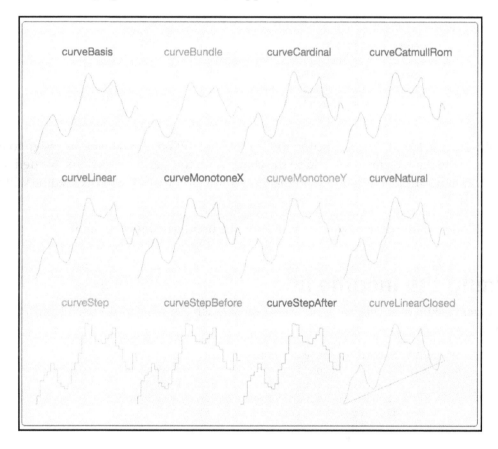

Most of these curves also allow specific configuration (for example, you can also close them by connecting the last point to the first one). More information on this can be found in the D3 API description on curves:

`https://github.com/d3/d3-shape/blob/master/README.md#curves`.

Now that we have the area, we also draw an additional line on top of this area to better show the values. If you look closely at the following code, you'll see it looks a lot like the code we used to add the area:

```
function addIndexedLine(xScale, yIndexedScale, adjustedIndexedData) {
    var line = d3.line()
        .x(function(d) { return xScale(d.date); })
        .y(function(d) { return yIndexedScale(d.indexed); })
        .curve(d3.curveCatmullRom.alpha(0.5));

    chart
        .append("path")
        .attr("d", line(adjustedIndexedData))
        .style("fill", "none")
        .style("stroke", "url(#line-gradient)")
        .style("stroke-width", "2");
}
```

For a line we use the d3.line function to generate the SVG path that we can assign to the d attribute of the path element we add to the chart. With the x and y functions, we define the points that make up this line, and with the curve function we define what the line will look like.

With the indexed line drawn, we can next draw the unadjusted income line.

Adding the income line

We'll quickly skim over this code, since it's pretty much the same as we used to add the indexed line:

```
function addIncomeLine(xScale, yIncomeScale, unadjustedCleaned) {
    var lineIncome = d3.line()
        .x(function(d) { return xScale(d.date); })
        .y(function(d) { return yIncomeScale(d.value); })
        .curve(d3.curveCatmullRom.alpha(0.5));

    chart.append("path")
        .attr("d", lineIncome(unadjustedCleaned))
        .style("fill", "none")
        .style("stroke", "steelblue")
        .style("stroke-width", "2");
}
```

The main change here is that we don't use a gradient for the `stroke` but use a fixed color. The chart at this point looks like this:

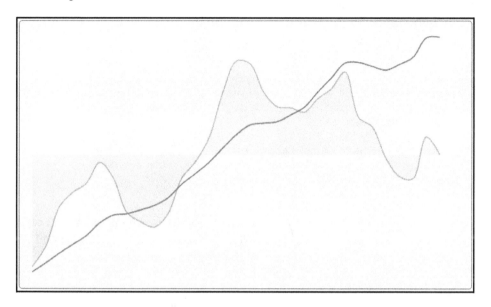

At this point we have visualized the data, but the chart doesn't really look nice yet, and we don't know what the different lines really mean. We'll add this information using a couple of axes.

Adding the axes

In the chart, we've got three axes:

- On the left side, we show the relative change from the income in 2014.
- On the right side, we show the absolute income.
- In the middle, we have an axis showing the years.

Besides that, we also have a number of thin lines shown at two index point intervals. First off, let's see what needs to be done to add the axis that shows the years.

Adding an x-axis with years

The first thing we need to do is add an axis that will show the years. We do this with the `addAxis` function:

```
function addAxis(yIncomeScale, yIndexedScale, xScale, xRangeAdjusted) {
    ...
    var bottomAxis = d3.axisBottom().scale(xScale).ticks(15,"f");
    var bottomAxisChart = chart.append("g")
        .attr('transform', 'translate( 0 ' + yIndexedScale(100) +  ')')
        .call(bottomAxis);

        bottomAxisChart.selectAll('text')
        .attr("transform", "translate(-16 14) rotate(-70)");
    ...
}
```

For the center axis, we use the `d3.axisBottom` function to create an axis based on our `xScale`. With the `ticks` function, we specify that we want to have 15 ticks (one for every two years), and we want to format the ticks with a **fixed point** notation (`f`).

D3 has an additional module that can be used to format numbers. You can use this library to specify scientific, fixed point, binary, octal, and many other types of notation. Besides notation types, it also contains a large set of other format options to make sure the number output looks exactly as you want. In this book, we'll not dive into the details of the different options. You can look at the excellent D3 API documentation to see what is possible: `https://github.com/d3/d3-format#locale_format`.

After defining the axis, we add it to a specific group, which we position at the center of the graph by setting the `transform` property and translating this element using `yIndexedScale(100)` to position it in the vertical center of the chart. The last thing we do is that we change the position of the `text` element of the axis so that they are rotated and moved a little bit (`translate(-16 14) rotate(-70)`). We do this to avoid the labels overlapping with the axis on the right side.

Next, we add the axis on the right side.

Adding a y-axis with absolute income

For this axis, we don't do anything special:

```
function addAxis(yIncomeScale, yIndexedScale, xScale, xRangeAdjusted) {
    ...
    var rightAxis = d3.axisRight().scale(yIncomeScale).ticks(20);
    var rightAxisSVG = chart.append("g")
        .attr('transform', 'translate( ' + (width + 4) + ')')
        .call(rightAxis);
    ...
}
```

We just create d3.axisRight based on the yIncomeScale, and ask for twenty ticks. When we add this axis, we position the axis using the transform attribute and position it a little bit farther to the right to leave some room for the labels of the x-axis.

The axis on the left side will take some more work, since we're going to customize that a bit.

Adding the y-axis with the index values and the horizontal marker lines

We've seen how we've already the x-axis and one of the y-axes. The final axis is the one showing the index values:

```
function addAxis(yIncomeScale, yIndexedScale, xScale, xRangeAdjusted) {
    ...
    var steps = d3.range(100-xRangeAdjusted, 100+xRangeAdjusted + 1, 2);
    var leftAxis = d3.axisLeft().scale(yIndexedScale).tickValues(steps);
    var leftAxisSVG = chart.append("g")
        .attr('transform', 'translate( 0 ' + yIndexedScale(100 +
xRangeAdjusted) + ')')
        .call(leftAxis);

    leftAxisSVG.selectAll('text')
        .text(function(d) {
            return d === 100 ? "no change" : d3.format("+")(d - 100);
        })
        .attr("stroke", "#aaa")
        .attr("dy", "-0.5em")
        .attr("dx", "1em")
        .style("font-weight", "100")
        .attr("text-anchor", "start");

    leftAxisSVG.selectAll('.domain').remove();
```

```
leftAxisSVG.selectAll('.tick line')
    .attr("x1", width)
    .attr("stroke", "#ddd")
    .attr("opacity", "0.6");
...
}
```

The first thing we do here is define the number of ticks we want to show. We use the
d3.range function for this, which returns an array from 100-xRangeAdjusted (90) to
100+xRangeAdjusted+1 (111), with a gap of two. So, in this case we get back an array with
values: 90, 92, 94 ... 108, 110. We use these values as parameters of the
tickValues function when we create the axis. This means we get steps.length ticks,
where each tick has its data set to the corresponding value from the steps array. Next, we
append the axis to the chart and position it correctly. However, we're not done yet. We next
select all the text elements of this axis, and change the text using d3.format. Negative
values will have a – prepended, and positive ones a +. If the value is 100, we set the tick
text to no change. At the same time, we also set some text styles to property format the text
(note that we've also could have done this directly through CSS). The final step we take here
is adding the horizontal marker lines. For this, we first remove the vertical axis (which can
be found by selecting the domain class), and after that we change the width, stroke, and
opacity of the ticks to transform them to the horizontal marker lines.

At this point, the complete chart is drawn, and by using the axis we can understand what
this chart represents:

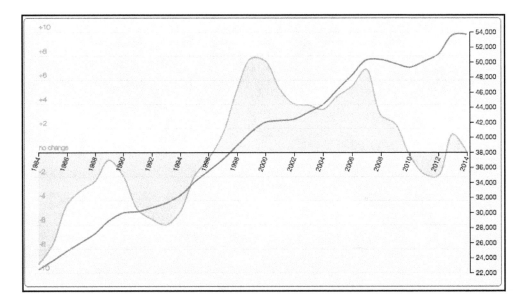

In the last section, we're going to add some interactivity to this chart.

Tracking the mouse

As a last step, we'll add the mouse support that highlights the data points, shows the values at that specific year, and adds a vertical line to make things more clear:

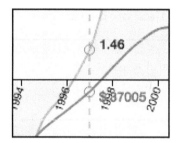

We do this in two steps. First, we create all the elements that make up the line and the markers, and after that we add a mouse listener, which will show these elements in the correct positions. Let's look at the elements:

```
function addMouseTracker(xScale, yIndexedScale, yIncomeScale,
adjustedIndexedData, unadjustedCleaned) {

    ...
    var focus = chart.append("g").attr("class", "focus").style("display",
"none");
        focus.append("circle").attr("id", "indexCircle").attr("r", 4.5);
        focus.append("circle").attr("id", "incomeCircle").attr("r", 4.5);
        focus.append("text").attr("id", "indexText").attr("x",
9).attr("dy", ".35em");
        focus.append("text").attr("id", "incomeText").attr("x",
9).attr("dy", ".35em");

    var verticalLineP = d3.line()([[0,-10],[0,height+10]]);
focus.append("path")
        .attr("d", verticalLineP)
        .attr("class", "verLine")
        .attr("stroke", "grey")
        .attr("stroke-dasharray", "6,6")
        .attr("stroke-width", "1");

    chart.append("rect")
        .attr("class", "overlay")
        .attr("width", width)
```

```
        .attr("height", height)
        .on("mouseover", function() { focus.style("display", null); })
        .on("mouseout", function() { focus.style("display", "none"); })
        .on("mousemove", mousemove);


    ...

}
```

We first add a group, which we hide (display: none), to which we add two circles, two text elements, and a vertical line. These are the elements we'll show when we move the mouse over the chart. We also add a rectangle that completely covers the chart. To this rectangle, we add our mouse listeners. As you can see, when we enter this rectangle, the focus g element becomes visible, and when we move out of the rectangle, the g element is hidden again. The interesting code, however, is in the mousemove() function:

```
function mousemove() {
    var x0 = xScale.invert(d3.mouse(this)[0])
    var xToShow = Math.round(x0);
    var d = adjustedIndexedData[xToShow-1984];
    var dIncome = unadjustedCleaned[xToShow-1984];
    var xPos = xScale(xToShow);
    var yIncomePos = yIncomeScale(dIncome.value);
    var yIndexPos = yIndexedScale(d.indexed);

    focus.select("#indexCircle").attr("transform", "translate(" + xPos +
"," + yIndexPos + ")");
    focus.select("#incomeCircle").attr("transform", "translate(" + xPos +
"," + yIncomePos + ")");
    focus.select(".verLine").attr("transform", "translate(" + xPos + "," +
0 + ")");

    var textOffset = (yIncomePos < yIndexPos) ? 5 : -5;

    focus.select("#indexText")
        .attr("transform", "translate(" + xPos + "," +
(yIndexedScale(d.indexed) + textOffset) + ")")
        .text(Math.round((d.indexed-100)*100)/100);
    focus.select("#incomeText")
        .attr("transform", "translate(" + xPos + "," +
(yIncomeScale(dIncome.value) - textOffset) + ")")
        .text("$ " + dIncome.value);

}
```

In this code, the following steps are taken whenever we move the mouse over the chart:

1. We get the positon of the mouse inside the rectangle we defined, and get the value of x from that position (`d3.mouse(this)[0]`). With this x position, we can determine the year we're working with by using the `xScale.invert` function. So, at this point we know which year corresponds to the position of the mouse.
2. Next, we get the relevant data (`d` and `dIncome`). With the year and these two values we can get the exact x and y positions of the data elements belonging to the year on the two lines: `xPos`, `yIncomePos`, and `yIndexPos`.
3. Now that we have the positions, we move the circles and line we created to those positions.
4. Finally, we move the text elements to the correct positions and set their values to the correct values.

And that's it. With this mouse listener added, we have a line and a set of circles that move to the correct points on the line whenever we move the mouse on the chart.

Population growth estimates using a stacked graph

For the final chart in this chapter, we're going to create a simple stacked chart, which shows the expected population growth in the US to 2060. We won't create too much interactivity or other advanced features for this graph, but will just show you how to create the following two graphs:

First, we'll create an area chart:

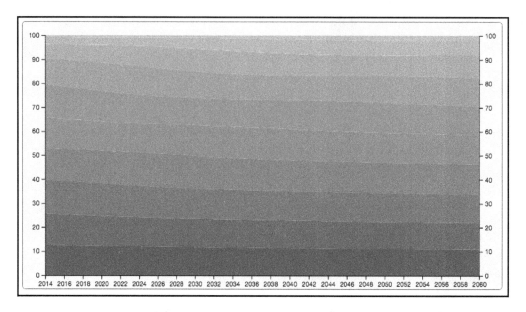

And then we'll use the same data to create a stacked bar chart:

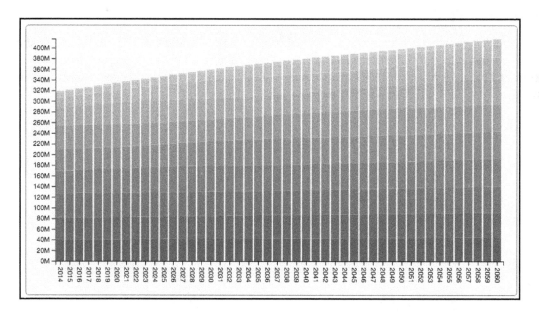

In the area chart we'll show the relative population distribution over the years, and in the bar chart, we'll show the absolute population, divided into age groups.

Getting and sanitizing the data

The US Census Bureau provides a number of files related to population growth and other projections. We'll use the CSV file you can find at this link:
`http://www.census.gov/population/projections/files/downloadables/NP2014_D1.csv`. There is also an accompanying document explaining the file structure available, which you can download from here:
`http://www.census.gov/population/projections/files/filelayout/NP2014_D1.pdf`.

Let's look at the data that is in there:

```
origin,race,sex,year,total_pop,pop_0,pop_1...
0,0,0,2014,318748017,3971847,3957864...
0,0,0,2015,321368864,4000831,3988161...
```

What you can see here is that we've got data that can be organized by `origin` (0 is *total*, 1 is *Not Hispanic*, and 2 is *Hispanic*), by `race` (0 is *all*, 1 is *White*, 2 is *Black*, and so on) and by `sex` (0, 1 is *Male* and 2 is *Female*). For each of these combinations we can get the total population, which is then further divided into the part of the population that has a specific age.

For this example, we'll just get the data where the first three columns are 0. So, we'll take the data for all origins, all races, and both sexes. Furthermore, we'll group the ages together so that we've got 11 groups: 0-9, 10-19, 20-29, and so on until we reach 90 and older. We'll write another small D3-based script to simplify this data so that we don't need to process 3 MB for our visualization.

In the `<DVD3>/src/chapter-02/data` directory, you can find a `cleanPopulation.js` script that cleans up the data:

```
var d3 = require('d3');
var fs = require('fs');

fs.readFile('./NP2014_D1.csv', function (err, fileData) {
    var rows = d3.csvParse(fileData.toString());

    var allPopulation = rows.filter(function (row) {
        return row['origin'] === '0'
            && row['race'] === '0'
            && row['sex'] === '0';
    });
```

```
        var mapped = allPopulation.map(function(row) {
            var populationGrouped = {};
            for (var i = 0 ; i < 10 ; i++) {
                var sum = 0;
                for (var j = 0 ; j < 10 ; j++) {
                    var indexName = i * 10 + j;
                    sum += +row['pop_' + indexName]
                }
                // for the last row we explicitly need to add the `pop_100`
                if (i == 9) sum += +row['pop_100'];
                populationGrouped.year = row.year;

            }

            populationGrouped[i] = sum;
            populationGrouped.total = row.total_pop;
            return populationGrouped;
        });

        fs.writeFile('./populationFiltered.csv',d3.csvFormat(mapped));
    });
```

In this script, we add the age population totals together in groups of ten years, and finally write the data to the `populationFiltered.csv` file. After running `node ./cleanBusinesses.js`, we've got data in the following format:

```
0,1,2,3,4,5,6,7,8,9,year
40419482,41715720,44901696,41419433,41411749,44054508,33905105,18995755,958
7628,2336941,2014
40427758,41681751,45213477,42005558,40994700,44122655,35187055,19626018,968
0443,2429449,2015
```

Each number contains the totals for that specific age group (for example, the 0 column is the data from zero to nine years).

Creating the stacked area chart

We've got two charts that use the same approach for creating the stacked data. The first one we'll look at is the area chart. We'll skip how the data is loaded, how the basic chart is set up, and how the axis are added, since we've done that a couple of times already:

```
{
    ... // setup and data loading isn't shown.. data is in the data
    variable

    var scaleX = d3.scaleLinear().domain([0, data.length-1]).range([0,
```

```
width]);
    var scaleY = d3.scaleLinear().domain([0, 100]).range([height, 0]);
    var scaleC = function(i) {return d3.interpolateWarm(i/9)};

    // we've got 10 year groups, right value is not inclusive
    var stack = d3.stack().keys(d3.range(0,10));
    var series = stack(data);

    var area = d3.area()
        .x(function(d, i) { return scaleX(i); })
        .y0(function(d) { return scaleY(asPercentage(d,d[0])); })
        .y1(function(d) { return scaleY(asPercentage(d,d[1])); });

    var serieG = chart.selectAll("g").data(series).enter().append("g");
    serieG.append("path")
        .style("fill", function(d) { return scaleC(d.key); })
        .attr("d", area);

    ... // adding axis isn't shown.
}

function asPercentage(row, value) {
    return (value/row.data.total * 100);
}
```

For the stacked area chart, we once again start with setting up the scales. We use a `d3.scaleLinear` function for the x and the y positions, and a simple interpolator wrapped around `d3.interpolateWarm` to determine the color for each age group. Next, we use the `d3.stack()` function to split our data into the series we want to stack. With the `keys` function we define the **key** that is used to group. In our case, our data looks like this:

```
0: 40427758
1: 41681751
2: 45213477
3: 42005558
4: 40994700
5: 44122655
6: 35187055
7: 19626018
8: 9680443
9: 2429449
total: 321368864
year: 2015
```

The keys of our data is an array with values from 0 to 9. So when we call
`d3.stack().keys(d3.range(0,10))` a stack is created which will group our data based
on these keys. Now when we call `stack(data)`, we'll get an array with ten elements, one
for each key. Each of these elements itself is also an array with 47 elements, one for each
row we passed in (so in our case, each of these 47 elements represents a single year). These
47 values contain the values from the row, but stored in a stacked format. This is easier to
explain by looking at the data. Let's look at the data for the first year:

```
> series[0][0]
  [0, 40419482]
> series[1][0]
  [40419482, 82135202]
> series[2][0]
  [82135202, 127036898]
> series[3][0]
  [127036898, 168456331]
```

In this screenshot, you can see that by calling `stack(data)`, D3 returns data that is already
stacked. The data for the first three series is returned nicely sequenced, and we can now use
the values to draw our chart using the area function:

```
var area = d3.area()
    .x(function(d, i) { return scaleX(i); })
    .y0(function(d) { return scaleY(asPercentage(d,d[0])); })
    .y1(function(d) { return scaleY(asPercentage(d,d[1])); });
```

You may remember from earlier in this chapter that the area is drawn using two lines. Here,
both lines use the same function for the x value (hence no separate x0 and x1 functions),
and base their y0 and y1 values on the first and second elements of an array. So, if we pass
in each of our series arrays (remember, these have 47 elements, which are arrays with the
two values we need), we can draw our area chart:

```
var serieG = chart.selectAll("g").data(series).enter().append("g");
serieG.append("path")
    .style("fill", function(d) { return scaleC(d.key); })
    .attr("d", area);
```

So, with this code, we add 10 g elements, in which we add a `path` element that represents our area. Each array of 47 elements is passed on to `area` function to create the SVG path. When you create the series using the `stack(data)` function, D3 also adds the `key` and `index` value to the resulting series. We use this `key` value to get the color we want for the fill.

In the next section, we'll use this same approach to create the stacked bar chart.

Creating the stacked bar chart

Just like we did for the previous example, we'll skip over loading the data and setting up the basic chart. In the following code snippet, you can see the steps we take to render the bar chart from the same data as we used in the area chart:

```
var scaleX = d3.scaleBand()
    .domain(data.map(function(d) {return d.year}))
    .range([0, width])
    .padding(0.15);

var scaleY = d3.scaleLinear().domain([0, d3.max(data, function(d) {return
d.total})]).range([height, 0]);

var scaleC = function(i) {return d3.interpolateCool(i/10)};
var stack = d3.stack().keys(d3.range(0,10));
var series = stack(data);

// append a g element for all the years.
var serieG = chart.selectAll("g").data(series)
    .enter().append("g")
    .attr("fill", function(d) { return scaleC(d.key); })
    .selectAll("rect").data(function(d) {return d})
    .enter().append("rect")
    .attr("x", function(d) { return scaleX(d.data.year); })
    .attr("y", function(d) { return scaleY(d[1]); })
    .attr("height", function(d)
    {
        return scaleY(d[0]) - scaleY(d[1]);
    })
    .attr("width", scaleX.bandwidth());
```

We start by setting up the scales again. `scaleY` and `scaleC` are the same as in the previous example. For `scaleX`, however, we use a different one: d3.scaleBand. With d3.scaleBand we can divide up the range into a set of bands that are evenly spaced. This is best explained by the following image (from `https://github.com/d3/d3-scale`):

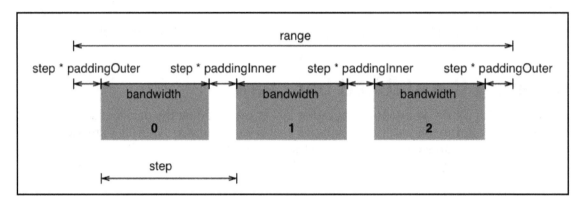

Here, you can see that instead of just dividing up the `range`, we can use it to create evenly spaced bands. In our case, we set all our available years as the domain, and set a slight spacing between the bands using the `padding` function. We'll use this scale to draw the individual rectangles that make up the stacked bar chart. We define the `series` in the same manner as we did previously, and use these `series` (remember, this is an array of 10 elements, one for each key, which contains 47 elements for each year) to create 10 g elements, and we set the `fill` property of these created elements to a color using the `scaleC` interpolator. Next, we're ready to create the individual `rect` elements for each series. For this, we use the `data` function to bind the array of 47 elements, and for the elements in that array, we create `rect`. We position the individual rectangles using the `scaleX` and `scaleY` scales, and set the height based on the data created by the `stack` function. Each rectangle's width is defined by the d3.scaleBand function we created earlier. By calling `scaleX.bandWidth()`, we get the correct size for the width of the rectangle.

Summary

In this chapter, we've looked at how you can use D3 to create basic chart types with lots of interactivity and information. While doing this, we learned a number of different D3 concepts. We've seen how we can use path generators to generate our arc segments for the donut chart and how you can add animations by using `d3.transition`.

In this chapter, we've also seen how easy it is with D3 to add axes to your chart, and how you can use the various scales provided by D3 to determine the size and position of your elements.

In the next chapter, we'll look at how you can visualize data that is in a hierarchical format.

3
Working with Hierarchical Data

In the previous chapter, we created some basic visualizations, a donut, a line chart, and some area charts. The data we visualized was rather simple, with no dependencies between the various data elements. In this chapter, we're going to look at how to visualize a different kind of data structure: hierarchical data. With hierarchical data, the data can be represented as a **tree** of data elements, where elements can have **parent** nodes and **child** nodes. D3 provides several different ways we can visualize this data. In this chapter, we're going to explore the following subjects:

- We're going to start by visualizing hierarchical data as a simple horizontal tree. Besides just showing the data, we'll also show you how you can **zoom** and **pan** around the visualization using standard D3 functionality.
- One of the disadvantages of using a standard horizontal tree to visualize data is that it can quickly become hard to read when you've got a deeply nested tree with lots of branches and leaves. An alternative way to visualize a hierarchical data structure is by creating a **radial** tree. In a radial tree, the data is projected into a circular representation. The second example will focus on creating such a radial tree, and we'll also show how to animate such a data visualization.
- Tree-based visualizations are great for visualizing the structure of a set of hierarchical data, but aren't a great fit when there is additional quantitative data at the nodes you'd like to visualize. For this, a **treemap** is often a better choice. We'll show you how to use the treemap and **partition** layouts provided by D3 to visualize a tree structure that has an additional quantitative dimension you want to represent.
- The final visualization we show in this chapter is an alternative to the treemap and pack visualizations called the **pack** layout. With the pack layout, we create a set of enclosing circles that represent the structure of the data, and where the size of the circles can be used to visualize the data's quantitative dimension.

The first one we'll focus on is the tree-based visualization.

Tree-based visualizations

While looking at data to use for this section, I stumbled upon a couple of samples where the **tree of life** was visualized. The tree of life contains a complete (or partial) taxonomy of all the living organisms in the world, from the smallest bacteria to apes and humans. The following image nicely shows what such a visualization could look like (from http://www.botany.wisc.edu/):

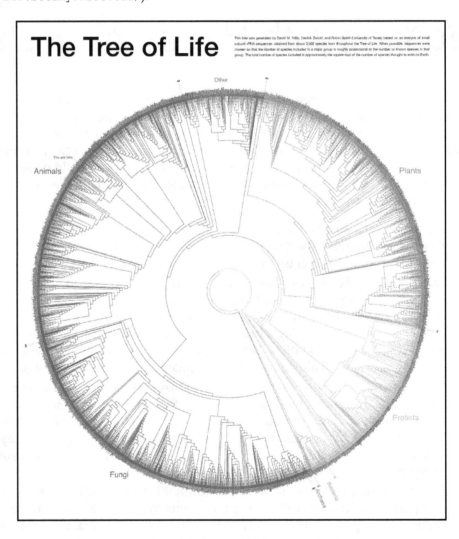

While this data is well-suited for visualizing in a tree, finding data in a form that can be visualized like this is a bit more difficult. Eventually, I found the **Integrated Taxonomic Information System** (**ITIS**), which provides much of the raw data for the **Encyclopedia of Life** (`http://www.eol.org`). While the Encyclopedia of Life provides a nice view on this data, it doesn't allow you to download trees or associated data. Luckily though, ITIS provides access to the raw data, and also allows you to download complete trees.

For this section on trees, we're going to use the hierarchy for felidae (or, in English: cats) to create a number of tree-based visualizations.

Getting and sanitizing the data

If you go to the ITIS website, you can find taxonomies for all different kinds of animal groups. For the felidae tree, open the following link:
`http://www.itis.gov/servlet/SingleRpt/SingleRpt?search_topic=TSN&search_value=1` `80580`.

At the top of the screen, you can find a download button, which allows you to download a | separated file. The contents of the file look like this:

```
...
[TU]|180581||Lynx|||||||valid||TWG standards
met|complete|2006|0|199...|552363
[TU]|180582||Lynx||rufus||||||valid||TWG standards
met|||0|1996-06-13...|180581
[TU]|180583||Lynx||rufus||rufus||||valid||TWG standards met|||0|1996-
...|180582
[TU]|180584||Lynx||lynx||||||valid||TWG standards met|||0|1996-06-13
...|180581
[TU]|180585||Lynx||canadensis||||||valid||TWG standards met|||0|1996-
...|180581
[TU]|180586||Felis|||||||valid||TWG standards
met|complete|2006|0|19...|552363
[TU]|180587||Felis||concolor||||||invalid|original name/combination|T...|0
...
```

We'll ignore most of the data and focus on the second row, which is the unique ID of that specific cat. The columns that follow the ID make up the taxonomy path, and we'll only process entries that have a `valid` value (column 12). In a column later in the data we also have a reference to the row's parent (column 19), so we'll also extract that one. So, for instance, in the preceding data, we have the following tree:

```
+-- lynx
|    +-- canadensis
|    +-- lynx
|    +-- rufus
|         +-- rufus
```

If you look further down this file, you can also find an `English` name for these elements:

```
[VR]||20776|bobcats|180581|English|N|
[VR]||111800|Bobcat|180582|English|N|
[VR]||86485|bobcat|180583|English|N|
[VR]||111798|Eurasian Lynx|180584|English|N|
[VR]||20778|lynx|180585|English|N|
[VR]||20756|small cats|180586|English|N|
[VR]||20760|mountain lion|180587|English|N|
```

Now we want to combine this data into a simple-to-use format for D3. We'll output the data in a format like this:

```
id,parentId,name,description
180580,,Felidae,cats
180581,552363,Lynx,lynxes
180582,180581,rufus,Bobcat
180583,180582,rufus,bobcat
180584,180581,lynx,Eurasian Lynx
180585,180581,canadensis,Canada lynx
```

Here, we list the ID of the node, the ID of a parent (and `''` for the root), and its name and description. We'll use `d3.stratify` later on to convert this automatically to a tree-like structure that we can visualize.

Like we did in the previous chapters, we create this data by writing a simple JavaScript file that loads in the CSV and, in this case, outputs the CSV file in the required format:

```
const d3 = require('d3');
const fs = require('fs');
const _ = require('lodash');

// read the data
fs.readFile('./felidae.csv', function (err, fileData) {
```

```
var FILTER_NAMES = ['Animalia','Bilateria',
    'Deuterostomia','Chordata','Vertebrata',
    'Gnathostomata','Tetrapoda','Mammalia','Theria',
    'Eutheria','Feliformia','Carnivora'];

// use parseRows since we don't have an header
var rows = d3.dsvFormat('|').parseRows(fileData.toString());

// do some initial filtering
var catsTree = rows.filter(function(row)
{
    return row[0] === '[TU]' && row[11] === 'valid'
});
var catsDescriptions = rows.filter(function(row)
{
    return row[0] === '[VR]' && row[5] === 'English'
});
// first map the catsDescriptions to an KV map for easy reference,
//not all have a reference.
var descriptionMap = catsDescriptions.reduce(
    function(kvs, row)
    {
        kvs[row[4]] = row[3];
        return kvs;
    },
{});

// Map the data from the row to an object array
var result = catsTree.map(function(row) {
    var id = row[1];
    var parent = row[18];
    var name = '';
    if (row[9].length > 0) { name = row[9]; }
    else if (row[7].length > 0) { name = row[7]; }
    else if (row[5].length > 0) { name = row[5]; }
    else if (row[3].length > 0) { name = row[3]; }
    var description = descriptionMap[id] ? descriptionMap[id] : '';
    // parent 552304 is our root, so ignore this one and set to ''
    if (parent === '552304') parent = '';
    return {
        id: id,
        parentId: parent,
        name: name,
        description: description
    }
});

var filtered = result.filter(function(row)
```

```
        {return FILTER_NAMES.indexOf(row.name) === -1});
    fs.writeFile('./cats.csv',d3.csvFormat(filtered));
});
```

The script takes the following steps to convert the incoming CSV file to the CSV file we want:

1. We first load the data and split it by the | delimiter by calling `d3.dsvFormat('|').parseRows(fileData.toString())`.

2. Next, we filter out the `[TU]` fields, which we use to create a tree, and the `[VR]` fields, which are used to add an English description (if available).

3. We convert the description fields to a *key/value* map (`descriptionMap`), where the key is the `id`. We can then use this as a simple lookup when creating the final rows.

4. Each row in the `[TU]` fields array is then converted into a simple JavaScript object with fields for `id`, `parentId`, `name`, and `description`. This last field is filled by looking up the `id` in the `descriptionMap`.

5. Before we write the output to the file, we remove the records (`FILTER_NAMES`) that are the ancestors of our requested root record, felidae (with an `id` of `552304`).

Now that we have the data, let's see what we can do with it.

Normal tree

With D3 we can create different types of tree visualization. We can create radial trees, such as the tree of life image shown in the previous section, but also create normal trees, which follow a horizontal (or a vertical) layout. We'll show how to do both, but in this section, we start with the normal horizontal tree:

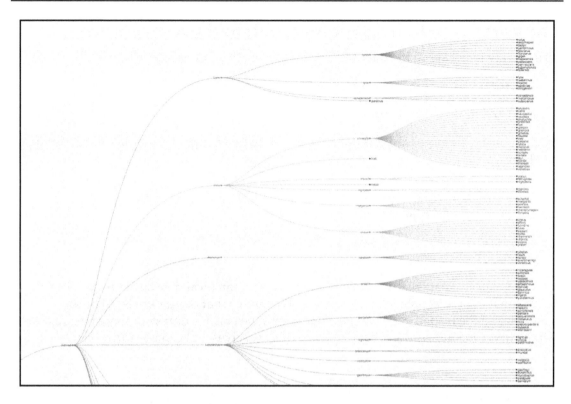

In this figure, you don't see the complete tree since it is too large to show, but only a small part. We'll also explain in this section how you can add **zoom** and **pan** functionality to your graph, to navigate large visualizations like this tree. To visualize this tree, we're going to take the following steps:

1. The first thing we need to do is load the data and convert it into a hierarchical data structure.
2. Once we have hierarchical data, we use the d3.tree function to convert this data to a set of x and y coordinates that we can use to draw the lines and the nodes.
3. When we have these coordinates, we can draw the line, the circle, and the text elements.
4. Finally, we'll add the zoom functionality to this visualization so that we can easily move around our visualized tree.

The first step is converting our CSV data to a hierarchical structure. Note that for this example we once again skip the standard setup where we define the main chart element. If you want to look at the complete code for this example, you can find it in <DVD3>/src/chapter-03/js/D03-01.js.

Converting data into a hierarchical data structure

Let's quickly look back at the data we're using for the tree examples:

```
id,parentId,name,description
180582,180581,rufus,Bobcat
180583,180582,rufus,bobcat
```

When we use `d3.csv` to load this data, the resulting JavaScript object will look something like this:

```
{
    "id": "180582"
    "parentId": "180582"
    "name": "180581"
    "description": "Bobcat"
}
```

You can see in this data that we don't really have a hierarchical data structure yet, but all the information is available to construct one. We know what our parent is, so by just processing all the loaded data elements, we should be able to convert the separate objects to a single tree. Luckily, we don't have to write this ourselves, but can use functionality provided by D3 for this:

```
d3.csv('./data/cats.csv', function(data) {
    var stratify = d3.stratify();
    var root = stratify(data);
    ...
}
```

Here, you can see that after loading the data, we use the `d3.stratify` function to convert our loaded data into a tree. With the default settings, `d3.stratify` will use the `id` property of the data array to identify a node and the `parentId` property to identify a node's parent. If your data has different properties you can use the `stratify.id('myId')` and the `stratify.parentId('myParent')` functions to change how `stratify` works. For our data, the properties match, so we just use the default `stratify` function. The result (`root`) looks like this:

```
▼ Node {data: Object, height: 4, depth: 0, parent: null, id: "180580"…} ▓
    ▼ children: Array[2]
        ▶ 0: Node
        ▶ 1: Node
          length: 2
        ▶ __proto__: Array[0]
    ▼ data: Object
          description: "cats"
          id: "180580"
          name: "Felidae"
          parentId: ""
        ▶ __proto__: Object
      depth: 0
      height: 4
      id: "180580"
      parent: null
    ▶ __proto__: Object
```

Here, you can see that our data is now converted to a tree structure. The original properties can be accessed through the `data` property, a node's children through the `children` property and a node's parent through the `parent` property.

Using D3 build-in functionality to create a tree

Now that we have our data in a hierarchical format, we need to convert it to a structure that has x and y coordinates that represent the position of each node in the tree:

```
var tree = d3.tree()
    .size([height*3, width*2])
    .separation(function(a, b) { return (a.parent === b.parent ? 5 : 13)});

tree(root);
```

Here, we use the d3.tree function to extend our hierarchical data with layout information (x and y), which we can use in the next section to draw the line, circle, and text elements. When you create a d3.tree() you can configure it by calling the following functions:

Operation	Description
tree.size([size])	Set the size of the complete tree to the provided two-dimensional array. When used with [width, height], the result will be a vertical tree. Note that these values can represent an arbitrary coordinate system (as we'll see in the following section where we create a radial tree).
tree.nodeSize([size])	With tree.size(), we set the size of the complete tree. With this function, it is also possible to set the [width, height] of an individual node.
tree.separation([separation])	This function allows you to set the separation between neighboring nodes. The separation is used to set the distance when nodes are rendered on the same level.

Looking at the previous table, we can see that we set the total size of our tree to [height*3, width*2]. This allows us to create a very large tree on which we'll use D3's zoom functionality to navigate. Also, note that we use [height,width] instead of [width,height]. The reason is that we want to draw a horizontally oriented tree and not a vertically oriented one. Finally, we define our separation based on whether the nodes have the same parent. If they do we set a separation of 5; otherwise, we set a separation of 13.

Before we move to the next section, let's see what our root element looks like now:

```
▼ 10: Node
  ▼ children: Array[1]
    ▼ 0: Node
      ► children: Array[2]
      ► data: Object
        depth: 3
        height: 1
        id: "621874"
      ► parent: Node
        x: 770.625
        y: 600
      ► __proto__: Object
        length: 1
    ► __proto__: Array[0]
  ► data: Object
    depth: 2
    height: 2
    id: "621781"
  ► parent: Node
    x: 770.625
    y: 400
```

Here, you can see that we've gained an x and y attribute, which we'll use in the following section.

Drawing the tree elements

The first elements we'll draw are the lines between the individual nodes. To draw these lines, we use the following JavaScript fragment:

```
var link = chart.selectAll(".link")
    .data(root.descendants().slice(1))
    .enter().append("path")
    .attr("class", "link")
    .attr("d", diagonal);
    ...
function diagonal(d) {
    return "M" + d.y + "," + d.x
        + "C" + ((d.y + d.parent.y) / 2) + "," + d.x
        + " " + ((d.y + d.parent.y) / 2) + "," + d.parent.x
        + " " + d.parent.y + "," + d.parent.x;
}
```

When we used the `stratify` function, D3 also provided us with a couple of helper functions for selecting specific. Here, we use the `descendants` function to get an array of all the nodes. We're going to draw lines from the a node to its parent, so we need to remove the first element from our array (`slice(1)`), which is our root node, which hasn't got a parent. We create a SVG path element (d) for all the nodes, which is set to the result of the `diagonal` function. In the `diagonal` function, we create a **Bezier** curve using SVG syntax. The easiest way to understand this function is by looking at its result:

```
M980,1454C735,1454 735,988 490,988
```

When drawing paths with SVG, we have to specify which type of line we want to draw and how to draw that line. The M in this string tells our browser to move to 980, 1454 and then draw a Bezier curve (identified by the C) from 980, 1454 to 490, 988, using two control points (735, 1454 and 735, 988). This results in the following curve:

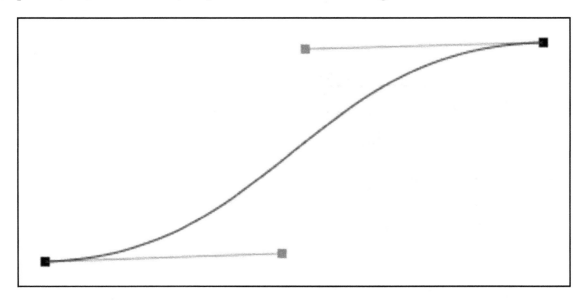

There are different ways we can create curves in SVG; Mozilla Developer Network has quite extensive documentation on paths and curves here:
https://developer.mozilla.org/en/docs/Web/SVG/Tutorial/Paths.

At this point we've got all our lines drawn, and it already starts to look like a tree:

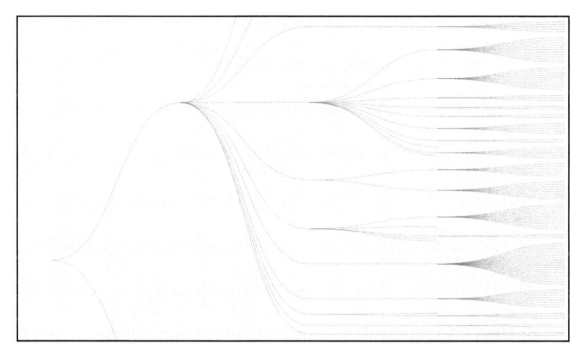

The only thing left to do is add the circles and the text elements:

```
var node = chart.selectAll(".node")
    .data(root.descendants())
    .enter().append("g")
    .attr("class", function(d) {
        return "node" + (d.children ? " node--internal" : " node--leaf");
    })
    .attr("transform", function(d) {
        return "translate(" + d.y + "," + d.x + ")"; });

node.append("circle").attr("r", 2.5);

node.append("text")
    .attr("dy", ".35em")
    .attr("x", function(d) { return d.children ? -4 :   4 })
    .style("text-anchor", function(d) { return d.children ? "end" :
"start"; })
    .text(function(d) { return d.data.name; });
```

Here, you can see that we add a g element for each of our nodes, which we position at the correct location, and we set a specific class based on whether it's an internal node or an end leaf. Note once again that we switch the x and y positions since we want to generate a horizontal tree instead of a vertical one. Finally, we add the text nodes, where we show the name from our initially loaded data:

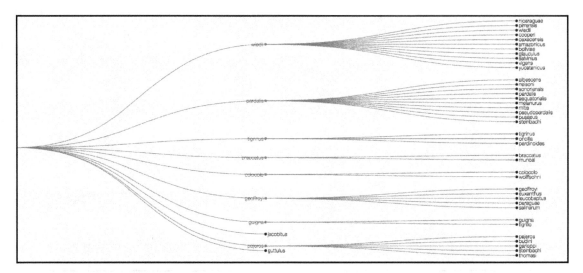

As you can see in this image, we've now got circles for the individual nodes, and also show the name. What you can also already see is that representing this complete structure in a tree results in a very large visualization. In the next section, we'll use d3.zoom to set up zooming and panning.

Adding panning and zooming to the visualization

Adding zoom and pan functionality to an existing chart is very easy. All the code required is shown in the following fragment:

```
var zoom = d3.zoom()
    .scaleExtent([0.1, 10])
    .on("zoom", zoomed);

d3.select(".chart").call(zoom);

function zoomed() {
    chart.attr("transform", d3.event.transform);
}
```

In this code fragment, we define the d3.zoom() we want to use. By setting the scaleExtent function, we define how far in and out we can zoom. So, our minimum scale value is 0.1, which means we can zoom out ten times, and the maximum scale factor is 10, which means we can zoom in ten times. Whenever a user zooms (or pans), we call the zoomed function. In this zoomed function, we can use the d3.event.transform property to set the new SVG transform property on our chart. This will zoom in and pan the chart to the required location. To make this work, we need to attach the zoom to our chart, which we do by calling d3.select(".chart").call(zoom). Now we can use the left mouse button to pan our tree, and the mouse wheel (or pinching when you're on mobile) to zoom in and out.

The d3.zoom functionality provides a lot of different functions. In this section, we've only used a small part of it. For more information on what can be done with d3.zoom, look at the API documentation: https://github.com/d3/d3-zoom/blob/master/README.md#_zoom.

As you've seen, a disadvantage of a tree like this is that it becomes difficult to visualize it in a compact manner. In the following section, we use a different approach. We create a radial tree using the same data.

Radial tree

A radial tree is pretty much the same as a normal tree, except we lay out the individual nodes in a radial manner. The tree that we'll create in this section looks like this:

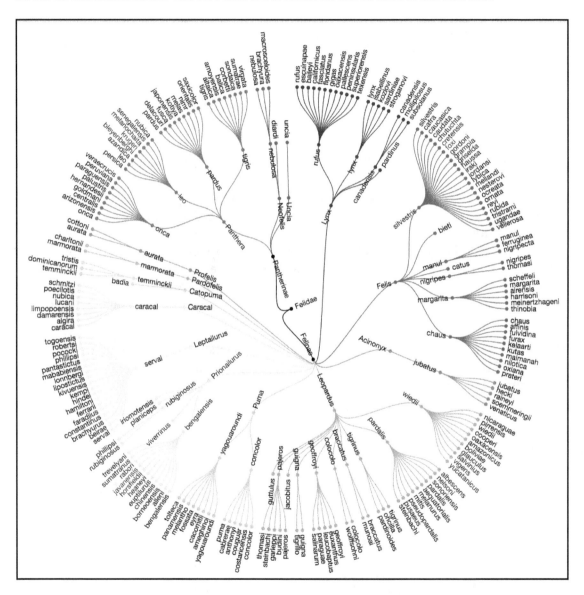

You can immediately see that we can represent much more data in a much more compact manner. When you open this example (`<DVD3>/src/chapter-03/03-02.html`), you can also see that we have animated this visualization:

- When first opened, all the lines, circles, and elements move to their correct positions.
- When you click on a node, it will collapse its children and the complete tree will be repositioned. When you click that node again, the collapsed tree will emerge again.

To accomplish this, we need a little bit more code, but, as you'll see, most of it is required to handle the animations. In the following sections, we'll explain these steps:

1. We need to load the data and convert it into an object that we can pass into our `d3.tree` function.
2. In this visualization, we color each of the branches to better visualize the various branches of our tree. To do this, we set up a `d3.scaleSequental` scale.
3. Next, we can render the individual lines, nodes and text elements.
4. For the elements we want to animate, we need to create transitions.
5. Finally, we register a mouse listener to trigger the animations.

We'll start with loading the data and parsing it into the correct format.

Loading the data

To load the data, we use the same approach as we did for the normal tree we saw previously:

```
var tree = d3.tree()
    .size([360, 300])
    .separation(function(a, b) { return (a.parent == b.parent ? 1 : 2) /
a.depth; });

var stratify = d3.stratify();

d3.csv('./data/cats.csv', function(loaded) {
    root = stratify(loaded);
    tree(root);

    // assign a group to descendants of level 2, which we use for coloring
    var colorGroups = root.descendants().filter(function(node)
    {
        return node.depth === 2
```

```
    });
    colorGroups.forEach(function(group, i) {
        group.descendants().forEach(function(node) {node.data.group = i;})
    });

    // the root and rootKV, are here merely for reference, to make sure we
    // have the correct number of records at any time. Let's clone the root
    // element, so we have a working copy.
    currentRoot =_.cloneDeep(root);

    // render the graph based on the currentRoot
    update();
});
```

Here you can see that we use d3.csv to load the data, convert it into a hierarchy by calling stratify(loaded), and we calculate the x and y values. In these visualizations we configure the d3.tree() function with size([360, 300]), where the first value represents the degrees on a circle (from 0 to 360 degrees), and the second value is the radius of the circle. We'll use these to values to position our node, line, and text elements correctly. We also use a different function for the separation, where the separation is not just based on whether nodes have the same parent, but we also take the depth into account.

 In this example, we create a full 360-degree circle, but you're of course free to use different values. A nice visualization might be where you only use 180 degrees instead of 360. Alternatively, you could also limit the degrees to 270, which would free up the upper-left corner, where you can add a legend explaining the colors used.

If you look at the tree shown in the beginning of this section, you can see that we color branches uniquely. We group nodes based on the nodes at depth level 2. So, all children of the nodes that are at level 2 use the same color. In this code, we prepare that by adding the group property to all the descendants of nodes with have a node.depth of 2. Finally, we make a copy of our data (root) that we can easily modify and work with, without modifying our loaded data. More on this later in this section, when we animate the nodes. At the end we call the update() function, which will render the tree.

Setting up a color scale

In our data, we have 12 nodes at a depth of 2. As we mentioned, we're going to color each branch from that level with the same color. For this, we create a simple sequential scale:

```
var stratify = d3.stratify();
var colorScale = d3.scaleSequential(d3.interpolateSpectral).domain([0,12]);
```

With this scale, our input domain is the values from 0 to 12, which is mapped to a range of 0 to 1, which are fed into the d3.interpolateSpectral interpolator. This way we get a nice set of colors back when we call colorScale(). In the previous section, we already set the group property for each node. Later on, we'll use this group property together with the colorScale to determine the color for the line, node, and text elements.

Rendering the lines, nodes, and text elements

We draw the tree in the update() function. Since this function is a bit large, we'll split it up for this discussion:

```
function update() {

    tree(currentRoot);

    // add the lines
    ...

    // add the nodes
    ...

    // add the circles
    ...

    // add the text elements
    ...
}
```

The first thing we do is enrich our data by calling the `tree()` function. This sets the x and y coordinates and adds the `descendants` function. Now let's first add the lines that connect the nodes with each other:

```
var links = chart.selectAll(".link")
    .data(currentRoot.descendants().slice(1));

var linksEnter = links.enter().append("path")
    .attr("class", "link")
    .style("stroke", function(d) {return colorScale(d.data.group)});

links.merge(linksEnter)
    .attr("d", diagonal);

...

function diagonal(d) {
    return "M" + project(d.x, d.y)
        + "C" + project(d.x, (d.y + d.parent.y) / 2)
        + " " + project(d.parent.x, (d.y + d.parent.y) / 2)
        + " " + project(d.parent.x, d.parent.y);
}

// convert the x,y to a position on the circle
function project(x, y) {
    var angle = (x - 90) / 180 * Math.PI, radius = y;
    return [radius * Math.cos(angle), radius * Math.sin(angle)];
}
```

As you can see, this is the standard *select, enter, update* scenario we often use in D3. In this case, we create new `path` elements for each of our nodes (except the root element, which is removed by the `slice(1)` function). We assign the `link` class to this element and set the color by passing its `d.data.group` value to the `colorScale` function. Finally, we set the d value to the result of the `diagonal` function. Remember that we set the size of the tree to `360, 300`. To draw our nodes in a circle we need to convert the coordinates to a circle. We do this in the project function. To convert the radius and the angle to the corresponding x and y coordinates for our radial treemap, we need some simple trigonometry: where x = r cos(angle) and y = r sin(angle). We do this in the `project` function. Also note that we use an offset of `-90` degrees to make sure the first element is positioned at the top of our radial treemap.

If we now render our treemap, it'll look like this:

You can already see the shape of our final tree, and you can see that because we have used the `project` function our treemap is now rendered in a circular layout. Next, we'll add the node groups (g) and the circles in those groups:

```
var nodes = chart.selectAll(".node").data(currentRoot.descendants());

var nodesEnter = nodes.enter().append("g")
```

```
    .attr("class", "node")

nodesEnter.append("circle")
    .attr("r", 2.5)
    .style("fill", function(d) {return colorScale(d.data.group)});

var nodesUpdate = nodes.merge(nodesEnter);

nodesUpdate
    .attr("transform", function(d)
    {
        return
        "translate(" + project(d.x, d.y) + ")";
    })
```

We again use the standard D3 approach for selecting, adding, and updating elements. In this case, we add a g element for each of our nodes and add a circle element, which we color using colorScale. Our treemap now looks like this (we only show part of the treemap):

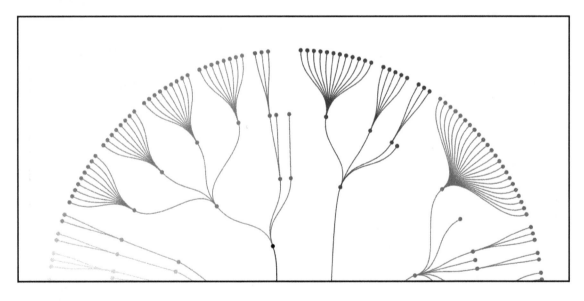

The last elements we need to add are the text elements:

```
// the same nodesEnter/nodesUpdate we used to add the circles
nodesEnter.append("text")
    .attr("dy", ".31em")

var nodesUpdate = nodes.merge(nodesEnter);
...
```

```
nodesUpdate.select("text")
    .attr("x", function(d) { return d.x < 180 === !d.children ? 6 : -6; })
    .text(function(d) {return d.data.name; })
    .style("text-anchor", function(d) {
        if (d.x < 180 && d.children) return "end"
        else if (d.x < 180 && !d.children) return "start"
        else if (d.x >= 180 && !d.children) return "end"
        else if (d.x >= 180 && d.children) return "start"
    })
    .attr("transform", function(d) {
        return "rotate(" + (d.x < 180 ? d.x - 90 : d.x + 90) + ")";
    })
```

When we add a `text` element, we need to take some additional steps to make sure the `text` elements are rendered correctly. The position is already correct, since we added the text element to the `g` group. For the text element, we need to determine where the text-anchor is available. We do this by looking whether we're at the right side or left side of the circle, and whether we have children or not. Finally, we do an additional rotation to make sure the text labels are correctly aligned on the circle. At this point we have all the elements in the correct position:

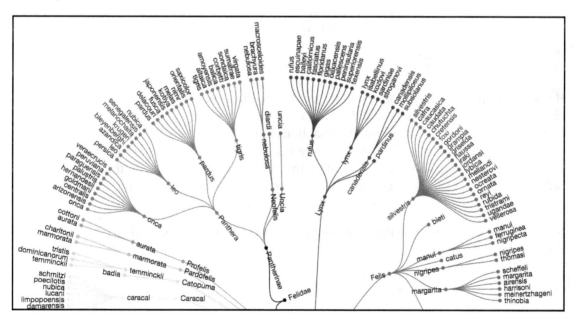

Now we need to add the animations.

Adding the animations

For this treemap, we're going to add two different kinds of animation:

1. When the treemap is initially loaded, we'll animate and move all the elements to their correct positions.
2. When you click on a node, we'll hide that node and reposition all the other elements.

We'll first set up the transitions for when we initially load the treemap.

Animating the treemap on initial load

Let's again start by looking at the lines:

```
var links = chart.selectAll(".link")
    .data(currentRoot.descendants().slice(1));

var linksEnter = links.enter().append("path")
    .attr("class", "link")
    .attr("d", diagonal({x:0, y:0, parent: {x:0, y:0}}))
    .style("stroke", function(d) {return colorScale(d.data.group)});

links.merge(linksEnter)
    .transition().duration(2000).attr("d", diagonal);
```

If you compare this, you'll notice that we've only made a couple of small changes. The first change we made is that we added the `.attr("d", diagonal({x:0, y:0, parent: {x:0, y:0}}))` line. This draws an initial lines (when we first add this `path`), from `0,0` to `0,0`. We need to do this, so that we can use a transition from the center of the circle, to the calculated position for this data element by the `tree()` function. We add this transition with the `.transition().duration(2000).attr("d", diagonal)` line. These two changes are enough to set up the animation for the lines.

Next, let's look at animating the `g` elements. The only thing we need to do for this is add a `transition` like this:

```
nodesUpdate.transition().duration(2000)
    .attr("transform", function(d)
    {
        return "translate(" + project(d.x, d.y) + ")";
    })
```

This will make sure the nodes (and thus the circles and the text elements) will animate from the center of the screen to their required positions. For the `text` elements, we need to add an additional animation, since we need to also do a rotation. To do this, we just replace the part where we defined the rotation:

```
.attr("transform", function(d) {
  return "rotate(" + (d.x < 180 ? d.x - 90 : d.x + 90) + ")";
})
```

Replace the previous code with this:

```
.transition().duration(2000)
    .attr("transform", function(d)
    {
        return "rotate(" + (d.x < 180 ? d.x - 90 : d.x + 90) + ")";
    })
```

Now when we open the treemap you'll see it exploding from the center, and slowly move into the correct positions:

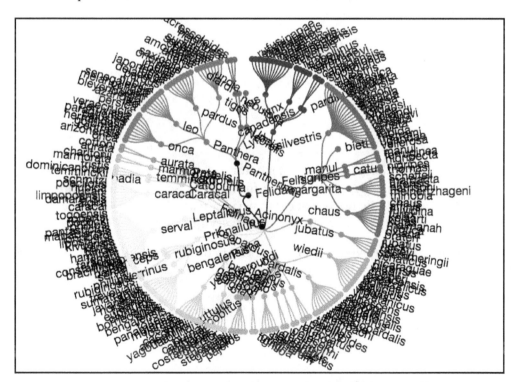

The last part we're going to animate is when a node is clicked.

Animating hiding a node

The first thing we need to do is add a listener that will listen to clicks on the node we want to collapse:

```
var nodesEnter = nodes.enter().append("g")
    .attr("class", "node")
    .on("click", click);

function click(d) {
    if (d.children) {
        d._children = d.children;
        d.children = null;

        // highlight the selected circle
        d3.select(this).select("circle").style("stroke", "red");
        d3.select(this).select("circle").style("stroke-width", "2");
    } else {
        d.children = d._children;
        d._children = null;

        // reset the highlight
        d3.select(this).select("circle").style("r", 2.5);
        d3.select(this).select("circle").style("stroke", "");
    }
    update();
}
```

Here we use the on function to define a listener for click events. When clicked the click() function will be called. In the click function, we set the nodes children to null and highlight the circle. If the node is one that we've already hidden, we do the opposite. Finally, we call the update() function to render everything again.

To correctly handle the removed children, we need to do some additional preprocessing before we render the data again:

```
function update() {
    // calculate the x,y coordinates of the currentRoot
    tree(currentRoot);

    // create KV for simple access
    var currentRootKV = currentRoot.descendants()
        .reduce(function(kv, el) {kv[el.data.id] = el; return kv},{});

    // we don't really want to remove the hidden nodes, we just want them
```

```
        // to be hidden.
    var toRender = root.descendants().map(function(el) {
        if (currentRootKV[el.data.id]) {
            var newNode = currentRootKV[el.data.id];
            return newNode;
        } else {
            // if the child is not in the KV map, it is hidden. We
            // now need to set its position to the calculated position of
            // the first visible parent. In other words, the first one
            // which is in the currentRootKV map.
            var fromRoot = _.cloneDeep(el);
            var parent = fromRoot.parent;

            while (!currentRootKV[parent.data.id])
            {
                parent = parent.parent;
            }
            var newParent = currentRootKV[parent.data.id];

            fromRoot.hidden = true;
            fromRoot.x = newParent.x;
            fromRoot.y = newParent.y;

            // we also set the parents x,y since the lines need to
            // be drawn from this position.
            fromRoot.parent.x = newParent.x;
            fromRoot.parent.y = newParent.y;

            return fromRoot;
        }
    });
    // animate the links, text and circles, like we seen before
    ...
}
```

This might seem a bit complex, that's why we left in the code comments. What we do here is create a new array of elements to render, `toRender`, (which is the same size as the original set). We do this with the following steps:

1. We first calculate the new x and y values for the tree where the children of the selected nodes have been hidden: `tree(currentRoot)`. This will have values for all the nodes, except for the hidden children. We also set up a key-value map for easy access to the nodes of this tree: `currentRootKV`.

2. If we just pass in the result from step 1, our tree will animate, but our removed children will just disappear. So, we don't really want to remove them, we want to move them to the position of their parent, and hide them. To do this, we walk through all the nodes from our initial tree:
   `root.descendants().map(function(el) {...}`

3. If a node from the root can be found in the `currentRootKV` map it means it hasn't been removed, and we can just copy the value from the `currentRootKV`.

4. If a node from the root can't be found in the `currentRootKV` map, it means it's one of the children of a node that has been removed. We now create a new node (`fromRoot`), where we set the x and y values to the position of the first visible ancestor and make sure to set the x and y of the parent correctly to make sure the lines are drawn correctly. To help in the animations, we also set the `hidden` property to `true`.

5. The result is that the `toRender` array contains the complete tree, including the hidden nodes, where all the x and y positions are correct.

If we now pass in the `toRender` array to the `data` functions instead of the `currentRoot`, the lines, circles, and text elements will move and rotate to the correct positions. If you stop here, however, we don't have the desired effect:

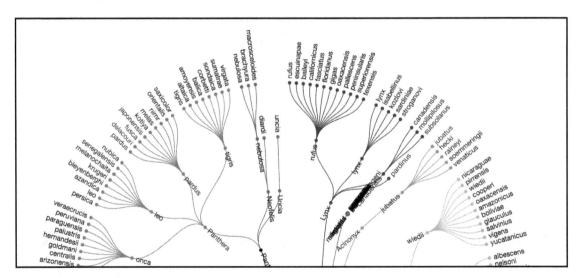

In this figure, you can see that the positions are correct, but the hidden elements aren't hidden. They're just moved. What we will do is the following:

- When the elements are being moved, we'll slowly lower the transparency to make them fade away
- When the transition is finished, we'll set their CSS display `style` to `none`, to hide them completely

For this, we need to update the transition for the `g` elements to this:

```
nodesUpdate.transition().duration(2000)
    .attr("transform", function(d)
    {
        return "translate(" + project(d.x, d.y) + ")"; })
        .style("opacity", function(d) { return !d.hidden ? 1 : 0} )
        .on("end", function(d) {d.hidden ? d3.select(this).attr("display",
"none") : ""})
        .on("start", function(d) {!d.hidden ?
        d3.select(this).attr("display", ""): ""
    });
```

Here, you can see that elements that have a `hidden` property will transition to an opacity of `0`, while elements that don't have this property will transition to an opacity of `1`. This way, when a node is clicked the first time, the elements will fade away, and when clicked again, they'll slowly appear. When a transition is run, it provides events you can listen on. The `end` event is called when the transition finishes and the `start` event is called when a transition is started. In this case, we use these events to set the `display` property to completely hide the node when `hidden` is `true`, and show the node when `hidden` is `false`.

And with this addition, we've completed this radial tree. We now have a tree where we can hide and show nodes by clicking on them:

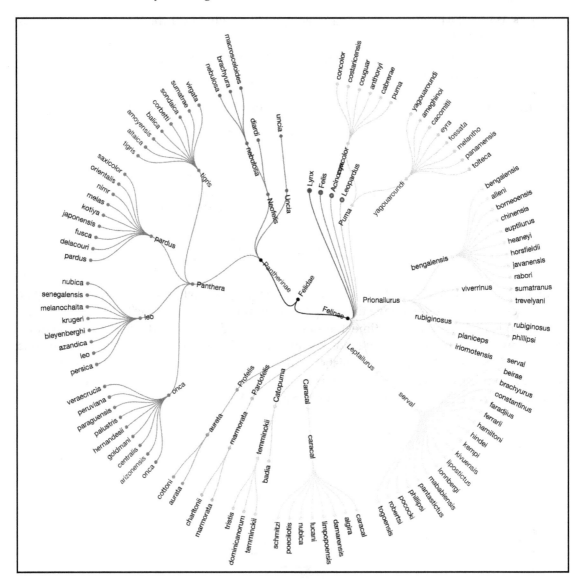

In this figure, you can see that we've hidden four nodes and their children, and that the other nodes have updated their position and rotation to reflex this new state.

In the next section, we'll look at two other visualizations: the treemap and the partition.

Treemap and partition

Trees work well for visualizing the nested structure of a taxonomy (or any other kind of tree), but what we can't easily visualize are the values attached to each of the node. Say, for instance, that each of our end nodes in our taxonomy had an additional value attached. This attached value would represent some information about that specific species (for example, the current total population). In a tree-based visualization, this would be difficult to represent. We could perhaps change their size, but then we'd quickly run out of space. When you have such a value that you want to represent besides the structure, a treemap or partition visualization might be better suited. The following figure shows the biggest cities in a large number of countries:

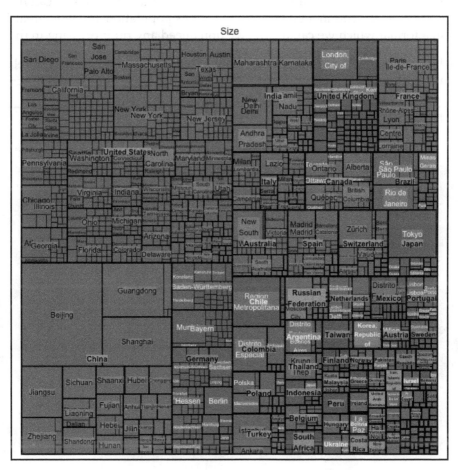

In this section, we're going to use these two visualizations to show some nested data. The data we used in the previous section doesn't have any quantitative data attached to the nodes we can use, so we'll use some other data for the examples in this section. We'll use population data, which can be downloaded from here:
`https://www.worlddata.info/downloads/`.

If you download the `countries.csv` file you'll see data that looks like this:

```
"Country (en)";...;"Country code";"Continent";...;"Population";"Area";...
"Afghanistan";...;"AF";"Asia";...;32564342;652230;...
"Egypt";...;"Misr";"EG";"Africa";...;88487396;1001450;...
```

We've left out some fields in the preceding snippet, but in this CSV file you can find the name of the country, the continent it belongs to, and its population and land area. This data is already in a format which we can use, so we don't need any preprocessing in this case.

With this data, we're first going to create a treemap where we can visualize the relative population of each country and continent (`<DVD3/src/chapter-03/D03-03.html>`):

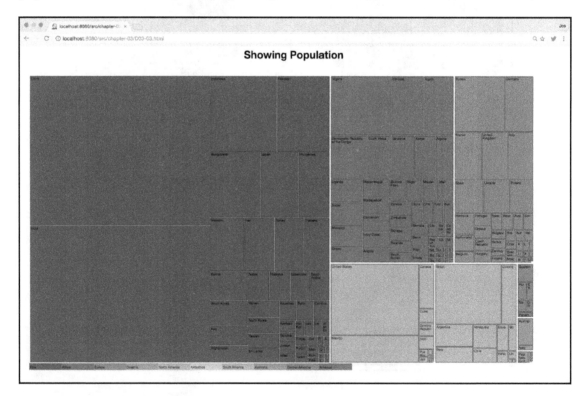

As you can see in this image, the treemap shows information grouped per continent. The size of the individual rectangles is based on that country's population. In this image, you can see that Asia has the largest population, and most people in Asia live in China and India.

We're also going to make this treemap a bit more interesting by adding the following:

- When the map is loaded, the rectangles will be animated to transition to their correct position and size.
- When you hover over a rectangle, we'll show a popup with some information about that country.
- If you click on the treemap, we'll switch between the following set of possible values: population, area size, and population density. This switch is, of course, animated.
- To better understand which continent is which, we add a simple legend to the bottom of the treemap.

The following image shows our cubes transitioning from displaying one dataset to another:

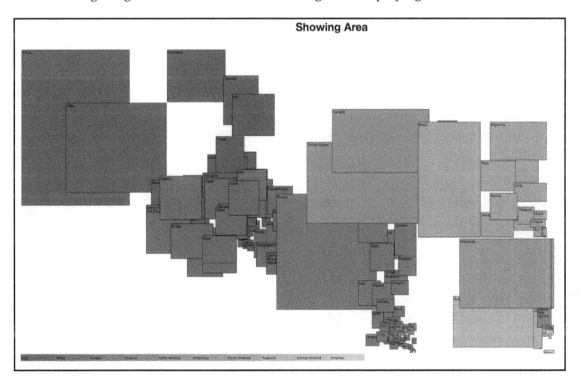

To create a treemap, we'll take the following steps:

1. Load the data from the CSV file and convert it into a nested structure.
2. Set up coloring for the different continents and draw the legend.
3. Draw and animate the rectangles for each country.
4. Add the text elements inside the rectangles with the names of the countries.
5. Set up the popup when you hover on top of a rectangle.
6. Add the click event listener to change the value that is represented by the size of the rectangle.

Loading the country data

The first thing we have to do is load the data and convert it into a structure we can work with. In the previous example we used `stratify()`; in this example, we'll use a different way we can automatically have D3 do the conversion for us, called `nest()`:

```
d3.text('./data/countries.csv', function(raw) {
    var data = d3.dsvFormat(";").parse(raw)

    // convert population and area to a number
    data = data.map(function(el) {
        el.Population = +el.Population;
        el.Area = +el.Area;
        el.Density = el.Population / el.Area;

        if (el.Density === Infinity) el.Density = 0;
            return el;
    });

    // group entries using nest and create hierarchy per continent
    var entries = d3.nest()
        .key(function (d) {return d.Continent; })
        .entries(data);

    // setup the tree generator
    var tree = d3.treemap()
        .size([width, height])
        .padding(2)
        .tile(d3.treemapSquarify.ratio(1))
```

Here you can see that we first load the data. Since this data isn't comma-separated but uses a ; to separate records, we use `d3.text()` to load the data, and `d3.dsvFormat` to convert the rows to JavaScript objects. Once the data is loaded, we convert the `Population` and the `Area` properties to numeric values and also calculate the `Density`. Next, we use the `d3.nest()` function to convert the data to a nested structure. With `d3.nest()`, we specify the values to group by using the `key` function. In this case, we group by the `Continent` property, which is available in each row. If we want to create a deeper nested structure, we could call `key` multiple times. When we've specified all the values to group by, we pass in our data array using the `entries` function. If we now look at the result of this call, we see that our data now looks like this:

```
▼ Array[10]  
  ▼ 0: Object
      key: "Asia"
    ▶ values: Array[51]
    ▶ __proto__: Object
  ▼ 1: Object
      key: "Africa"
    ▼ values: Array[59]
      ▼ 0: Object
          Area: 1001450
          Birthrate: "22.9"
          Capital: ""
          Coastline: "2450"
          Continent: "Africa"
          Country (de): "Ägypten"
          Country (en): "Egypt"
          Country (local): "Misr"
          Country code: "EG"
```

Note that the output is an array of twelve elements, one for each continent, where the name of the continent is set to the `key` property. We can now use this nested structure to calculate the x and y values for the rectangles by calling the `d3.treemap()` function. Just like the `tree()` function we saw earlier, the `treemap()` function can be configured by calling a number of functions:

Operation	Description
`treemap.size([width, height])`	Sets the size of the complete treemap to the provided two-dimensional array.
`treemap.round([boolean])`	When `round` is set to `true`, the resulting x and y coordinates will be rounded to the nearest decimal value.

`treemap.padding([padding])`	Sets the inner and outer padding of each rectangle to the provided value or function. When it is a function, the function will be called for each data element.
`treemap.paddingOuter([padding])`	Sets the outer padding to the specified value. You can also set the `top`, `right`, `bottom` and `left` padding separately by calling the `paddingTop`, `paddingRight`, `paddingBottom` and `paddingLeft` functions.
`treemap.paddingInner([padding])`	Sets the inner padding. The inner padding is the padding used to separate a node's children.
`treemap.tile`	Defines the tiling algorithm to use. The tiling algorithm determines how the squares from the treemap are drawn. D3 comes with six different tiling algorithms you can use: `d3.treemapBinary`, `d3.treemapDice`, `d3.treemapSlice`, `d3.treemapSliceDice`, `d3.treemapSquarify` (the default), and `d3.treemapResquarify`. We'll show how these render the rectangles further in this chapter. `d3.treemapSquarify` and `d3.treemapResquarify` can be further configured by calling the `ratio()` function. For a more in-depth explanation of these algorithms, take a look at the D3 API for hierarchies: `https://github.com/d3/d3-hierarchy#treemap`.

A quick overview of the difference in `tile` options is shown in the following image:

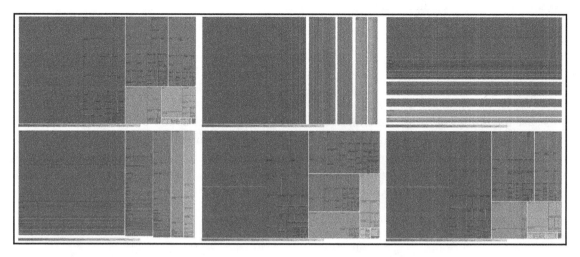

In this figure we have (clockwise, starting from the top left) the following `tile` algorithms: `d3.treemapBinary`, `d3.treemapDice`, `d3.treemapSlice`, `d3.treemapSliceDice`, `d3.treemapResquarify` with a ratio of 1 and `d3.treemapSquarify` with a ratio of 2.

For our example, we use `d3.treemap` like this:

```
var tree = d3.treemap()
    .size([width, height])
    .padding(2)
    .tile(d3.treemapSquarify.ratio(1))
```

So we'll get a `d3.treemap()` with the size of our chart, which uses a `padding` of 2 and uses the `d3.treemapSquarify` algorithm with a `ratio` of 1. Before we use this `tree` to calculate the x and y values for our treemap, we'll first set up the colors and draw a simple legend that explains which color is used for which continent.

Setting up coloring and draw a legend

We're going to add colors for each continent and draw a legend that looks like this:

This legend just draws the colors for each continent and adds the name. The first thing we need to do is set up a color scale:

```
var colorScale = d3.scaleOrdinal()
    .domain(entries.map(function(el) {return el.key}))
    .range(d3.range(0,entries.length + 1)
        .map(function(i) { return d3.interpolateWarm(i/entries.length);}))
```

In this case, we use a d3.scaleOrdinal function. This scale maps a set of input values, in this case the names of the continents (which were mapped to the key property by the d3.nest() function), to an output range of the same size. For the output, we call the d3.interpolateWarm function interpolator to create the twelve domain values. The result is that we can now call colorScale('Asia') to get the color for that continent. With these colors, we can now quickly draw our legend:

```
var legend = chart.append("g")
    .attr("class","legend")
    .attr("transform", "translate(0 " + height + ")" )

legend.selectAll("rect")
    .data(colorScale.domain())
    .enter()
        .append("rect")
        .attr("x", function(d,i) {return i * 100})
        .attr("fill", colorScale)
        .attr("width", 100)
        .attr("height", 20)

legend.selectAll("text")
    .data(colorScale.domain())
    .enter()
    .append("text")
    .attr("x", function(d,i) {return i * 100})
    .attr("dy", 15)
    .attr("dx", 2)
    .text(function(d) {return d})
```

Nothing too special here. We just use the colorScale.domain function to get an array of all the names of the continents, and use that, together with the colorScale, to draw the colored rectangles and add a text element to each individual rectangle. Together, this makes up the legend.

Drawing and animating the rectangles

We mentioned at the beginning that we want to be able to switch between three different types of visualization. The name of the property that we want to show (Population, Area, or Density) is passed into the update function, which will use those values to render the rectangles:

```
function update(property) {
    var root = d3.hierarchy({values: entries}, function(d) { return
d.values; })
        .sum(function(data) { return data[property]; })
        .sort(function(a, b) { return b.value - a.value; });
    tree(root);
        ...
}
```

The first thing we do is that we convert our nested structure entries (the result of the d3.nest() function) to an D3 hierarchical object by calling d3.hierarchy(). We pass a new root object, where we set our entries as the children. We also tell D3 that our children can be found by looking at the values property. For D3 to be able to correctly determine the size and position of the rectangles, we also need to define the sum and the sort functions. The result from the call to d3.hierarchy() can be passed to the tree() function we defined earlier. The result is an object that looks like this:

```
▼ Node {data: Object, height: 2, depth: 0, parent: null, children: Array[10]…}
  ▼ children: Array[10]
    ▼ 0: Node
      ▼ children: Array[51]
        ▼ 0: Node
          ▶ data: Object
            depth: 2
            height: 0
          ▶ parent: Node
            value: 1367485388
            x0: 4
            x1: 561.9180548350575
            y0: 4
            y1: 447.8769874386519
          ▶ __proto__: Object
        ▶ 1: Node
        ▶ 2: Node
```

In this figure, you can now see that we've got `x0`, `y0`, `x1`, and `y1` properties. These properties define the boundaries of the rectangles we need to draw.

We now take all the `leaves` of this object (the nodes that have no children) and use these values to draw our groups:

```
function update(property) {
    ...

    var groups = chart.selectAll(".node")
        .data(root.leaves(), function(d) {return d.data['Country code']})

    var newGroups = groups
        .enter()
        .append("g")
        .attr("class","node")
        .on("mouseover", mouseover)
        .on("mousemove", mousemove)
        .on("mouseout", mouseout)
        .on("click", onclick);
    ...
```

The one thing to note here is that instead of just passing an array to the `data` function, we pass in an additional function: `function(d) {return d.data['Country code']}`. This function returns an additional key with which our data can be identified. What this means is that the next time we pass in data, this function will be used to select the elements to update, instead of using the index of each element in the array. So even if the `leaves()` function returns country elements in a different order, this function will make sure that the correct data elements are updated.

Next, let's add the rectangles to these groups:

```
newGroups.append("rect")
    .style("fill", function(d) {return colorScale(d.parent.data.key)})
    .style("stroke", "black")
    .attr("width", function(d, i) {return d.x1 - d.x0})
    .attr("height", function(d, i) {return d.y1 - d.y0});

var allGroups = groups.merge(newGroups)

allGroups.transition().duration(2000)
    .attr("transform", function(d) {return "translate(" + d.x0 + " " + d.y0
+ ")"})

allGroups.select("rect")
    .transition().duration(2000)
    .attr("width", function(d, i) {return d.x1 - d.x0})
```

```
            .attr("height", function(d, i) {return d.y1 - d.y0})
            ...
    }
```

Here, we first use the x0, y0, x1 and y1 properties to draw the rectangles. Next, we merge the updated and new elements together, and use a transition to animate them to their correct position. At the same time, we select all the added rect elements and use another transition to animate them to their correct size. When we open the visualization at this point, we can already see the correct colors, the animation of the positions, and the size of the rectangles:

The next step to do, is add text to the rectangles.

Add the text elements

While this might seem easy, and looks like something we already did earlier, there are some aspects of SVG we need to take into account. When we add a normal text element it is rendered either on top of the rectangles we drew or behind it, depending on whether we add it before or after the rectangle. If you've done some CSS you might know about the z-index property, which you can use to determine which element is rendered before another. This, however, doesn't apply to SVG elements. From the SVG specification: *"Elements in an SVG document fragment have an implicit drawing order, with the first elements in the SVG document fragment getting "painted" first. Subsequent elements are painted on top of previously painted elements."*

Now, how does this apply to this visualization? Well, we want to add some text to our rectangles (the name of the country), but don't want it to overflow on top of the other rectangles. We want the text to be contained to the rectangle it belongs to. To accomplish this, we'll use a feature of SVG where we can embed HTML inside SVG objects. You can do this by adding an element called `foreignObject`. The following fragment shows how we use this fragment, to create a nested HTML `div` element. Inside this element, we add a `p` element where we write out our text.

```
newGroups.append("foreignObject")
    .append("xhtml:body")
    .style("margin-left", 0);

...

allGroups.select("foreignObject")
    .transition().duration(20000)
    .attr("width", function(d) {return d.x1 - d.x0})
    .attr("height", function(d) {return d.y1 - d.y0})

allGroups.select("foreignObject").select("body")
    .style("margin-left", 0)
    .transition().duration(20000)
    .tween("custom", function(d, i) {

        // need to get the current height. We get this from the element
        // itself, since the bound data can be changed.
        var oldHeight = 0;

        // this can be undefined for the first run
        var currentDiv = d3.select(this).select("div").node();
        if (currentDiv) {
            var height = currentDiv.getAttribute("data-height");
            oldHeight = height ? height : 0;
        }

        // calculate the new height and setup a interpolator
        var newHeight = (d.y1 - d.y0);
        var interpolator = d3.interpolateNumber(oldHeight, newHeight);
        // assign to variable, so we can access it in the custom tween
        var node = this;
        return function(t) {
            d3.select(node).html(function(d) {
                var newHeight = interpolator(t);
                return '<div data-height="' + newHeight +
                '" style="height: ' + newHeight + '"
                class="node-name"><p>' + d.data
                ['Country (en)'] + '</p></div>'
```

```
            })
        }
    });
```

In the previous code, we add `foreignObject` to the `newGroups` selection. When we add `foreignObject`, we get the following DOM elements:

```
<foreignObject>
    <body><div></div></body>
</foreignObject>
```

To animate this `foreignObject` we need to use a custom `tween` function, since the standard tweens provided by D3 don't know how to handle this specific use case. When we write a custom `tween` function, we need to return a function that is called at intervals (from 0 to 1), and we need to return the correct `div` element with the correct size. In this `tween` function, we first determine the current `height` and store it in the value `oldHeight`. Then we create an interpolator from the `oldHeight` to the `newHeight`. This interpolator is then used in the function that is returned to calculate the correct `newHeight`, which is set as a CSS style property on the `div` element that contains the text. This way, the size of our `div` will nicely grow and shrink when the transition is running. If you now run this, you'll already see this kind of working:

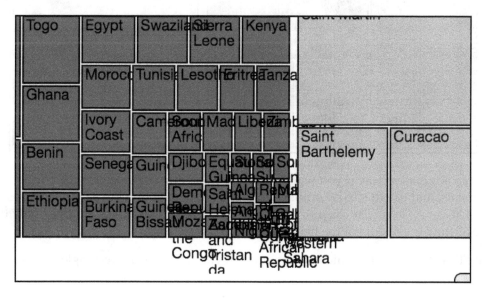

As you can see, some of the text elements already look correct, but for the very small rectangles, the text overflows to the left and to the right. The nice thing is, though, that since this is a standard p element inside `div`, we can use simple CSS to hide the overflowing text. In the code fragment we saw earlier, we added the `node-name` class to the `div`. In our CSS file, we now can hide the overflowing text by setting these CSS properties:

```
.node-name {
    ...
    overflow-x: hidden;
    overflow-y: hidden;
    ...
}
```

Now, when we look at the treemap, we write text contained in the rectangle, and the overflow is nicely hidden:

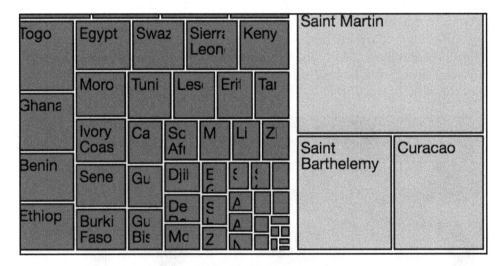

There is an alternative way if you want to stick to SVG. You can calculate the width of the text elements, and use that to determine when to draw a new line. An example of this can be found at `http://bl.ocks.org/mbostock/7555321`. Note that in this example, only the width overflow is solved, not the height overflow.

Next, we'll add the popup, which is shown when you hover over a rectangle.

Setting up the popup

The popup we show is just a simple `div` element, which we add to the page like this:

```
var div = d3.select("body").append("div")
    .attr("class", "tooltip")
    .style("display", "none");
```

By default, we set the `display` to none, which hides this element. To show this element we use a number of mouse event listeners, which we added when we created the g elements containing the country rectangles:

```
var newGroups = groups
    .enter()
    .append("g")
    .attr("class","node")
    .on("mouseover", mouseover)
    .on("mousemove", mousemove)
    .on("mouseout", mouseout)
    .on("click", onclick);
```

The `mouseover, mousemove,` and `mouseout` listeners look like this:

```
function mouseover(d) {
    div.style("display", "inline");
    div.html("<ul>" +
        "<li><strong>Name:</strong> " + d.data['Country (en)'] + " </li>" +
        "<li><strong>Population:</strong> " + d.data['Population'] + "
</li>" +
        "<li><strong>Area:</strong> " + d.data['Area'] + " </li>" +
        "</ul>")
}

function mousemove(d) {
    div
        .style("left", (d3.event.pageX ) + "px")
        .style("top", (d3.event.pageY + 20) + "px");
}

function mouseout() {
    div.style("display", "none");
}
```

In the listeners, we use the `mouseover` function to change the `display` style of the popup `div` and set the inner value to the specified HTML with the `html` function. The popup is positioned to the correct location by the `mousemove` listener. We hide the `div` again when we move out of a rectangle, and that's all you need to do to create the popup:

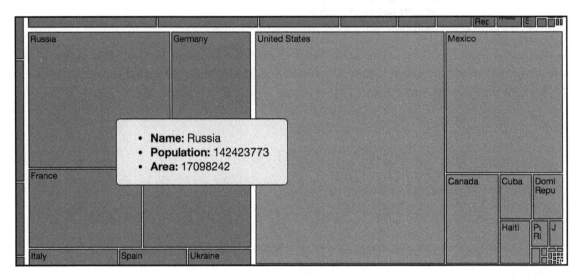

The final step we need to do is add the listener that switches the data to be shown in the treemap.

Adding the click event listener to switch the value shown

We've seen in the previous section how to add the click listener. When you click on a rectangle, we run the following click listener:

```
var properties = ['Population', 'Area', 'Density'];

function onclick(d) {
    var currentProp = properties.shift();
    properties.push(currentProp);
    update(currentProp);
    mouseout()
}
```

As you can see, we just select the next value from our properties array, which determines the property to show. Since we set up our code in the previous sections to correctly handle updated values, this is all that is needed to trigger the transitions we defined on the elements.

And that's it. Now we've got an animated treemap that changes the data that is visualized whenever the map is clicked.

Alternative visualizations using partition and pack layouts

Besides the treemap visualization, D3 also provides a couple of other ways of visualizing hierarchical data in approximately the same way. With a *partition* layout, the rectangles aren't nested but are shown together; and the *pack* layout uses circles instead of rectangles.

We won't go into too much detail in the following two sections, since the steps shown for the treemap layout are the same as for the pack and partition layouts.

Data visualized using a partition layout

The following image is an example of visualizing the same data, but this time in a pack layout:

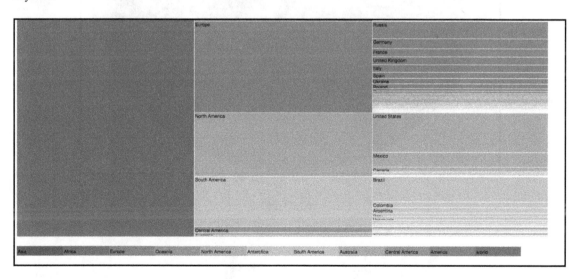

The code for this example can be found in the `DVD3/chapter-03/D03-04.js` file.

Data visualized using a pack layout

Another way to visualize the same data is by using circles. The code, once again, looks pretty much the same as the previous examples. This time, however, we create `circle` elements based on a provided radius, instead of rectangle elements:

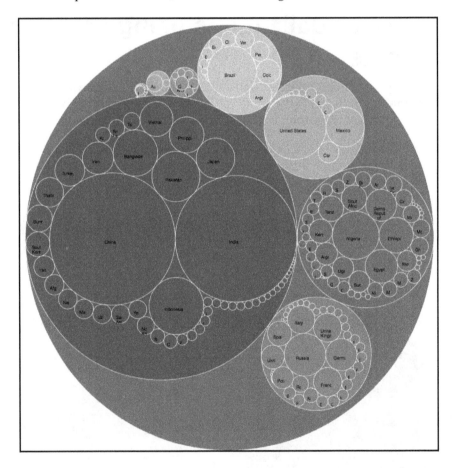

We won't go into the details here on how to use this layout type. If you want to explore this example further, look at the `DVD3/chapter-03/D03-05.js` file.

Summary

That wraps it up for this chapter on visualizing hierarchical data. With D3, we can easily visualize this kind of data through different visualizations. Once you've got your data, you first need to create a nested structure of it. D3 offers helper functions for this (`d3.nest` and `d3.stratify`) that take care of converting row-based data to a structure that can be passed into the chart functions (such as `tree` and `treemap`). We've also seen that not all data can be visualized properly with the available visualizations. The normal `tree` works well for visualizing trees, but can quickly result in very large charts. Luckily, D3 offers a `d3.zoom` function, which allows you to pan and zoom around the chart. We've also seen that by changing how the x and y coordinates are projected, we can quickly change the way the chart looks. With our *radial* tree, we showed that large tree structures can be visualized in a concise way. We've also made the charts interactive and more visually appealing by adding user interaction. When a start is opened the first time, the elements animate to their correct positions, and we've seen that data changes (hiding a node, changing the value visualized) can be easily animated.

One of the very nice things about D3 is that the approach for all these charts is the same. Select the data, add the elements, and (if you want animations) set up the transitions. Whether you're creating a *tree*, a *treemap*, or any of the other examples shown in this chapter, the approach is the same. We use one of D3, provided chart functions to calculate the coordinates (and, in some cases, the radius), and use those to create the SVG elements.

In the next chapter, we're going to move it one step further and look at how to visualize graphs using *chord* and *forces* diagrams.

4
Visualizing Graphs

So far, we've seen a number of different data structures. We've visualized linear data with bar, pie, and line charts, and have shown how to visualize nested data using trees and treemaps. An important data structure that we haven't looked at yet is the graph. With a graph, we have a number of nodes which are connected to each other to form a network. In this chapter, we'll look at a couple of different approaches you can use to visualize these kinds of structures.

In this chapter, we'll show the following D3 supported visualizations:

- We'll start with the **force** layout. With a force layout, we can create force-directed graphs. In a force-directed graph, the nodes are connected to each other with links. All the nodes and links can exact forces on one another which will result in visually pleasing network of nodes. We will visualize this using data from the Simpsons, where we show characters' interaction with each other per episode.
- We'll make a **bubble chart** of the most used words of the main Simpsons characters, with the size equivalent to the number of times, and colored per person: https://bl.ocks.org/ctufts/f38ef0187f98c537d791d24fda4a6ef9.
- An alternative way to visualize a network of relations is by using a **chord** layout. This visualization results in a circular layout, where various parts of the circle are connected with one another to show the relation between the nodes.
- If you've got a large network you need to visualize, a force layout or a chord layout can quickly become unreadable. A static alternative is a **matrix** diagram. We will use this diagram to visualize the interactions between a very large number of Simpson characters.

The first layout we'll look at is the force layout.

Force layout

A force layout renders a graph as a set of nodes and interconnected links. It's easiest to visualize by looking at an example. The following graph is a very simple example of what you can create with a force layout:

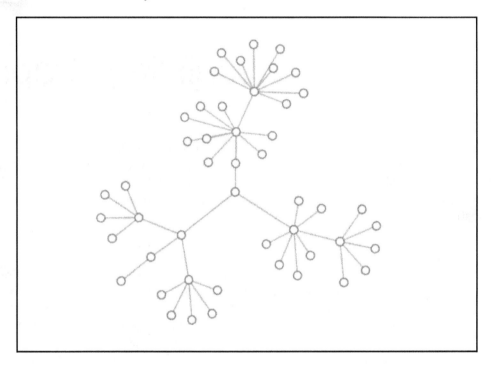

While this is a very simple example, if you have the time, you can create beautiful layouts. An especially beautiful one is the one created by (amongst others) the creator of D3:

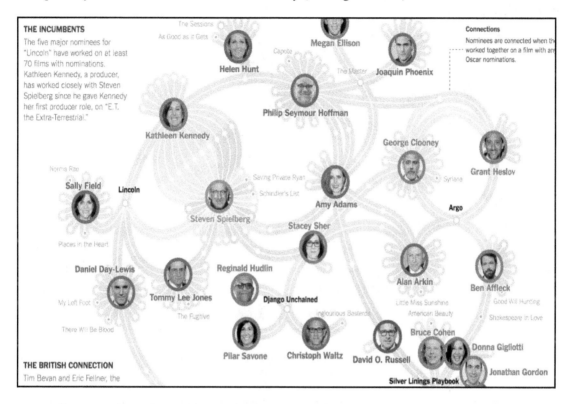

You can interact with this visualization here:

`http://www.nytimes.com/interactive/2013/02/20/movies/among-the-oscar-contenders`
`-a-host-of-connections.html`

For our first visualization in this chapter, we're going to create a force layout that uses information from the Simpsons. We're going to show which characters appear in a specific location in an episode. The final result looks something like this:

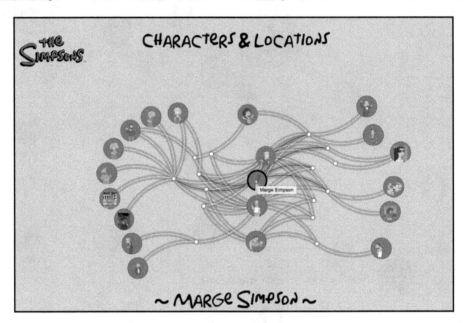

Here we have a force layout (which you can see in DVD3/src/chapter-04/D04-01.html) with the following features:

1. We have two different kinds of node. The small circles in the previous figure represent locations, and the large circles shows the characters.
2. The links between a character and a location means that that character, in the specific episode (we used the first one of season one), appeared in that location.
3. When you hover over a node, it'll highlight all the outgoing connections and show the name of the location at the bottom of the screen.
4. And finally, you can reposition nodes by dragging them.

The first thing we need to do is get the data behind this visualization.

Getting the raw Simpsons data

For the visualizations, we're going to work with data from the Simpsons. There is a number of online resources that offer a lot of information regarding this TV series, but getting and converting that data into an easy-to-use form is hard to do and very time consuming. Luckily, somebody has already done the hard work, and provided a way to get access to most of the data we'll be using in this chapter.

Todd Schneider created a GitHub project (`https://github.com/toddwschneider/flim-springfield`) in which he provides a tool to gather information from a set of online resources and store it in a PostgreSQL database. You can see some of the things he did with this data at `http://toddwschneider.com/posts/the-simpsons-by-the-data/`. You can either run this for yourself or use the PostgreSQL dump that's provided in the data directory of this chapter. If you want to do this for yourself you can follow the instructions from the GitHub link, and if you want to restore the PostgreSQL dump, just run the following command:

```
psql dbname < <DVD3>/src/chapter4/data/simpsons_db.dmp
```

Note that it isn't necessary to actually set up the database to work with the examples from this chapter, since we'll use exports from specific SQL queries as input for our data preparations scripts. If you didn't load the data into PostgreSQL, you can skip the following section and go directly to the section titled *Converting the data from the database*.

Getting the relevant information from the database

When you've either imported the database dump or run the steps from Todd Schneider's GitHub project yourself, we can now export a couple of tables from the database, which we'll process using a JavaScript file, like we did in the previous chapters. We're interested in the `characters` table, the `locations` table, and a selection from the `script_lines` table:

```
COPY(SELECT * FROM characters) TO 'characters.csv'
    WITH CSV DELIMITER ',' HEADER ;
COPY(SELECT * FROM locations) TO 'locations.csv'
    WITH CSV DELIMITER ',' HEADER ;
COPY(select episode_id, character_id, location_id, raw_character_text,
    raw_location_text FROM script_lines s1
    WHERE s1.character_id IS NOT NULL
    AND  episode_id = 1801) TO 'simpsons-s18e01.csv'
    WITH CSV DELIMITER ',' HEADER ;
```

The preceding SQL commands will export the relevant data to a set of CSV files, which we'll process further using a simple JavaScript file, which we run using Node.js. The content of the files looks something like this:

```
# characters.csv
id,name,normalized_name,gender,created_at,updated_at
7,Children,children,,2016-09-29 15:24:20.372136,2016-09-29 15:24:20.372136
12,Mechanical Santa,mechanical santa,,2016-09-29 15:24:20.690947,2016-09-29
15:24:20.690947
...

# locations.csv
id,name,normalized_name,created_at,updated_at
1,Street,street,2016-09-29 15:24:20.189358,2016-09-29 15:24:20.189358
2,Car,car,2016-09-29 15:24:20.213079,2016-09-29 15:24:20.213079

# simpsons-s18e01.csv
episode_id,character_id,location_id,raw_character_text,raw_location_text
1801,1,2,Marge Simpson,Car
1801,2,2,Homer Simpson,Car
1801,2,2,Homer Simpson,Car
1801,1,4,Marge Simpson,Auditorium
1801,2,4,Homer Simpson,Auditorium
...
```

By analyzing the output from this last file, we can determine which character appeared at a specific location. With the raw content extracted, we need to convert it so that we can easily load it into D3 and use it as a basis for our visualization.

Converting the data from the database

To create the visualization we saw at the beginning of this section, we need the data in a different format. We need to determine which people appear in a specific location. For that, we're going to create a single JSON file that looks like this:

```
{
    "links": [
    {
        "source": "c_1",
        "target": "l_2",
        "value": 1
    },
    {
        "source": "c_2",
        "target": "l_2",
        "value": 2
```

```
        },
        ...
    ]
,
"characters": [
    {
        "id": "c_16",
        "name": "DOCTOR ZITSOFSKY",
        "normalized_name": "doctor zitsofsky",
        "gender": "",
        "created_at": "2016-09-29 15:24:21.041002",
        "updated_at": "2016-09-29 15:24:21.041002",
        "type": "character"
    },
    ...
],
"locations": [
    {
        "id": "l_2",
        "name": "Car",
        "normalized_name": "car",
        "created_at": "2016-09-29 15:24:20.213079",
        "updated_at": "2016-09-29 15:24:20.213079",
        "type": "location"
    },
    ...
    ]
}
```

This JSON file shows which character appeared (and how often) in a specific location (the links array). To make processing in D3 easier, we also add all the locations and characters that are referenced from the links array to this file. We can accomplish this by running the groupSimpsons.js script in the data directory of this chapter:

```
const d3 = require('d3');
const fs = require('fs');
const _ = require('lodash');


d3.queue()
    .defer(d3.csv, "file:simpsons-s18e01.csv")
    .defer(d3.csv, "file:locations.csv")
    .defer(d3.csv, "file:characters.csv")
    .await(function (error, season, locations, characters) {
        process(season, locations, characters)
    });

function process(rows, locations, characters) {
```

```
// handle duplicate locations
var sanitizeLocations = {
    "21": "20",
    "23": "20",
    "18": "17",
    "11": "10" };

// Remove unwanted characters
var removeCharacters = [ "7", "12", "13", "20",
                         "24", "27", "34", "35",
                         "36", "37", "33", "21", "28",
                         "32", "4", "19", "23"];
var rows = rows.filter(function(d) {return
    !_.includes(removeCharacters, d.character_id)});

// first group the characters at the location
var locationGroups = {};
rows.forEach(function(d) {
    // we check if we need to replace the key
    var checkId = sanitizeLocations[d.location_id] ?
        sanitizeLocations[d.location_id] : d.location_id;
    if (!locationGroups[checkId]) {
        var location = {
            id: checkId,
            name: d.raw_location_text,
            persons: []
        };
        locationGroups[checkId] = location;
    }
    locationGroups[checkId].persons.push(d.character_id);
});

// when we have the locations we can generate our links
var links = Object.keys(locationGroups)
    .map(function(groupKey) {
    var data = locationGroups[groupKey];
    var counts = _.countBy(data.persons);

    return Object.keys(counts).map(function(key) {
        return {
            source: "c_" + key,
            target: "l_" + data.id,
            value: counts[key]
        }
    });
});

// flatten, since we've got an array of arrays
```

```
var finalLinks = _.flatten(links);

// based on these links, we can filter the characters and the locations
var uniqCharacters = _.uniqBy(finalLinks, 'source')
    .map(function(el) {return el.source});
var filteredCharacters = characters.filter(function(loc) {
    return _.includes(uniqCharacters, "c_" + loc.id);
}).map(function(el) {
    el.id = "c_" + el.id;
    el.type = "character";
    return el;
});

// finally remove the links that have only a single record
var counted = _.countBy(finalLinks, function(d)
    {return d.target});
var locationsToRemove = _.filter(Object.keys(counted),
    function(d) {return counted[d] === 1});

var filteredFinalLinks = _.filter(finalLinks, function(d) {
    return !_.includes(locationsToRemove, d.target);
})

// create reference to the locations that are in the array
var uniqLocations = _.uniqBy(filteredFinalLinks, 'target')
    .map(function(el) {return el.target});
var filteredLocations = locations.filter(function(loc) {
    return _.includes(uniqLocations, "l_" + loc.id);
}).map(function(el) {
    el.id = "l_" + el.id;
    el.type = "location";
    return el;
});

var output = {
    links: filteredFinalLinks,
    characters: filteredCharacters,
    locations: filteredLocations
};

fs.writeFile('./graph.json', JSON.stringify(output));
};
```

The comments in this script pretty much explain what is going on, so we won't go into detail here. The main steps taken by this script are the following:

1. Use `d3.queue()` to load the three CSV database exports.
2. Next, we group all the rows (the script lines) based on their location.
3. This gives us enough information to create the `links` array for output JSON.
4. Next, we filter out the isolated locations, that is locations that only appear once.
5. We select the referenced locations and characters that need to be added to the final JSON.
6. At this point, we have all the data for our output file and write it to `graph.json`.

You can apply this same setup to other episodes. For this, use the SQL `copy` queries shown earlier to get the correct information from the `script_lines` table, and make sure to update the `sanitizeLocations` and `removeCharacters` from this script to represent the input data.

Creating the force layout

Now that we have the input data, we can create a force layout. For this, we're going to take the following steps:

1. Before we do anything with the force layout, we'll set up the fonts, the title at the top of the screen, and the Simpsons logo.
2. We start by setting up the force simulation. This will define how the various nodes and links interact with each other.
3. Next, we're going to load the data and draw the circles and the lines.
4. Next, we're going to run the simulation and see the effect this has on our layout.
5. In the screenshot at the beginning of this chapter, you can see that we had images for the characters. We'll add these next.
6. Finally, we'll add the mouseover effects that highlight the paths and the nodes, set the text at the bottom of the screen, and allow you to drag nodes around.

We start by loading the Simpsons logo, which is an SVG file in itself.

Loading the fonts, setting up the title, and loading the Simpsons logo

A feature of SVG that we haven't looked into yet is the option to store SVG in an external file that you can either use directly in an `img` HTML element or load through D3 and attach at a specific location. We're going to do the latter. In the following code sample, we load an external SVG image and add it to the main chart. At the same time, we also add some text explaining what is shown in this visualization:

```
// part of the standard setup we do each example.
var svg = d3.select(".chart")
        .attr("width", width + margin.left + margin.right)
        .attr("height", height + margin.top + margin.bottom)
        .append("g")
        .attr("transform", "translate(" + margin.left +
            "," + margin.top + ")");

// Load the simpsons logo as svg
d3.xml("data/simpsons_logo.svg").mimeType(
    "image/svg+xml").get(function(error, xml) {
    var logoAndText = svg.append("g")
        .attr("class", "title")
    logoAndText.node().appendChild(xml.documentElement);
    logoAndText.select("svg g").attr("transform",
        "translate(-55 -140) scale(0.4)")

    // also append some text
    logoAndText.append("text").text("Characters & Locations")
        .attr("text-anchor", "middle")
        .attr("transform", "translate(" + (width/2) + ", 50)")
});
```

Using `d3.xml`, we load an SVG image. Once it's loaded, we create a new g to hold this image, and use `appendChild(xml.documentElement)` to attach the loaded SVG file to this newly created group. This results in a DOM structure that looks like this:

```
▼<svg class="chart" width="1100" height="750">
  ▼<g transform="translate(20,20)">
    ▼<g class="title">
      ▼<svg xmlns:dc="http://purl.org/dc/elements/1.1/" xmlns:cc="http://creativecommons.org/ns#" xmlns:rdf="http://www.w3.org/1999/02/22-rdf-syntax-ns#"
       xmlns:svg="http://www.w3.org/2000/svg" xmlns="http://www.w3.org/2000/svg" xmlns:sodipodi="http://sodipodi.sourceforge.net/DTD/sodipodi-0.dtd"
       xmlns:inkscape="http://www.inkscape.org/namespaces/inkscape" height="133" width="300" version="1.1" id="svg2" inkscape:version="0.91 r13725"
       sodipodi:docname="The_Simpsons_Logo.svg">
        ▶<metadata id="metadata52">…</metadata>
        <defs id="defs50"></defs>
        <sodipodi:namedview pagecolor="#ffffff" bordercolor="#666666" borderopacity="1" objecttolerance="10" gridtolerance="10" guidetolerance="10"
        inkscape:pageopacity="0" inkscape:pageshadow="2" inkscape:window-width="1920" inkscape:window-height="980" id="namedview48" showgrid="false"
        inkscape:zoom="3.5595182" inkscape:cx="145.19177" inkscape:cy="65.719167" inkscape:window-x="0" inkscape:window-y="34" inkscape:window-maximized=
        "1" inkscape:current-layer="g4"></sodipodi:namedview>
        ▶<g transform="translate(-55 -140) scale(0.4)" id="g4">…</g>
      </svg>
    </g>
```

Here, you can see that the loaded XML is added as a new `svg` element in the group we just created. The image in itself is a bit large, so we use a `transform` attribute on the nested `g` element (`logoAndText.select("svg g")`) to scale and position it in the top-left corner. In the preceding code fragment, we also add an additional `text` element, which shows the title of our visualization. The font we use isn't a standard one available on each browser, so we need to specify the following CSS to use a custom font (from `D04-01.css`):

```
@font-face {
    font-family: 'simpsons';
    src:    url('../data/fonts/simpsons.woff2') format('woff2'),
            url('../data/fonts/simpsons.woff') format('woff'),
            url('../data/fonts/simpsons.ttf')  format('truetype');
}

g.title text {
    font-size: 40px;
    font-family: 'simpsons'
}
```

With all this in place, we've got the title image and text for this example:

Next, we'll get to the interesting part of the section: defining the force simulation.

Setting up the force simulation

With the `d3-force` module, we can simulate forces between the nodes and the links of a graph. To use this module, we define a `simulation` object and add a number of forces to that object. When the simulation is started, D3 will apply the defined forces, and we can use the results from that to render a force layout on screen. A note before we dive into the details: working with forces isn't really an exact science. The way your layout will eventually look often requires a lot of experimentation with different forces and different force configurations.

For our example, let's start by looking at the `simulation` definition we used for this visualization:

```
var simulation = d3.forceSimulation()
    .force("link", d3.forceLink().id(function(d) { return d.id; }))
```

```
.force("charge", d3.forceManyBody().strength(function(d) {
    return d.type === "location" ? -40 : -40;
}))
.force("collide", d3.forceCollide(function(d) {
    return d.type === 'character' ? 50 : 20; }
).iterations(16))
.force("y", d3.forceY(height/2).strength(0.2))
.force("x", d3.forceY(height/2).strength(0))
.force("center", d3.forceCenter(width / 2, height / 2))
```

You create a force layout by instantiating a d3.forceSimulation. On this force simulation, we can define a number of forces (or write one ourselves, which we do in the next visualization). For this visualization, we defined a number of forces, which are explained in the following table. In this table, we only explain the most commonly used properties. For a more detailed explanation of what the forces do, you can check out the D3 API documentation at https://github.com/d3/d3-force#links.

Force	Description
d3.forceLink	d3.forceLink can be used to push linked nodes together or apart. The length of the link can be set by calling distance(). A link object needs to have a source and a target property and needs to have a unique identity (whose accessor can be set using the id() function). You can also use the strength() function to set the strength of the link. You specify the links you want to simulate by calling the links(...) function.
d3.forceManyBody	With this force, we can define whether nodes attract or repel each other. You can set this force through the strength() function. Negative values causes nodes to repel each other, and positive values cause nodes to attract each other. You can also specify the distance (through the distanceMin() and distanceMax() functions) at which these forces apply to one another. Only nodes between distanceMax() and distanceMin() affect each other.
d3.forceCollide	With the forceCollide force we can avoid nodes overlapping one another. By setting the radius() we can specify the required free space we want around a node. We can also specify the strength of this force through the strength() function.
d3.forceX / d3.forceY	With these two forces, we can push the nodes to a specific x or y location. Just like with the other forces, we can set the strength with the strength() function.

d3.forceCenter(x,y)	The final function used in this example is the forceCenter force. This force creates a centering force on the providing x and y coordinates.

Besides the individual forces, the simulation object also provides a number of properties and functions. Before we go into the properties, a quick note on how D3 forces work.

The forces we've seen in the previous table are simple functions that take a value that indicates how far along the simulation we are and calculate the position of the nodes (or links) based on that value. It can position the node using the following properties, which are assigned when the simulation starts:

- **index**: the node's index in the array
- **x**: the node's current x coordinate
- **y**: the node's current y coordinate
- **vx**: the node's current x velocity
- **vy**: the node's current y velocity

An example function, which slowly decreases the speed of a node, might look like this:

```
function force(alpha) {
    for (var i = 0, n = nodes.length, i < n; ++i) {
        node = nodes[i];
        node.vx -= node.x + (0.1 * alpha);
        node.vy -= node.y + (0.1 * alpha);
    }
}
```

An important aspect here is the alpha that is passed in. This alpha decrements each time a step (a tick) in the simulation runs. A simulation provides a number of properties that we can use to control this rate. Those properties, along with other properties on the simulation object, are shown here:

Property/function	Description
nodes(...)	Sets the array of nodes to run this simulation on. When you specify these nodes, the simulation will start and simulate all the specified forces.
restart()	You can specify the simulation to rerun based on the current state of the nodes by calling this function.
stop()	Using stop(), you can halt a currently running simulation.

force(name, force)	With force, you add a specific force (see the preceding code snippet) to this simulation. This force can be referenced through the specified name by calling simulation.force(name).
alpha(n)	Sets the alpha to the specified value in the range of 0 to 1. If not specified, the alpha at the beginning is 1.
alphaMin(n)	Sets the minimum value the alpha property can have. This value, together with the alphaDecay, determines how long (how many iterations) this simulation will run. The default is 0.001. When the alphaMin is reached, no new steps will be simulated.
alphaDecay(n)	Each step in the simulation decreases the alpha with this value. Its default is 0.0228, which results in approximately 300 iterations.
alphaTarget(n)	By default, the alphaTarget is 0. This means that the simulation stops at an alpha of 0, since after an alpha smaller then alphaMin we don't have additional simulation steps. You can also specify an alphaTarget larger than the alphaMin, which would cause the simulation to run forever at that alpha.
velocityDecay(n)	By setting the vx and vy properties, we can specify the velocity of the nodes. By default, each step/tick the velocity is decreased by multiplying the values by 0.4. You can use this value to make the simulation stop moving at a quicker rate.
find(x, y, radius)	This is a helper function that you can use to find nodes at a specific location that falls within the provided radius.
on(event, callback)	This is a listener that you can use to listen to tick events. There are two types of event you can listen to. tick, which is called whenever we simulate a step; and end, which is called at the end of the simulation. In this example, we use tick to update the nodes' and links' positions in each step of the simulation.

As we said earlier, the result of a force layout isn't easy to predict. To make it easier to experiment with some of the forces in this example, we added a small menu in the top-right corner. With this menu, you can experiment with different values.

After changing a value, hit **simulate**, and you can see the effect in action:

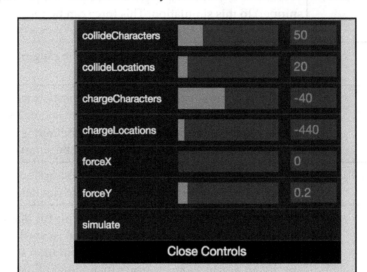

At this point, we've configured the simulation, but haven't run it yet. We'll first set up the nodes and links, and after that we'll show you how to run the simulation.

Loading the data and drawing the circles and the lines

To add the nodes and the lines, we use the same approach as we've used for all the chapters. We use d3.json to load the data, and then just add them to the SVG chart:

```
d3.json("./data/graph.json", function(error, graph) {
    // we create one big array of the characters and the locations
    graph.nodes = graph.characters.concat(graph.locations);

    // draw the links in two steps, the inner line
    var link = svg.append("g")
        .attr("class", "links")
        .selectAll(".links")
        .data(graph.links)
        .enter().append("path")
            .attr("class", "links");
    // and the outer line
    var link2 = svg.append("g")
        .attr("class", "links2")
        .selectAll(".links2")
        .data(graph.links)
        .enter().append("path")
```

```
        .attr("class", "links2");

    // draw the nodes and add listeners
    var node = svg.append("g")
        .attr("class", "nodes")
        .selectAll("g")
        .data(graph.nodes)
        .enter().append("g")

    // draw the circle
    node.append("circle")
        .attr("r", function(d) { return d.type === 'character' ? 25 : 5;
})
        .attr("class", function(d) {return d.type})
        .attr("stroke", "black");
}
```

You can see that we add `circle` for the nodes, where the `character` circle has a radius of 25 and a `location` circle a radius of 5. Besides that, we also define the `path` elements for the links. We draw the links in two steps, and style them with CSS:

```
path.links {
    fill:none;
    stroke: steelblue;
    stroke-width: 12;
    opacity: 0.5;
    stroke-linecap: round;
}

path.links2 {
    fill:none;
    stroke: white;
    stroke-width: 1;
    stroke-linecap: round;
}
```

This results in the following effect for the lines:

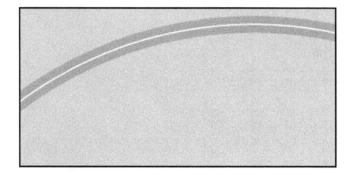

Now that we've added the lines and the nodes, we can run the simulation.

Running the simulation

To start the simulation, we just need to add the nodes to the simulation and the links to `force` with the `name` link:

```
simulation.nodes(graph.nodes).on("tick", ticked);
simulation.force("link").links(graph.links);

function ticked() {
    link.attr("d", linkArc)
    link2.attr("d", linkArc)
    node.attr("transform", function(d) {return
        "translate("+ d.x +" " + d.y + ")"})
}

function linkArc(d) {
    var cX = (d.source.x + d.target.x) / 2;
    var cY = Math.abs(d.source.x - width/2) > Math.abs(d.target.x
        - width/2) ? d.target.y : d.source.y;    return "M" + d.source.x +
"," + d.source.y + "Q" +
        cX + "," + cY  + "," + d.target.x + "," + d.target.y;
}
```

As you can see in this code, we've specified an `on` callback that listens to the `tick` event. In this callback, we set the location of the nodes (which is a `g` element) by setting the `transform` attribute. For the paths, our data element contains the source and target nodes (accessible through the `source` and `target` properties).

So, we use the positions of the source and target elements to draw a curved path. For the curved path, we use the `linkArc` function. This function draws a *Quadratic Bezier Curve*. In contrast to the *Cubic Bezier Curve* we saw earlier, this one only requires a single control point:

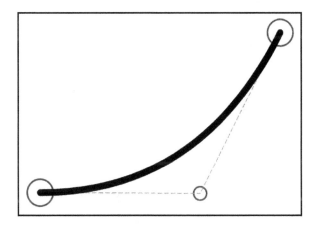

When we run this simulation you'll see something like this. The actual results might differ a bit based on OS, browser, and so on:

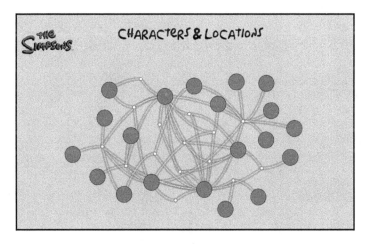

We're getting somewhere, but it looks a bit boring, without the faces of the Simpsons characters in there. In the next section, we'll show you how to get the images and add them to the circles.

Adding images to the circles for the characters

Before we can look at the JavaScript needed to add the images to the visualization, we first need to get the images. We could use Google and get the images manually, but that's too much work. So, we've written a script that pulls down the images from *WikiSimpsons* (`https://simpsonswiki.com`). WikiSimpsons has a detail page for each episode, in which they list appearances and show a nice image of that character.

The script (which can be found in `DVD3/src/chapter-04/data/downloadAppearances.js`) looks like this:

```javascript
var https = require('https');
var cheerio = require('cheerio');
var idl = require('image-downloader');

var mapping = {
    "waylon smithers, jr.": "waylon smithers",
    "charles montgomery burns" : "c. montgomery burns",
    "abraham simpson" : "grampa simpson",
    "irving zitsofsky" : "doctor zitsofsky"
}

var options = {
    host: 'simpsonswiki.com',
    path: '/wiki/Simpsons_Roasting_on_an_Open_Fire/Appearances'
}
var request = https.request(options, function (res) {
    var data = '';
    res.on('data', function (chunk) {
        data += chunk;
    });
    res.on('end', function () {
        // parse the incoming data and get all the names and image urls
        var allNames = loaded('ul.gallery.mw-gallery-
traditional').first().find('div.gallerytext a').map(function(i, d)
        {return loaded(d).text()}).toArray();
        var allImageUrls = loaded('ul.gallery.mw-gallery-
traditional').first().find('img').map(function(i, d)
        {return loaded(d).attr("src")}).toArray();

        allNames.forEach(function (d, i) {

            var name = mapping[d.toLowerCase()] ? mapping[d.toLowerCase()]
    : d.toLowerCase();

            var options = {
                url: allImageUrls[i],
```

```
                dest: './images/' + name + ".png",
                done: function(e, filename, image) {
                    if (e) {
                        console.log("Error while downloading ' "+ filename
+" ': "  + e.message);
                    }
                    console.log('File saved to', filename);
                },
            };
            idl(options);
        });
    });
});

request.on('error', function (e) {
    console.log("Error while getting wikisimpsons data: " + e.message);
});
request.end();
```

We won't go into too much detail about what this script does, but the main steps it takes are as follows:

1. It looks for a set of names at a specific location and stores these in the `allNames` property.
2. Next, it applies a mapping to make sure the names match the names for the characters we already have.
3. And then, it'll download the image of each character and stores these in the `images` directory, with the character name in the filename.

This results in a directory containing character images:

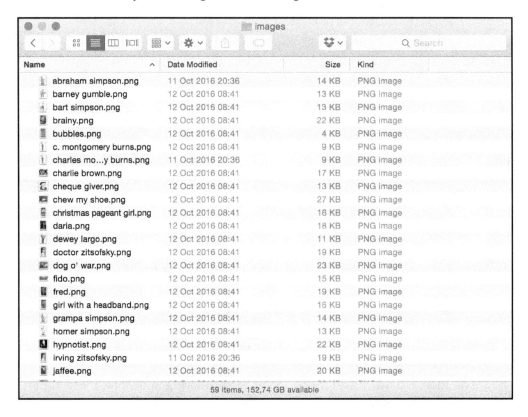

If you want to use this yourself, be sure to update the page where the appearances are downloaded from, and check whether the names used in the other sources match the names of the downloaded files. If there is a mismatch, use the `mapping` array to update the filenames before writing them to disk.

Now that we've got our images, we can add them to the node groups (the `g` elements) we've already created:

```
node.filter(function(d) {return d.type === 'character' })
    .append("image")
    .attr("xlink:href",  function(d) { return "./data/images/" +
d.name.toLowerCase() + ".png"; })
    .attr("height", 50)
    .attr("width", 50)
    .attr("transform", "translate(-25 -15)")
```

As you can see, we add an `image` element, and point the `xlink:href` attribute to the location where our images are stored. We do the final `transform` to center the top half of the image in the middle of the circle. Now we already have something that looks a lot better:

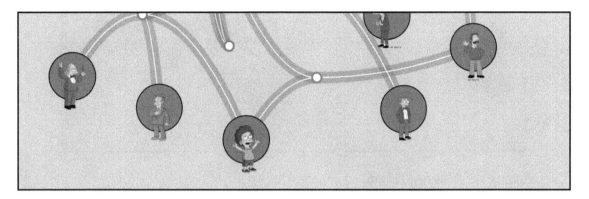

But, as you can see in this image, the image isn't contained inside the circle, but overflows. Luckily, with SVG (and also with CSS) we can use clip paths to determine the drawable area for an element. What we need to do is define a clip path that matches the size of our character node (a circle with a radius of 50) and assign this clip path to our node group.

Defining the clip path works in the same way as you'd use to create a circle. This time, however, we wrap it in a `clipPath` element and put it in the `defs` section of our chart:

```
d3.select(".chart").append("defs").append("clipPath")
    .attr("id","clip-1")
    .append("circle")
    .attr("r", 50)
```

Now we just need to assign this clip path to our nodes:

```
var node = svg.append("g")
    .attr("class", "nodes")
    .selectAll("g")
    .data(graph.nodes)
    .enter().append("g")
        // the line below is added
        .attr("clip-path","url(#clip-1)")
```

And this way, the content of all these `g` groups are limited to the circle rendered in our `clipPath` with `id` set to `clip-1`. Now when we show the layout, we see that the images are nicely contained within the circles:

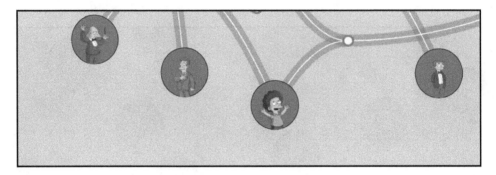

The last thing we need to do is add some interactivity.

Adding a mouseover effect for selecting and dragging.

In this last section for this visualization, we're going to add support for dragging nodes. We'll add a highlight when you select either a location or a character, and add a simple text at the bottom showing the name and location of the selected node.

We're aiming for something that looks like this:

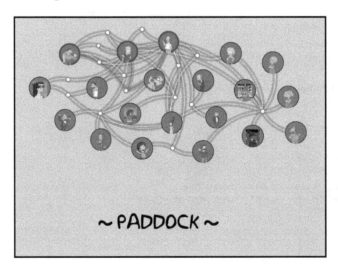

The first thing we need to do is add the correct listeners. Luckily, D3 provides standard functionality for this. To add the listener to our nodes, we extend the creation of the nodes with following code:

```
var node = svg.append("g")
    .attr("class", "nodes")
    .selectAll("g")
    .data(graph.nodes)
    .enter().append("g")
    .attr("clip-path","url(#clip-1)")
    .on("mouseover", mouseOver)
    .on("mouseout", mouseOut)
    .call(d3.drag()
        .on("start", dragstarted)
        .on("drag", dragged)
        .on("end", dragended));

// helper groupings
var groupedCharacterLinks = _.groupBy(graph.links, "source");
var groupedLocationLinks = _.groupBy(graph.links, "target")


var svgGroup = svg.append("g").attr("class","output-text")
    .attr("transform", function(d, i) { return "translate( " + (width/2) +
" " + (height-50) + ")"})
    .append("text").attr("text-anchor", "middle").text("");
```

Here, we add two mouse effects, the `mouseover` and the `mouseout`, and we use the `d3-drag` module to add drag support to the nodes. Whenever a node is dragged or we hover over it with the mouse, the relevant callbacks are called. Besides defining the callbacks, we also specify the output `text` element for the text (`svgGroup`), and create a key-value map for our links so that we can easily select the links and nodes we need to highlight (more on this later).

We'll start by looking at the `mouseOver` and `mouseOut` callbacks. First, let's see the `mouseOver` function:

```
function mouseOver(d) {
    // when you hover over a node, draw a circle and set some text
    d3.select(this).select("circle").attr("stroke-width","8");
    d3.select('.output-text text').text("~ " + d.name + " ~");

    if ((d.id[0]) === 'c') { // for a character
        // select the lines that leave from this node and set the style.
        var links = groupedCharacterLinks[d.id].map(function (el) { return
el.target.id });
        var selected = d3.selectAll("path.links2").filter(function (pp) {
```

```
                return _.includes(links, pp.target.id) && pp.source.id === d.id
            }).style("stroke","blue")
        } else { // for a location
            // select the lines that leave from this node and set the style.
            var links = groupedLocationLinks[d.id].map(function (el) { return
    el.source.id });
            var selected = d3.selectAll("path.links2").filter(function (pp) {
                return _.includes(links, pp.source.id) && pp.target.id === d.id
            }).style("stroke","green")

            // also highlight the relevant characters
            d3.selectAll(".nodes circle").filter(function (pp) {
                return _.includes(links, pp.id)
            }).attr("stroke-width", "8")
                .attr("stroke", "red");
        }
    }
```

The first thing we do in this function is highlight the node we're hovering over by setting its `stroke-width` to 8. Next, we set the name of the character or location in the `text` element we created for this, and which is positioned at the bottom of the screen. Next, we check whether we're dealing with a character or a location. We then use the key-value maps to quickly get the locations or characters connected to this node, and highlight the link between them. We do this by using the `filter` function on the selection of all the links (`d3.selectAll("path.links2")`), and on the result of this filter we use the `style` function to change the `stroke` style. If we're dealing with a location, we also select all the connected characters and replace the small black border with a thick red one.

In `mouseOut` we do the opposite:

```
function mouseOut(d) {
    // remove the text
    d3.select(this).select("circle").attr("stroke-width","0");
    d3.select('.output-text text').text("");
    // reset highlighting styles
    d3.selectAll("path.links2").style("stroke","white");
    d3.selectAll(".nodes circle")
        .attr("stroke", "black")
        .attr("stroke-width", 2);
}
```

Here, we just reset the `stroke` property of all the links and the `stroke` and `stroke-width` property of all the nodes back to their original state.

The last feature to implement is handling the three drag events: `dragstarted`, `dragged` and `dragended`:

```
function dragstarted(d) {
    if (!d3.event.active) simulation.alphaTarget(0.8).restart();
    d.fx = d.x;
    d.fy = d.y;
}

function dragged(d) {
    d.fx = d3.event.x;
    d.fy = d3.event.y;
}

function dragended(d) {
    if (!d3.event.active) simulation.alphaTarget(0);

    if (!d3.event.sourceEvent.shiftKey) {
      d.fx = null;
      d.fy = null;
    }
}
```

The event handlers are rather simple. In the `dragstarted` function we restart a simulation that will eventually keep the simulation running at an alpha of `0.8` (because the `alphaTarget` is larger than the `alphaMin`). When we drag the node (`dragged`), we use the `fx` and `fy` properties to fix the dragged node to the location we're dragging it to. Finally, in the `dragended` function, we set the `alphaTarget` to 0, which will make the simulation end normally, and we remove the fixed positions.

If you keep the shift key pressed when releasing the dragged node, we'll keep it fixed in that position:

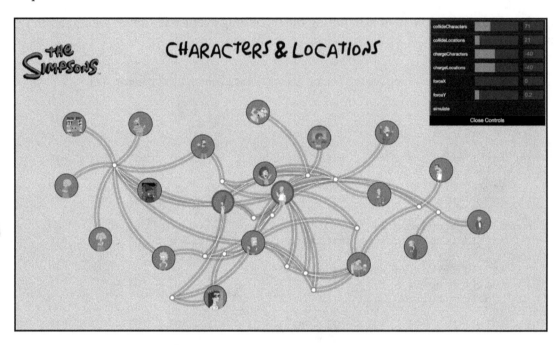

So now we've got a force layout that uses the data we prepared in the beginning of this chapter, uses the images downloaded from WikiSimpsons, and responds to mouse events.

As you can see, the force layout works well for showing a graph of connections. With the different forces you can apply, you can quickly get an interactive layout where you can drag and place the nodes. However, the force layout can also be used without links. In the next section, we'll use the force layout to create a *bubble chart* that shows the most frequent word used per Simpson character.

Bubble chart

In this section, we're going to create the following bubble chart. This chart shows which word throughout all the Simpsons episodes is spoken the most by a specific character:

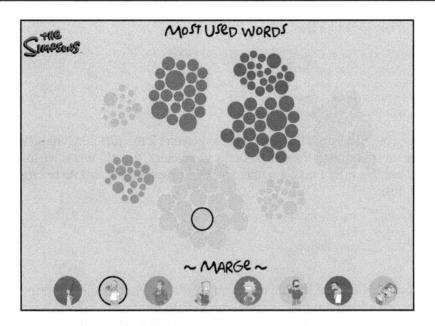

This bubble chart has the following features:

- The size of a circle represents how often that word is spoken
- It uses a force layout to position the bubbles
- We use a custom force function to group the words together for each character
- You can drag and drop individual words
- When you hover over a word, the word is shown at the bottom, and the character who said it is highlighted

But first we need to create the data that we'll use for this chart.

Getting the data

For this data, we're going to use the same database we used in the beginning of this chapter. This time we're going to use the data in the script_lines table, but only for the main characters that we want to show. In this case, we'll use Marge, Homer, Skinner, Bart, Lisa, Ned, Moe, and Millhouse.

The words we'll use look like this:

```
character_id,raw_character_text,normalized_text
1,Marge Simpson,ooo careful homer
2,Homer Simpson,theres no time to be careful
2,Homer Simpson,were late
1,Marge Simpson,sorry excuse us pardon me
```

We've got a very big file, with all the sentences spoken by the different characters. We could read in this big file and match the words to the characters directly when we load the visualizations, but this might take a while. So, we'll preprocess this data to create a CSV file that looks like this:

```
character,word,count,characterName
1,ooo,49,marge simpson
1,homer,1358,marge simpson
...
```

This CSV file contains a list of the most spoken words per character. The script we'll use to create this uses one additional file, stopwords.csv, to remove words such as I, it, the, and so on, so that we're left with real words. The script that counts everything is shown here:

```
d3.queue()
    .defer(d3.csv, "file:words.csv")
    .defer(d3.csv, "file:characters.csv")
    .defer(d3.csv, "file:stopwords.csv")
    .await(function (error, words, characters, stopwords) {
        process(words, characters, stopwords)
    });

function process(words, characters, stopwords) {

    var characterKV = characters.reduce(function(res, el) {
        res[el.id] = el;
        return res;
    }, {});

    var stopWordsMap = stopwords.reduce(function(res, el) {
        res[el.word] = el.word;
        return res;
    }, {});

    var characterWords = {};

    words.forEach(function(row, i) {
        // if character is new, add it to the mapping
```

```
        if (!characterWords[row["character_id"]]) {
            characterWords[row["character_id"]] = {};
        }
        var processFor = characterWords[row["character_id"]];

        var wordsInLine = row["normalized_text"].split(" ");
        wordsInLine.forEach(function(word) {
            if (!stopWordsMap[word] && word.length > 2) {
                if (processFor[word]) {
                    processFor[word] = processFor[word] + 1;
                } else {
                    processFor[word] = 1;
                }
            }
        });
    })

    var output = [];
    // filter out the single usages and the 'stopwords'
    Object.keys(characterWords).forEach(function(key) {
        Object.keys(characterWords[key]).forEach(function(wkey) {
            if (characterWords[key][wkey] > 20)  {
                output.push({
                    character: key,
                    word: wkey,
                    count: characterWords[key][wkey],
                    characterName: characterKV[key]
                        .normalized_name
                });
            }
        });
    });

    fs.writeFile('./words_filtered.csv',d3.csvFormat(output));

};
```

There isn't anything special in this script, we just iterate over all the words, and keep track of how often a word is spoken by a specific character. To limit the size of the resulting list, we filter out words that have been used less than twenty times (if
(characterWords[key][wkey] > 20)). With the list of words per character, we can now start creating the bubble chart.

Create the bubble chart

To create the chart, we're going to take the following steps:

1. Loading and preparing the data.
2. We start by setting up the simulation and the forces that will group the nodes together.
3. Then we'll load the data, and create the circles for each word.
4. We'll also need to add a legend at the bottom to show who said a specific word.
5. Finally, we add the mouse handlers to support drag and drop and highlight the correct character and word.

Even though the data is already in a usable format, we'll need to group the data together and determine the min and max. We'll start with that.

Loading and preparing the data

The following code shows how the raw CSV lines are converted into groups, which are easier to show in our visualization:

```
d3.csv("./data/words_filtered.csv", function(row) {
    row.count = +row.count;
    return row;
}, function(error, words) {

    // Only show top 20 words per character, and group them
    // together.
    var groups = _.groupBy(words,"character");
    var res = Object.keys(groups).map(function(key) {
        return _.sortBy(groups[key], "count").reverse().slice(0, 20)
    });

    // determine max in group
    var groupMax = {};
    res.forEach(function(d) {
        var groupMax =  _.maxBy(d, "count");
        groupMax[groupMax.character] = groupMax;
    });

    // and add them to a single array
    var mostUsed = _.flatten(res);

    var max = d3.max(mostUsed, function(d) {return d.count});
    var min = d3.min(mostUsed, function(d) {return d.count});
```

```
    var scaleRadius = d3.scaleLog().base(2).domain([min, max]).range([5,
30]);

    // and use the scale to determine the radius
    mostUsed.forEach(function(d) {
      d.r = scaleRadius(d.count);
    });
    ...
```

In this fragment, we first select the top twenty most used words per character to avoid too much bubbles in the chart, and create a `groupMax` object, which contains the row with the word that occurs the most in that group. We also create an array of all the words (`mostUsed`) by flattening the `res` array and use that to calculate the maximum and minimum values with the `d3.max()` and `d3.min()` functions. With the min and the max values, we setup a `d3.scaleLog` scale, which we can use to determine the size of circles we're going to create. We use a `d3.scaleLog` instead of a `d3.scaleLinear` here in order to have a more even distribution of circle sizes among all the characters.

At this point, we've got a list of nodes (`mostUsed`) that contains all the information we need to draw the word circles. First, though, let's set up the simulation.

Setting up the simulation

The simulation is set up in pretty much the same way as we did in the previous section:

```
simulation = d3.forceSimulation()
    .velocityDecay(0.07)
    .alphaDecay(0.006)
    .force("charge", d3.forceManyBody().strength(-13))
    .force("x", d3.forceX(width/2).strength(0.020))
    .force("y", d3.forceY(height/2).strength(0.03))
    .force("collide", d3.forceCollide(function(d)
        {return d.r + 2}))
    .force("center", d3.forceCenter(width / 2, height / 2))
    .force("cluster", clusteringForce)
```

The main change, however, is that we haven't specified a `link` force because our nodes aren't linked together. We have also added a `velocityDecay` and an `alphaDecay` to tune how quickly the velocity of the nodes drop, and to make the simulation run a bit longer. This gives the nodes time to position themselves together. What you'll also see is that the `collide` force uses the radius of the nodes to avoid overlapping nodes.

The interesting part here is the `clusteringForce` function, which applies a custom force. This force moves the smaller circles to the largest one in a cluster of words:

```
function clusteringForce(alpha) {
    mostUsed.forEach(function(d) {
        var cluster = groupMax[d.character];
        if (cluster === d) return;

        // determine the distance between this node and the
        // cluster node
        var x = d.x - cluster.x;
        var y = d.y - cluster.y;
        var l = Math.sqrt(x * x + y * y);

        // we need to take into account the nodes radii to avoid
        // overlapping. Note that this only avoid overlapping with
        // the main node, doesn't avoid running over other nodes.
        var r = d.r + cluster.r ;

        // as long as we're still not touching
        if (l > (r)) {

            // move the smaller nodes towards the main node
            l = (l - r) / l * (alpha);

            d.vx -= (x*l)/40;
            d.vy -= (y*l)/40;
        }
    });
}
```

In this custom force function, we calculate the distance between this node and the biggest node in the cluster. If the circles aren't touching, we change the speed to move this node towards the location of the biggest node. With `/40`, we can set the relative speed of the smaller nodes. You can also see that we use the `alpha` value to slow down the speed of the nodes. When our alpha decreases, so will our additions to the speed vector.

With our simulation set up, we can add some nodes.

Adding the nodes and running the simulation

Adding the nodes follows the same principle we've used in all the visualizations:

```
var color = d3.scaleOrdinal().domain(Object.keys(groups))
    .range(d3.schemeCategory20);

var node = svg.append("g")
    .attr("class", "nodes")
    .attr("transform", "translate(0 -60)")
    .selectAll("circle")
    .data(mostUsed)
    .enter().append("g")

node.append("circle")
    .attr("r", function(d) {return scaleRadius(d.count)})
    .attr("fill", function(d) { return color(d.character); })
    .attr("stroke", function(d) { return
        d3.rgb(color(d.character)).darker(0.2); });
```

In this fragment, we create g elements and append a circle to each element. The color of this circle is determined by the color scale, which maps the character IDs to one of the colors of the d3.schemeCategory20 scale. The stroke around this circle is a slightly darker version of the fill color, which we create by using the d3.rgb(..).darker(0.2) function. With this function, we can create a darker version of a specific color. The 0.2 value determines how much darker we want the color to be (if you want a lighter function, you can use lighter instead). At this point, we can already run the example, if we call the following:

```
simulation
    .nodes(mostUsed)
    .on("tick", ticked);

function ticked() {
    node.select("circle")
        .attr("transform", (function(d) {return "translate(" + d.x + " " +
d.y + ")"}))
    }
```

We take the same approach as we did in the previous example, and use the x and y values from the bound data element (which are set by the simulation) to move the circles to the correct location. Now we'll see the circles being moved into place using the forces we specified:

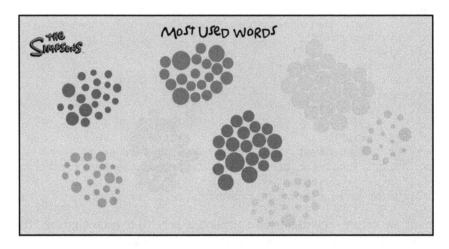

This is already starting to look better, but without a legend, we don't really know which circle belongs to which Simpsons character.

Adding the legend

To add a legend, we'll create a new g element and bind the res value (remember, these are the grouped elements):

```
var scalePoint = d3.scalePoint().domain(Object.keys(
    groups)).range([0, width]).padding([5]);

d3.select(".chart").append("defs").append("clipPath")
    .attr("id","clip-1")
    .append("circle")
    .attr("r", 40)
    .attr("width","20")
    .attr("height",100);

var legendGroups = svg.append("g").attr("class","legend")
    .selectAll("g").data(res)
    .enter().append("g")
    .attr("clip-path","url(#clip-1)")
    .attr("transform", function(d, i) { return "translate(" +
        scalePoint(d[0].character) + " " + (height-30) + ")"})
```

```
legendGroups.append("circle")
    .attr("fill", function (d,i) {return (color(d[0].character))})
    .attr("class", function(d,i) {return "legend-" +
       d[0].character})
    .attr("r", 40)

legendGroups.append("svg:image")
    .attr("xlink:href",  function(d) { return "./data/images/" +
       d[0].characterName.toLowerCase() + ".png";})
    .attr("height", 90)
    .attr("width", 70)
    .attr("transform", "translate(-30 -30)");
```

We determine the location of each element by using a d3.scalePoint scale. This scale can be used to divide the range into equal segments for each domain object, just like the d3.scaleBand. But instead of returning the position of the band, we get the value of the center of the band. The fill of each circle is set to the color scale we saw earlier, and we add a custom class, which we'll use in the next section to highlight this circle. In this code fragment, you can also see that we use a clipPath to further contain the images within the size of the circle. The result is that we get a nicely drawn row of characters:

The final step to do is add some interactivity.

Adding interactivity

We'll add the functionality to drag the nodes, just like we did for the previous visualization, and we'll use mouseover to highlight which character said that specific word, and also show the word just above the legend. We won't show the code here that handles the drag events, since that is exactly the same as we saw in the previous visualization.

The mouseover and mouseout events are pretty straightforward:

```
// Shows the word that is hovered over
var svgGroup = svg.append("g").attr("class","output-text")
    .attr("transform", function(d, i) { return "translate( "
       + (width/2) +  " " + (height-80) + ")"})

svgGroup.append("text")
```

```
              .attr("text-anchor", "middle")
              .text();

    node.append("circle")
              .attr("r", function(d) {return scaleRadius(d.count)})
              .attr("fill", function(d) { return color(
                 d.character); })              .attr("stroke", function(d) { return
    d3.rgb(
                 color(d.character)).darker(0.2); })
              .on("mouseover", function(d) {
                 d3.select(this).attr("stroke", "black")
                 d3.select(this).attr("stroke-width", "4")
                 d3.select(".legend-" + d.character).attr(
                    "stroke", "black")              d3.select(".legend-" +
    d.character).attr(
                    "stroke-width", "8")              var toShow =
    d.word.charAt(0).toUpperCase() +
                    d.word.slice(1);              d3.select(".output-text
    text").text( "~ " + toShow
                    +  " ~")
              })
              .on("mouseout", function(d) {
                 d3.select(this).attr("stroke", "")
                 d3.select(".legend-" + d.character)
                    .attr("stroke", "")
                 d3.select(".output-text text").text("")
              })
```

In the `mouseover` event, we highlight the current circle, and set the current `d.word` as the value of the `output-text` group. In the `mouseout`, we reset everything again.

And that's it. We now have an interactive visualization, which automatically groups words together:

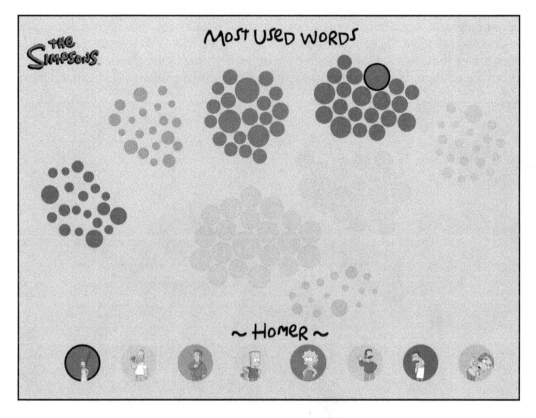

That's it for the force diagrams in this chapter. In the next section, we'll look at an alternative way of visualizing graphs, and that is through a *chord diagram*.

Chord diagram

The force layout we've seen at the beginning of this chapter can nicely be used to show the relations of a graph. An alternative way we can show relations is in a chord diagram. With a chord diagram, all the nodes are moved to the edge of a circle, and ribbons are drawn between nodes that have a relation with each other. The size of the ribbon reflects the weight of the relation. In this section, we're going to create the following chord diagram:

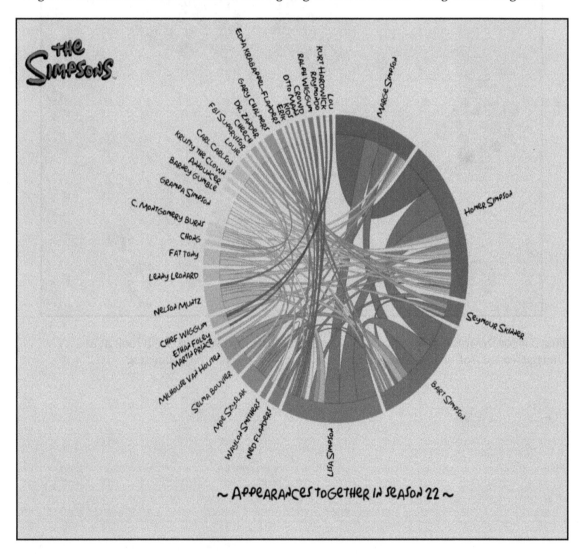

In this diagram, we show when specific characters appeared together in a specific location. We don't do this for a single episode, but show this for a complete season. In this case, we used season 22. When you open this example (`<DVD3>/chapter04/D04-03.html`), you can see that the chord diagram also responds to mouse events. When you hover over an edge, the chord diagram will only show the outgoing connections from this specific edge and make the other ribbons and edges transparent:

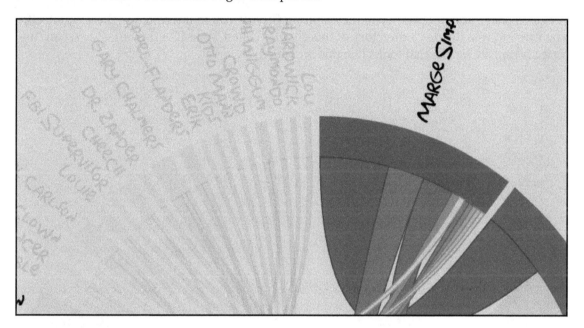

In the next sections, we'll explain how to set up a chord diagram. The first thing we need to do is get the data.

Preparing the data

We use the same approach for sanitizing the data as we did in the previous sections. We get the data from the database and use a simple JavaScript file to convert and prepare the data. The output from this script is a CSV file that we can then load with D3.

We'll skip the script used to sanitize the data (since it looks pretty much the same as the previous ones), and just show you the resulting CSV. If you're interested in the script itself, you can find it in the `data` directory of this chapter called `appearTogether.js`. When this script is run, a CSV file that looks like this is created:

```
from,to,value
1,2,104
1,8,47
1,9,55
1,11,8
1,15,6
1,17,8
1,22,12
1,31,10
1,71,7
1,568,7
2,3,7
2,8,83
2,9,64
2,11,13
2,15,11
2,17,17
2,18,6
2,22,11
2,31,17
2,33,9
2,71,11
2,139,9
```

Each row indicates two characters (`from` and `to`) appearing together. The `value` columns indicate how often the characters appeared together in the same location. Each connection will only appear once, so that's why we have a connection from 1 to 2, but you don't see this one from 2 to 1.

With this data, we can next load it in D3 and create the data structure D3 expects.

Loading and converting the data in D3

The first step we need to take is to load the data. We load the CSV we saw in the previous section, and also load the `characters.csv` file we created at the beginning of this chapter so we can show the names in the chord diagram instead of the `id`. Before we look at the code, it's important to understand the format D3 expects.

For a chord diagram (and also for the matrix diagram we'll show in the next section), D3 expects data in the form of a matrix:

```
      "1"   "2"   "3"
"1"   0     5     8
"2"   5     0     4
"3"   8     4     0
```

In this 3x3 matrix, you can see how D3 expects the data. In this example, we have three IDs, so we created a matrix with 3 rows and 3 columns. The value of each matrix cell corresponds to the number of times the IDs appear together. So, in this case, ID 1 and ID 2 appear together 5 times, 1 and 3 appear eight times, and 2 and 3 appear four times.

The following code fragment shows how we create this matrix:

```
d3.queue()
    .defer(d3.csv, "./data/appear_together.csv")
    .defer(d3.csv, "./data/characters.csv")
    .await(function (error, words, characters) {
        process(words, characters)
    });

// first thing to do is setup the matrix
function process(data, characters) {

    // use for easy referencing
    var characterKV = characters.reduce(
      function(res, el) { res[el.id] = el; return res; }, {});

    // the target matrix.
    var matrix = [];

    // we need to get the from, to, put them in an array and use that for
the size.
    var toIds = data.map(function(d) {return d.from});
    var fromIds = data.map(function(d) {return d.to});

    // these are the unique ids and define the dimensions of the matrix.
    var uniqueIds = _.uniq(toIds.concat(fromIds));
```

```
        // initialize the array with zero values
        uniqueIds.forEach(function(id, i) {
            // initialize an empty matrix with zeros
            matrix[i] = Array.apply(null,
    Array(uniqueIds.length)).map(Number.prototype.valueOf,0);
        });

        // now walk through the rows, and fill the specific rows
        data.forEach(function(d) {
            var n = uniqueIds.indexOf(d.from);
            var m = uniqueIds.indexOf(d.to);

            matrix[n][m] = +d.value;
            // do we need to way back?
            matrix[m][n] = +d.value;
        });

        ...
```

In this code fragment, we first determine the number of unique IDs we have in our dataset. The number of unique IDs determines the size of our target matrix. When we've got our unique IDs, we create an empty n by n matrix, filled with zeros. Next, we'll walk through each row in the `data` array (the information from the CSV file) and set the corresponding values in the matrix. Because we prefilled the matrix with zeros, all matrix cells will contain a value. The following screenshot shows what this matrix looks like:

```
▼ Array[37]
    ▶ 0: Array[37]
    ▶ 1: Array[37]
    ▶ 2: Array[37]
    ▶ 3: Array[37]
    ▶ 4: Array[37]
    ▶ 5: Array[37]
    ▼ 6: Array[37]
        0: 0
        1: 0
        2: 0
        3: 0
```

In this example, we've got a `37x37` matrix, where the values from the CSV files are stored in the correct positions. Now that we've got the data, we can use D3 to create our diagram.

Create a chord diagram from the data

To create a chord diagram from the matrix, we use the d3.chord() function. This function will convert our matrix to a set of SVG paths. Before we add the elements to the graph, we're first going to set up some d3.js helpers:

```
var color = d3.scaleOrdinal()
    .domain(d3.range(uniqueIds.length))
    .range(d3.range(uniqueIds.length)
        .map(function(i) { return
d3.interpolateRainbow(i/uniqueIds.length);}));

var chord = d3.chord()
    .padAngle(0.03);

var arc = d3.arc()
    .innerRadius(innerRadius)
    .outerRadius(outerRadius);

var ribbon = d3.ribbon()
    .radius(innerRadius);
```

We set up a color d3.scaleOrdinal that creates a unique color for each of our unique IDs. Next, we create a d3.chord. With this function, we can convert the matrix to a set of objects that can be used to draw the arc segments and the ribbons. The following table shows what can be configured on the chord():

Property/function	Description
.padAngle([angle])	Sets the spacing between the individual groups (the arc segments).
.sortGroups([func])	Determines the order in which the arc segments appear.
.sortSubGroups([func])	Determines the order in which the ribbons leave the individual arc segments.
.sortChords([func])	Set the sorting for the chords to the provided function. You can use this function to determine the order in which the ribbons are drawn.

Besides d3.chord, we also set up a d3.arc generator that we use to draw the arc segments, and finally a d3.ribbon generator, which can be used to create the connecting paths between the arc segments.

With the setup of the generators done, let's draw the chord diagram:

```
var g = svg.append("g")
    .attr("transform", "translate(" + width / 2 + "," + height / 2 +
")")
    .data (chord(matrix));

# the ribbons
g.append("g")
    .attr("class", "ribbons")
    .selectAll("path")
    .data(function(chords) { return chords; })
    .enter().append("path")
    .attr("d", ribbon)
    .style("fill", function(d) { return color(d.target.index); })
    .style("stroke", function(d) { return
d3.rgb(color(d.target.index)).darker(); })

# groups for the arc segments and texts
var group = g.append("g")
    .attr("class", "groups")
    .selectAll("g")
    .data(function(chords) { return chords.groups; })
    .enter().append("g");

# draw the arc segments
var paths = group.append("path")
    .style("fill", function(d) { return color(d.index); })
    .style("stroke", function(d) { return color(d.index); })
    .attr("d", arc)
```

The first thing we do is we add a g element to which we bind the result of the chord(matrix) function. When we call this function, our matrix is converted to an object that looks like this:

```
▼ Array[70] 🔘
  ▼ 0: Object
    ▼ source: Object
        endAngle: 0.2544991825670184
        index: 0
        startAngle: 0
        subindex: 1
        value: 104
      ▶ __proto__: Object
    ▼ target: Object
        endAngle: 0.9305355690832959
        index: 1
        startAngle: 0.6760363865162775
        subindex: 0
        value: 104
      ▶ __proto__: Object
    ▶ __proto__: Object
  ▼ 1: Object
    ▶ source: Object
    ▶ target: Object
    ▶ __proto__: Object
  ▶ 2: Object
  ▶ 3: Object
```

With this data bound to the g element, we first draw the individual ribbons. We can draw each ribbon by creating a path element and setting the d property to the result of calling ribbon(d), where d is one of the elements from the result of the chord(matrix) function. We also set the fill and the stroke properties using the color scale. Next, we add a number of groups that will contain the arc segments, and later on, the names of the characters. To draw the arc segments, we set the d property of each added path to the result of the arc(d) function.

When we render the chord diagram at this point, we see the following:

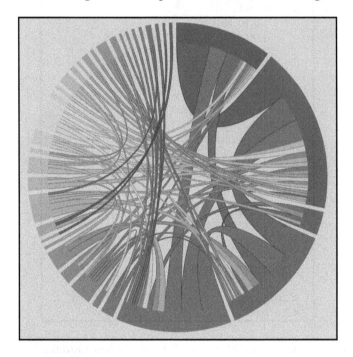

Now that we've got basic chord ready, we can add the character names by just adding a `text` element to the previously created groups:

```
group.append("text")
    .each(function(d) { d.angle = (d.startAngle + d.endAngle) / 2; })
    .attr("dx", function(d) {return arc.centroid(d)[0] >
        0 ? "1em" : "-1em"})
    .attr("dy", "0.3em")
    .attr("transform", function(d) {
        return "rotate(" + (d.angle * 180 / Math.PI - 90) + ")"
            + "translate(" + (innerRadius + 26) + ")"
            + (d.angle > Math.PI ? "rotate(180)" : "");
    })
    .style("text-anchor", function(d) { return d.angle >
        Math.PI ? "end" : null; })
    .text(function(d, i) { return characterKV[uniqueIds[i]].name});
```

This is the same approach we used in the previous chapter when positioning the labels of the radial tree. The last step is to add some interactivity.

Adding a mouseover effect

We'll add the mouseover effect on the arc segments. The following code fragments show what we need to do:

```
var paths = group.append("path")
    .style("fill", function(d) { return color(d.index); })
    .style("stroke", function(d) { return color(d.index); })
    .attr("d", arc)
    .on("mouseover", function(d) {
        var index  = d.index;

        var invalidInces = [];
        d3.selectAll(".ribbons path")
            .filter(function(dRibbon) {
                var isValid = (dRibbon.source.index == index ||
                dRibbon.target.index == index);
                if (isValid) {
                    invalidInces.push(dRibbon.source.index);
                    invalidInces.push(dRibbon.target.index);
                };
                return !isValid;
            })
            .style("opacity", "0.1");

        d3.selectAll(".groups path")
            .filter(function(dPath) { return !_.includes(
                invalidInces, dPath.index); })
            .style("opacity", "0.1");

        d3.selectAll(".groups text").filter(function(dPath) {
            return !_.includes(invalidInces, dPath.index); })
            .style("opacity", "0.1");

    })
    .on("mouseout", function(d) {
        d3.selectAll(".ribbons path").style("opacity", "1");
        d3.selectAll(".groups path").style("opacity", "1");
        d3.selectAll(".groups text").style("opacity", "1");
    });
```

On the `mouseover` event, we first determine which elements should be hidden and store them in the `invalidInces` array. Next, we use `d3.selectAll(..).filter()` to select the elements for which we need to change the opacity. On the `mouseout` event, we simply reset the opacity of all the elements to 1 to show them again.

The result of this is that we can now quickly see which characters appear together by just hovering over one of the arc segments:

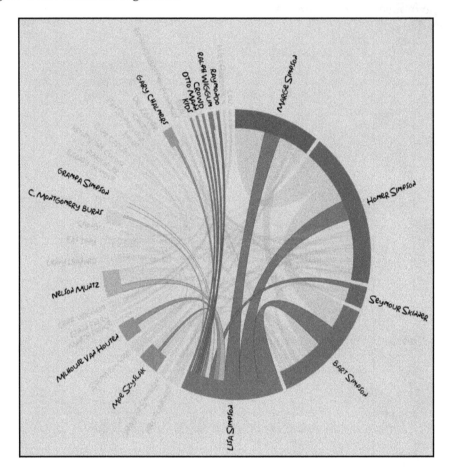

For a last example, we're going to visualize the same matrix as a *matrix diagram*.

Matrix diagram

For the last visualization of this chapter, we're going to create a matrix diagram. With a matrix diagram, we visualize the graph of nodes as a single matrix. For this example, we'll visualize the most important Simpsons characters as they appear together in a scene.

The result that we'll create is this:

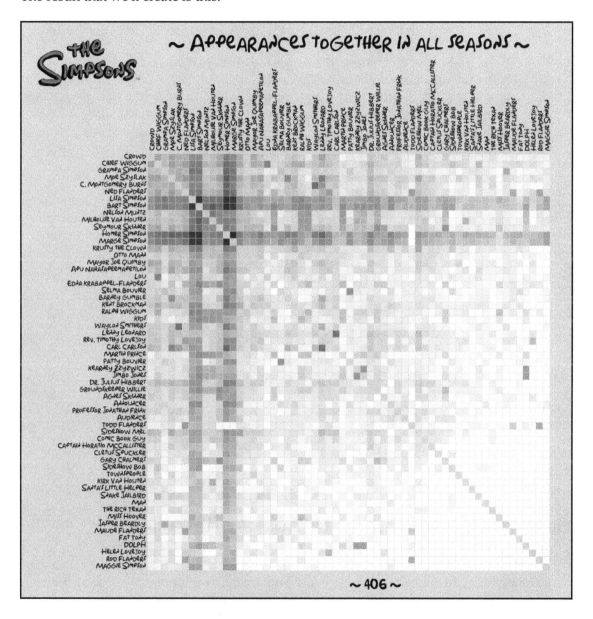

This visualization provides the following features:

- It shows a matrix where the intensity of the color reflects how often characters appear together in a location.
- When you hover you mouse, it changes the opacity of the row and column to better identify the two characters the value applies to.
- When you click on the visualization, it changes sorting order. By default, the sort order is on the total amount of appearances a character has. If you click, it changes to sort on the number of unique characters the character appears with.
- At the bottom, the value of a specific matrix cell is shown. This represents the appearances the two characters at this intersection have.

We'll skip over preparing the data, because we use the same data as we did for the previous example. This time, however, we parse the episodes of all the seasons. The resulting data file that we'll work with is located in the `DVD3/chapter-04/data` directory and is named `appear_together_all.csv`:

```
from,to,value
1,2,3726
1,3,141
1,8,2179
1,9,2203
1,10,116
1,11,291
1,14,83
1,15,173
1,17,243
1,18,71
```

In the next section, we'll load the data and prepare it a little bit before presenting it in the matrix diagram.

Setting up the data and the standard D3 components

In the following code fragment, we're going to prepare the data for use. We'll also set up a number of scales we'll use for laying out and coloring the individual rectangles:

```
// load the required information sources
d3.queue()
    .defer(d3.csv, "./data/appear_together_all.csv")
```

```
    .defer(d3.csv, "./data/characters.csv")
    .await(function (error, words, characters) {
        process(words, characters)
    });

// first thing to do is setup the matrix
function process(data, characters) {

    // create a KV for lookups
    var characterKV = characters.reduce(function (res, el) {
        res[el.id] = el;
        return res;
    }, {});

    // to we need to get the from, to, put them in an array and use
    // that for the dimensions size.
    var toIds = data.map(function (d) { return d.from });
    var fromIds = data.map(function (d) { return d.to });
    var uniqueIds = _.uniq(toIds.concat(fromIds));

    // count the max, which we use to set up the color scale
    var max = d3.max(data, function (d) { return +d.value });
    var cv = d3.scaleLog().base(10).domain([1, max]).range([0, 1]);
    var color = function (v) {
        return v == 0 ? d3.rgb(255, 255, 255) :
d3.interpolateBlues(cv(v));
    };
    // use a scaleBand to draw the individual records
    var x = d3.scaleBand().range([0, width]).domain(
            d3.range(0, uniqueIds.length)).paddingInner([0.05]);

    // Setup the values we'll be sorting on
    var uniqueCounts = determineTotalValue(uniqueIds, data);
    var uniqueTargets = determineTotalCount(uniqueIds, data);

    // zip up everything in a single object
    var idsEnriched = uniqueIds.map(function (d, i) {
        return { id: d, total: uniqueCounts[i], counts: uniqueTargets[i]}
    });

    // now that we've got the values to sort on, lets define two sort
methods
    var sorts = [sortTotal, sortCounts];

    ...
```

We load the data using d3.queue(), since we use information from multiple sources. Once loaded, we create a key-value map to look up character names (characterKV), and determine the unique characters IDs that are in our data (uniqueIds). Based on these IDs and the max value of the data elements, we set up the following scales:

- cv: A logarithmic scale. We use this because the values for the main Simpsons characters are much higher than for the rest. With a normal scale, the color distribution wouldn't look as nice.
- color: This is a simple function where we interpolate over a set of blue colors using the cv scale. If the value is 0, we return a white color.
- x: For positioning the rectangles, we use d3.scaleBand with a small padding. In the next section, we'll use the bandWidth property of this scale to determine the width and height of our rectangles.

Besides the scales, we count the total amount of connections for each ID (uniqueCounts) and the distinct characters each character has a connection with (uniqueTargets):

```
function determineTotalValue(uniqueIds, data) {
    var uniqueCounts = uniqueIds.map(function (d) {
        var toCount = _.filter(data, {to: d})
            .reduce(function (initial, d) {
            return initial + +d.value
        }, 0);
        var fromCount = _.filter(data, {from: d})
            .reduce(function (initial, d) {
            return initial + +d.value
        }, 0);

        return toCount + fromCount;
    });

    return uniqueCounts;
}

/**
 * Count number of unqiue connections
 */
function determineTotalCount(uniqueIds, data) {
    var uniqueTargets = uniqueIds.map(function (d) {
        var toCount = _.filter(data, {to: d}).length
        var fromCount = _.filter(data, {from: d}).length

        return toCount + fromCount;
    });
```

```
        return uniqueTargets;
    }
```

With these values, we create a single object called `idsEnriched`. Finally, we set up an array
(`sorts`) with the two sort options we provide:

```
function sortCounts(data) { return _.sortBy(data, ["counts"]).reverse() }
function sortTotal(data) { return _.sortBy(data, ["total"]).reverse() }
```

Now that we've done our generic preparation, we can fill the matrix.

Filling the matrix with data

We will fill the matrix by calling the `prepareData` function, with our raw data (the rows
loaded from the CSV file), the enriched IDs, and the sort function we want to apply:

```
        // based on the raw data, the enriched ids and a sort function
        // we create the matrix to show
        var toShow = prepareData(data, idsEnriched, sorts[0]);

        function prepareData(data, idsEnriched, sort) {
            // determine the sort order
            var idsEnriched = sort(idsEnriched);
            // the target matrix.
            var matrix = [];
            // initialize the array with zero values
            uniqueIds.forEach(function (id, i) {
                matrix[i] = Array.apply(null,
    Array(uniqueIds.length)).map(Number.prototype.valueOf, 0);
            });

            // now walk through the rows, and fill the specific rows
            data.forEach(function (d) {
                var n = _.findIndex(idsEnriched, {id: d.from});
                var m = _.findIndex(idsEnriched, {id: d.to});
                matrix[n][m] = +d.value;
                matrix[m][n] = +d.value;
            });

            // we want to keep track of which data belongs where so add an
    id.
            var mappedData = idsEnriched.map(function (d, i) {
                return {id: d.id, row: matrix[i]}
            });

            return mappedData;
```

```
    }
```

In the `prepareData` function, we sort the `idsEnrichted` based on the provided `sort` function. The order of `idsEnrichted` will determine the order in which the matrix is constructed. The matrix is first filled with 0 values, and then the `value` property of each `data` row is set at the correct location in the matrix. Before returning the matrix, we add an additional `id` to each matrix row. We need this to make adding transitions and updating data later on easier. The data at this point looks like this:

```
▼ Array[59]
  ▼ 0: Object
      id: "2"
    ▶ row: Array[59]
    ▶ __proto__: Object
  ▼ 1: Object
      id: "8"
    ▶ row: Array[59]
    ▶ __proto__: Object
  ▼ 2: Object
      id: "1"
    ▼ row: Array[59]
        0: 3726
        1: 2179
        2: 0
        3: 2203
        4: 243
```

Next up, we can start drawing the rectangles and the labels.

Drawing the visualization

We draw the visualization in the `show` function:

```
show(toShow);

function show(toShow) {
    ...
}
```

Drawing this matrix is done in a couple of steps:

1. First, we create the matrix rows as g elements.
2. For each element in a matrix row, we create a rectangle.
3. Once the rectangles are drawn, we add the text elements at the top.
4. And finally, we add the text elements at the bottom.

The first thing we do is drawing the individual rows:

```
// we first select all the rows and map the data based on id
var row = svg.selectAll(".row")
    .data(toShow, function (d) { return d.id });

// for the newly added rows, we add a group to contain the name and the
rectangles
var newRows = row.enter()
    .append("g")
    .attr("class", "row")
    .on("click", function (d) {
        // change the sort order, and reshow everything.
        sorts.reverse();
        show(prepareData(data, idsEnriched, sorts[0]));
    })

// merge with the rows that are updated and set the properties.
newRows.merge(row)
    // determine the position of the row
    .transition().duration(2000)
        .attr("transform", function (d, i) {
            return "translate(0," + x(i) + ")";
        })
    // we want to process each data element separately. So we do an
each.
    .each(function (d, i) {
        // here we add the rectangles
        ...
    });
```

Here, we follow the basic D3 approach of selecting elements, adding new elements using enter, and setting the positional and data driven values after a merge. Note that when we call data we provide an additional function that tells D3 that, when updating, data should be identified by the id property instead of the array index. When we first append a g element we also add a mouse listener, which, when the row is clicked, reverses the sorts array, recreates the matrix by calling prepareData, and refreshes the visualization by calling show. A new D3 function, which we haven't seen before, is the each() function.

This function allows us to process each bound data element separately. In our case we use this to add the individual rectangles (the following code fragment is contained within the each() function):

```
            // select all the existing rectangles in this row. And bind a single
            // data row.
            var rectangles = d3.select(this).selectAll("rect").data(d.row)

            // for the new rectangles, just create a new rect
            rectangles.enter().append("rect")
                .merge(rectangles)
                // set the position and size of each rectangle.
                .attr("x", function (d, j) { return x(j)})
                .attr("height", x.bandwidth())
                .attr("width", x.bandwidth())
                // add the row and column as data property for easy reference in
    the
                // mouse listeners
                .attr("data-r", function(e, j) {return i})
                .attr("data-c", function(e, j) {return j})
                // register mouse listeners to highlight the rows/columns
    currently selected
                .on("mouseover", mouseOver)
                .on("mouseout", mouseOut)
                // colors can change so we transition those.
                .transition().duration(2000)
                    .attr("fill", function (e, j) {
                        return i == j ? d3.rgb(200, 200, 200) : color(e);
                });
```

In the each function, we use d3.select to select the current row (which is a g element), and once again do the standard enter(), append(), and merge() steps. We use the scales we set up at the beginning of this section to position the rectangles, and use the color function to set the fill of the rectangles. We also add a data-r and data-c attribute to each added rectangle. We'll use these later on for our mouseover and mouseout event listeners.

If we run the visualization with the code at this point, we already have a visualization:

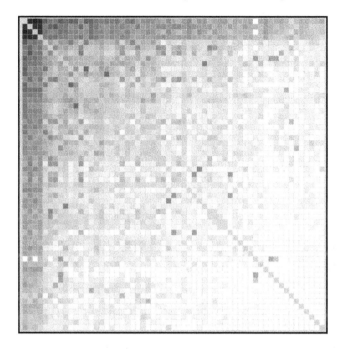

Adding the text is done like this:

```
// also bind the data to the text at the top of the matrix
var topText = svg.selectAll(".top").data(toShow, function (d) { return
d.id })

// set the standard values when creating new elements
topText.enter()
    .append("text")
    .attr("class", "top")
    .attr("dx", "0.5em")
    .text(function (e, j) { return characterKV[toShow[j].id].name})
    .attr("text-anchor", "begin")
    .merge(topText)
    // set the position on new and updated elements using a transition
    .transition().duration(2000)
        .attr("transform", function (d, j) {
            return "translate(" + (x(j) + (x.bandwidth())) + " 0)
rotate(-90)"
        });

// set the text on the left
```

```
        newRows.append("text")
            .attr("dy", "0.8em")
            .attr("dx", "-0.3em")
            .attr("fill", "black")
            .attr("class", "left")
            .attr("text-anchor", "end")
            .text((function (d, i) {
                return characterKV[d.id].name
            }));

        // finally add the legend at the bottom
        svg.append("text")
            .attr("class","legend")
            .attr("transform", "translate(" + (width/2) + " " + (height+100) +
    ")")
            .text("")
    }
```

This is the standard method D3 uses whenever we want to add elements. The final step is to look at the mouse handlers we defined in this section.

Add mouse handlers

With the mouse handlers, we want to create the following effect:

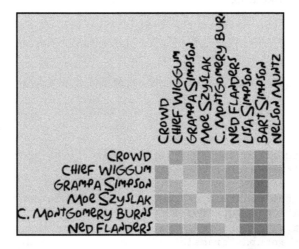

As you can see, the rows and columns preceding the selecting rectangle are made transparent to make it easier to see which characters we're talking about. We also add a simple legend at the bottom showing the value of the selected rectangle:

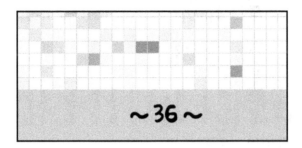

The mouse handlers look like this:

```
function mouseOver(d) {
    var r = +d3.select(this).attr("data-r");
    var c = +d3.select(this).attr("data-c");

    d3.selectAll("rect").filter(function(e) {return
+d3.select(this).attr("data-c") === c})
        .filter(function(e) {return +d3.select(this).attr("data-r") < r})
        .attr("opacity","0.3")
    d3.selectAll("rect").filter(function(e) {return
+d3.select(this).attr("data-r") === r})
        .filter(function(e) {return +d3.select(this).attr("data-c") <
c}).attr("opacity","0.3")
    d3.selectAll(".legend").text("~ " + d + " ~")
}

function mouseOut(d) {
    d3.selectAll("rect").attr("opacity", "1")
    d3.selectAll(".legend").text("")
}
```

The `mouseOut` handler just resets the default values. The `mouseOver` handler uses the `data-r` and `data-c` attributes that we've set on each rectangle to determine which rectangles need to have their opacity lowered. And with that, we've got our matrix working. When you hover over a rectangle, you can see the opacity changes and the value appearing at the bottom.

When you click, you can see the transitions that have been set up, moving the labels and rows around, and changing the colors:

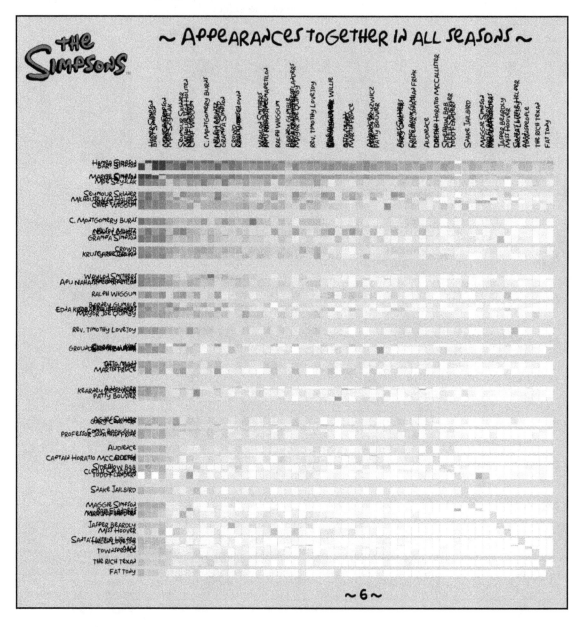

And that's it for this chapter on visualizing graphs of data.

Summary

In this chapter, we've explored a number of different ways you can visualize graphs of data. D3 provides a number of different standard tools and techniques to visualize these data structures. A very versatile one is the `d3.force` layout. With this layout, you specify how the various parts of the graph (the nodes and the edges) influence each other, and by running the simulation, D3 moves the elements to their correct positions. While very versatile, it can quickly become unreadable when the number of interconnections increases. For an alternative to the force layout, D3 provides a chord layout. With the chord layout, we can easily visualize more complex interactions in a compact visualization. The last visualization we showed in this chapter uses a matrix layout, where we created a big table that allows you to quickly see the links between elements without having to follow lines or ribbons.

So far, we've mostly looked at visualizing standard data structures. D3 also provides extensive support for visualizing geo-related information. In the next chapter, we'll show you how D3 can help with creating interactive maps and visualizing geographic shapes.

5
Working with Geo Data

In the previous chapters, we've created a number of visualizations based on various data sources. One type of data that we haven't looked at yet is geographic data (or geo data for short). In this chapter, we'll show the support D3 has for visualizing and manipulating geographic data.

We'll create the following visualizations in this chapter:

- **Election visualization**: The first visualization we'll create is one where we show the 2016 US presidential election results. We'll show a map of the USA, where each county is colored based on how it voted.
- **Earthquake map**: D3 can display in a number of different projections. We'll create a map that visualizes the location and magnitude of earthquakes. We'll also provide a way you can quickly switch between projections to see what they look like.
- **3D Globe**: With D3 we can create a fake 3D globe on which we can plot data and information. For this example, we'll create a globe on which we show the percentage of Internet users per country.

We start with the election map of 2016.

Elections 2016 choropleth

For our first example, we're going to create an election map for the 2016 presidential election. In this map, we'll color the results of each individual county based on whether they voted democrat or republican. The map we create will look like this:

Additionally, we'll also show a list of small cubes below the map that show the results of the individual counties. These counties are ordered per state (as they already appear like that in our source data). Before we can do all this, we first need to collect the data, and prepare it for use in D3.

Preparing data

As we'll see in this chapter, when working with geo-related data, a lot of time is spent on preparing the data, and representing it is rather straightforward. For this first example where we're going to create an election map, we first need to get create a JSON file containing the geometries for all the individual states, counties and districts.

To get those geometries in the correct format, we're going to take the following steps:

- Getting the geometry from the US Census Bureau and explore these in QGIS. Note that while we use these geometry sources, there are many other sources for geometries online.
- Converting the shapefiles to TopoJSON.
- Getting the results per county, state and district.

We start by getting the shapefiles.

Getting the geometries from the US Census Bureau and exploring these in QGIS

The shapefiles can be downloaded from the US Census Bureau. Go to the `https://www.census.gov/geo/maps-data/data/tiger-cart-boundary.html` website and download the 500k file, which is the most precise one (we've also included this one in the `data` directory for this chapter). When you unpack this zip file, you'll see a number of files, of which the interesting one is the `cb_2015_us_county_500k.shp` file. This is a shapefile in **ArcGIS** format, which contains all the polygons (and some additional data) representing all the individual districts in the US.

To better understand what is in these files it would be nice if we could open and visualize this shape. Luckily, there is an open source tool which can help you with that called QGIS. Installing QGIS is beyond the scope of this book, but if you go to `http://www.qgis.org/en/site/forusers/alldownloads.html?highlight=installation` you can find detailed installation instructions for every OS. Note that you don't need to install QGIS, we just use it to familiarize yourself with the shapefiles we've downloaded.

When you've started QGIS and dragged the shapefile to the QGIS window, it will open the shape, and show the contents. This looks a bit like this after some zooming in:

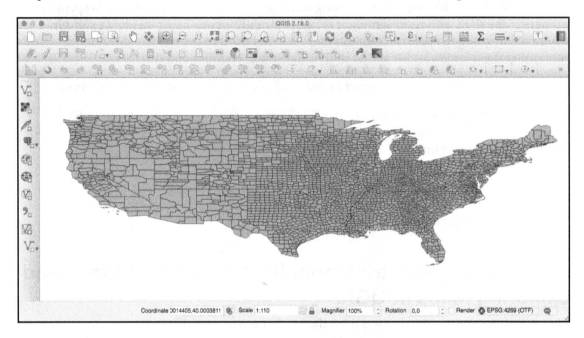

In this image, you can already see the USA and all the individual districts. You might notice that this shows the USA differently than you normally see. That is caused by the projection that QGIS uses to render the information from the shapefile. This doesn't just occur in QGIS but is also something you see in other projections. For instance, when you look at the Mercator projection, which is used in most web-based map services, the sizes of the continents are also incorrect. In this case, the data in the shapefile is stored in the **North American Datum 1983 (NAD83) geographic coordinate system (GCS)**, and QGIS uses a **projected coordinate system (PCS)** to translate these points and render them in 2D. By changing this PCS we can change how this map is represented. The main thing to remember is that, by changing the projection (the PCS), we can change how the map is rendered.

If you want to know more about these systems, ArcGIS has some great resources on this:

More information on GCS: `http://help.arcgis.com/en/arcgisdesktop/10.0/help/index.html#/What_are_geographic_coordinate_systems/003r00000006000000/`.

More information on PCS: `http://help.arcgis.com/en/arcgisdesktop/10.0/help/index.html#/What_are_projected_coordinate_systems/003r0000000p000000/`.

In QGIS these two different types of systems are consolidated in a **Coordinate Reference System** (**CRS**), which defines the GCS as well as the PCS. By setting the project CRS we can change how the data is projected. Click on the label that says **ESPG** on the right bottom, and you'll see the following screen:

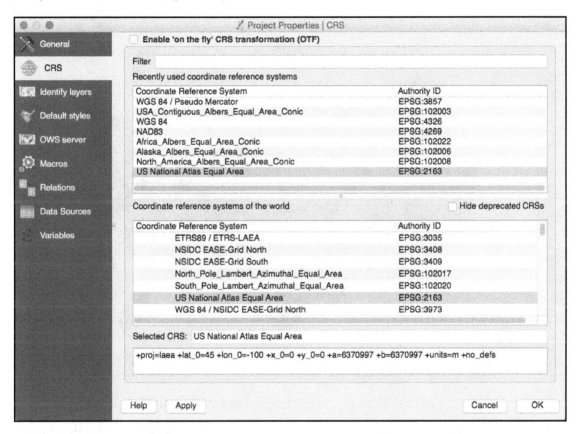

On this screen select the **US National Atlas Equal Area** projection (**EPSG:2163**) and click **OK**. This will render the US outline as you would normally expect to see it:

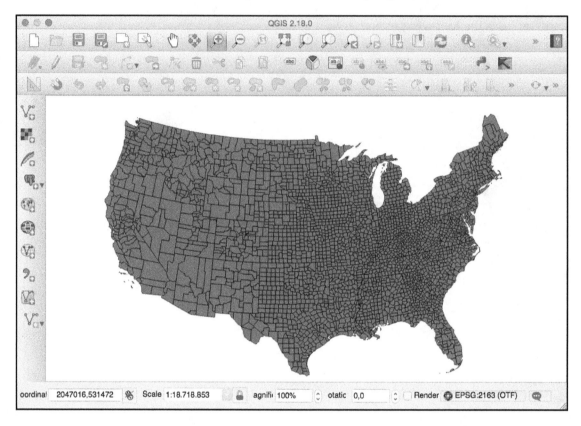

Later in this section, we'll use this same projection to render the individual counties in D3.

With QGIS, we can also explore what additional information is available besides the shape of the district. Select the icon in the top bar with the small **i**, and click on a district. This will show you the additional information stored together with the shape:

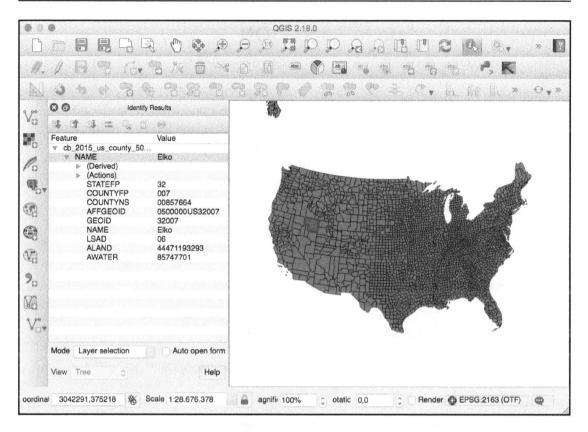

For our example, we're especially interested in the **GEOID** feature, since that uniquely identifies a county, and also happens to be the ID which is used to communicate election results. So now that we now what shapes we have, and that we've identified the associated data we need, we can take the next step and convert this file into a format we can use with D3.

Converting the data to TopoJSON

When visualizing data there are two formats we can use with D3: **GeoJSON** and **TopoJSON**. Both of these formats can be used to encode geographic data structures containing `Points`, `LineStrings`, `Polygons`, `MultiPoints` and `MultiLineStrings` as a JSON file. GeoJSON (`http://geojson.org/`) is the de facto standard for encoding data in JSON, and TopoJSON is an extension of GeoJSON, which tries to eliminate redundancy and create smaller files and speed up processing. TopoJSON (`https://github.com/topojson/topojson`) was created by Mike Bostock, the man behind D3. In this section, we'll convert the shapefile we explored in the previous section to a TopoJSON file which we can read in D3.

TopoJSON isn't just a data format, it also comes with a set of tools you can use to convert shapes files (and existing GeoJSON files) to TopoJSON. The first thing to do is install TopoJSON. The TopoJSON tools come as NPM modules, so we can just install it using the following command (since we installed NPM in the first chapter of this book):

```
$ npm install -g topojson topojson-simplify
```

This installs the `TopoJSON` and the `topojson-simplify` packages. These tools, however, work on GeoJSON files as their input. Since we have a shapefile, we first need to convert the shapefile to a GeoJSON file. We could use QGIS for this, but there is another simple NPM package that can help us with this called `mapshaper`. Let's install that package as well now:

```
npm install -g mapshaper
```

To test whether the installs were successful, we can run the `geo2topo -V`, `toposimplify -V`, and `mapshaper -v` commands:

```
$ geo2topo -V
2.0.0
$ toposimplify -V
2.0.0
$ mapshapser -v
0.3.37
```

We'll use **mapshaper** to convert the shapefile to a GeoJSON file, and we'll also extract the unique ID (GEOID) that we identified when exploring the shape in QGIS. Before we do that, let's use mapshaper to get some more information about our shapefile:

```
mapshaper -i cb_2015_us_county_500k.shp -info
Layer name: cb_2015_us_county_500k
Records: 3,233
Geometry
    Type: polygon
    Bounds: -179.148909 -14.548699 179.77847 71.365162
```

```
        Proj.4: +proj=longlat +datum=NAD83
    Attribute data
        Field       First value
        AFFGEOID    '0500000US01005'
        ALAND       2291820706
        AWATER        50864677
        COUNTYFP    '005'
        COUNTYNS    '00161528'
        GEOID       '01005'
        LSAD        '06'
        NAME        'Barbour'
        STATEFP     '01'
```

As you can see, it gives information about the coordinate systems used (longlat as the
PCS and NAD83 as the GCS), and more importantly, it shows the data associated with each
record. Here, we once again see the **GEOID** field, which we'll use to identify the records in
our GeoJSON and TopoJSON files. To limit the size of the resulting file, we'll also remove
all the other attributes except the **NAME** and **GEOID** one. We use the following command
for this:

```
$ mapshaper cb_2015_us_county_500k.shp -filter-fields GEOID,NAME -o id-
field=GEOID cb_2015_us_county_500k.geojson
Wrote cb_2015_us_county_500k.geojson
This will result in a GeoJSON file, identified by the GEOID field:
$ ls -l cb_2015_us_county_500k.geojson
-rw-r--r--  1 jos  staff  29251019 Nov 18 09:57
cb_2015_us_county_500k.geojson

$ head cb_2015_us_county_500k.geojson
{"type":"FeatureCollection","features":[
{"type":"Feature","geometry":{"type":"Polygon","coordinates":[...]},"proper
ties":{"GEOID":"01005","NAME":"Barbour"},"id":"01005"},
...
```

This file now contains all the correct data, but the file 29 MB so we'll use the TopoJSON
tools to shrink this file to a more acceptable size.

```
$ geo2topo -q 20000 cb_2015_us_county_500k.geojson | \
        toposimplify -F -S 0.3 >
cb_2015_us_county_500k.simplified.topojson \
    && ls -l cb_2015_us_county_500k.simplified.topojson

$ ls -l cb_2015_us_county_500k.*.topojson
-rw-r--r--  1 jos  staff  1948305 Nov 18 11:59
    cb_2015_us_county_500k.simplified.topojson
```

With the conversion to TopoJSON we've reduced the size from 29 MB to 2 MB. We first used `geo2topo` to convert the input to TopoJSON. By playing around with the `-q` value we can define the coordinate precision we want to keep in the result. This means that the lower this value, the less distinct coordinates we're left with. After this conversion we pipe the data to `toposimplify` where we further reduce the size. We can once again play around with the `-S` parameter, to specify how aggressive the simplification should be. Usually it is a good idea to experiment with these values to get a topology that suits your purpose. If you're interested in the technologies behind these two tools, you can look at the article from here:
`http://zevross.com/blog/2014/04/22/spatial-data-on-a-diet-tips-for-file-size-re`
`duction-using-topojson/`.

While 2 MB might still seem like a large file, if you serve this file using a web server that support `gzip` file format, the actual file size further drops to around 400 KB. Before we start with D3 to visualize this TopoJSON, lets open it in QGIS, to see what the map looks like after this simplification:

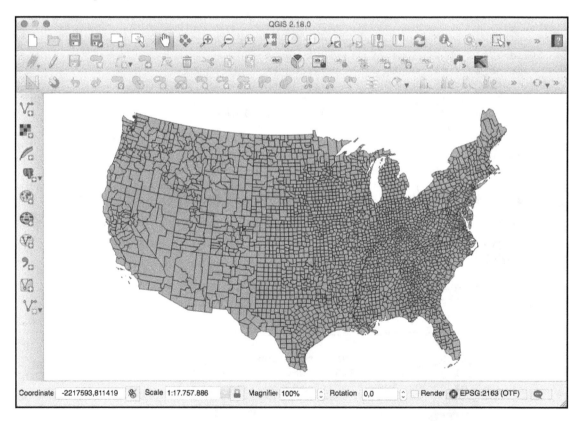

It still looks very detailed and more than sufficient for our purpose. Now that we have the map, the next step is to get the election results per district.

Getting the results per county

At the time of writing, there wasn't an official source for the county-level election results. Luckily, though, there is a project on GitHub, which collected all the results from various sources and combined them in a single download:

`https://github.com/tonmcg/County_Level_Election_Results_12-16`.

From this GitHub repository, you can download the `2016_US_County_Level_Presidential_Results.csv` file, which contains all the results for each individual district. One thing to note is that, for Alaska there are no county specific results, since the State of Alaska doesn't provide these. So we'll use the state-wide results for those specific counties. Looking at the data we see the following:

```
,votes_dem,votes_gop,total_votes,per_dem,per_gop,diff,per_point_diff,state_
abbr,county_name,combined_fips
...
3135,644.0,3409.0,4297.0,0.149872003724,0.793344193623,"2,765",64.35%,WY,Su
blette County,56035
3136,3233.0,12153.0,16661.0,0.194045975632,0.729428005522,"8,920",53.54%,WY
,Sweetwater County,56037
3137,7313.0,3920.0,12176.0,0.600607752957,0.321944809461,"3,393",27.87%,WY,
Teton County,56039
3138,1202.0,6154.0,8053.0,0.149261144915,0.764187259406,"4,952",61.49%,WY,U
inta County,56041
```

As you can see from the header, we've got a lot of information we can work with. For this example, we'll use the `per_dem`, `per_gop` fields to determine the color of each county. The higher the difference, the more pronounced will be the color blue for the democrats and the color red for the republicans.

Drawing the visualization

We visualize the data in two different way. We show it as a map, and as a set of small cubes. First, we'll look at the steps you need to take to show the map:

The first thing we do is to set up some scales and helper functions:

```
// setup the projection
var projection = d3.geoAlbersUsa();
var path = d3.geoPath()
```

```
    .projection(projection);

// add the scales
var scale = d3.scaleLinear().domain([-0.8, 0, 0, 0.8])
    .range(["blue", "#A6D8F0", "#FFB3A6" ,"red"]);
```

Here we see two features provided by D3 that help in showing geo data. With the `d3.geoAlbersUsa` function, we tell D3 that we want the geometry rendered using the `Albers USA` projection coordinate system. With the `d3.geoPath()` function, we convert JSON in GeoJSON format to a set of SVG paths (or HTML5 canvas instructions as we'll see later). In the next example, we'll give an overview of which projections are supported by D3. Besides the geo-specific parts, we also create a scale, which we use to map the percentile difference between democratic and republican votes. For example, if there are 40 percent more republic votes the value is 0.4, if there are 30 percent more democratic votes the value is -0.3. We use four colors in the scale, so that the democratic colors are always blueish, and the republican ones are always reddish.

The map-related data is already in the correct format, and we don't need to change much for the election results:

```
d3.queue()
    .defer(d3.json, "./data/cb_2015_us_county_500k.simplified.topojson")
    .defer(d3.csv, "./data/2016_US_County_Level_Presidential_Results.csv")
    .await(function (error, topo, data) {
        process(topo, data)
    });

function process (topo, data) {
    // make the ids the same in both files, by converting them to numeric
values
    topo.objects['cb_2015_us_county_500k']
        .geometries.forEach(function(d) { d.id = +d.id; });
    data.forEach(function(d) {
        d['combined_fips'] = +d['combined_fips'];
        d['per_gop'] = +d['per_gop'];
        d['per_dem'] = +d['per_dem'];
    });
    // lookup map.
    var dataKV = data.reduce(function(res, el) { res[el.combined_fips] =
el; return res; }, {});
    ...
}
```

The only thing we do here, after loading the data using `d3.queue()` (which allows you to wait for multiple data sources to be loaded asynchronously), is convert some values to numeric ones. We also create a key-value map, so that we can get to the data by just using the ID.

Once all these preparations have been done, drawing the map is really simple:

```
function process (topo, data) {

  ...
  svg.append("g").attr("class","map").selectAll(".county")
    .data(topojson.feature(topo, topo.objects[
      'cb_2015_us_county_500k']).features)
    .enter()
    .append("path")
    .attr("class","county")
    .attr("id",function(d) {return "cid-" + d.id})
    .attr("fill", function(d) {
      var electionData = dataKV[d.id];
      return electionData
          ? scale(electionData["per_gop"] - electionData["per_dem"])
          : "#ccc"
    })
    .attr("d", path)
  ...
};
```

In this code fragment we bind the TopoJSON data, we created at the beginning of this section. By calling `topojson.feature(topo,` `topo.objects['cb_2015_us_county_500k']).features` we convert the TopoJSON data to GeoJSON. By just calling `path(d)` we can now convert the GeoJSON feature to a SVG path, which can be assigned to the d attribute. The color of each district is based on the `scale` we defined.

We do use an additional check, when we can't find the ID of the geometry in our `dataKV` map, we return a gray color (`#ccc`). At this point, when we run this example, we can already see our map:

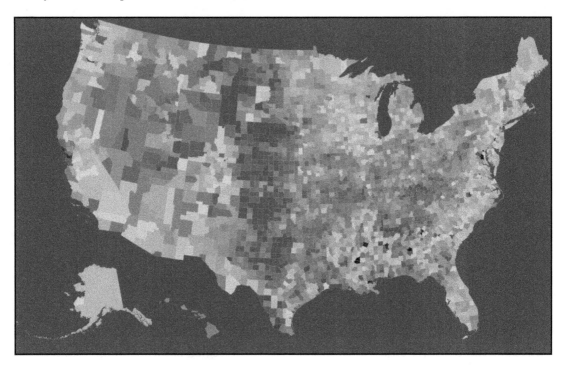

The next part we add are the cubes at the bottom:

```
function process (topo, data) {
    ...

    // based on the loaded data create a scaleband
    // we want 200 elements per row
    var gridBand = d3.scaleBand().domain(
        d3.range(0,100)).range([0, width]);
    var grid = svg.append("g")
        .attr("class","grid")
        .attr("transform", "translate(0 " + 550 + ")")
        .selectAll("rect").data(data).enter()
        .append("rect")
        .attr('fill',function(d) {return scale(
            d["per_gop"] - d["per_dem"])})
        .attr("x", function(d, i) { return gridBand(i % 100) })
        .attr("y", function(d, i) { return Math.floor(
            i / 100) * gridBand.bandwidth() })
```

```
    .attr("width", function(d) { return gridBand.bandwidth() })
    .attr("height", function(d) { return gridBand.bandwidth() })
    .attr("data-state", function(d) {return d['state_abbr']});
    ....
};
```

Here we first create a d3.scaleBand which we use to correctly position 100 cubes next to one another. Next, we just iterate over all the election data (data), and draw the rectangles, based on the gridBand. Note that we also add a data-state attribute to the rect we create. We'll use this in the next section to add some interaction. When we now run this example, you'll also see a set of rectangles at the bottom:

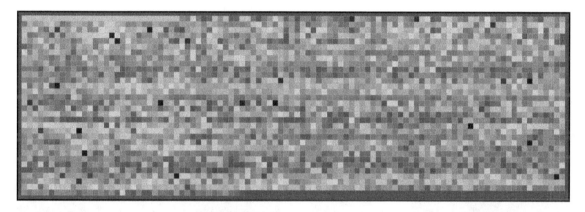

Just having those rectangles at the bottom doesn't really add much. So let's add some interaction. We'll add the following:

- When you hover over a rectangle, it'll show the name, and the percentages in a text element.
- When you hover over a rectangle, we'll fade out all the rectangles of the other states.
- When you hover over a rectangle, we'll add a black outline to the state in the map.

To add interactions we add a number of listeners to the rect we just created:

```
.on("mouseover", function(d) {
  d3.select(this).attr("class","selected")

  svg.select('#cid-'+d['combined_fips']).attr("class", "selected");
  svg.selectAll('rect').attr("style","opacity: 0.3")

  var sel = svg.selectAll('rect[data-state="' + d['state_abbr'] + '"]');
```

```
        sel.attr("style","opacity: 1")

        svg.select("g.text  text").text(d['state_abbr']
            + ": " + d['county_name']
            + " (Dem: " + (parseFloat(d['per_dem']).toFixed(2))
            + " Gop: " + (parseFloat(d['per_gop']).toFixed(2)) + ")");
    })
    .on("mouseout", function(d) {
        d3.select(this).attr("class","")
        svg.selectAll('rect').attr("style","opacity: 1")
        svg.select('#cid-'+d['combined_fips'])
            .attr("class", "county");
    })
```

In the `mouseover` listener, we first add the `selected` class to the element we're hovering over, which adds a black outline (see the CSS file for this example for more details). We also select the element with ID `#cid-` and then the unique ID of that county. This will select the correct county from our map and also set the `selected` class to that element. Next, we change the `opacity` attribute of all the rectangles to `0.3`, and directly change the `opacity` attribute of the rectangles that have the correct `data-state` value to 1. This will result in all the rectangles that belong to the state we're hovering over to be highlighted:

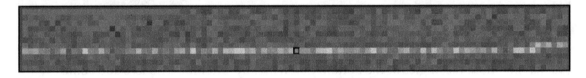

Finally, in `mouseover`, we add some output text, showing the details of the selected county. In `mouseout` we just reset the values we made in `mouseover`. The result is an interactive map which you can use to see the election details of specific counties:

In this example, we used the `Albers USA` projection. In the next example, we'll explore what other kinds of projections are available in D3.

Earthquake data on a flat map

For this example, we're going to plot earthquake data on a map. This visualization will have the following features:

1. A slider at the bottom can be used to select the year to be shown.
2. A dropdown at the top allows you to switch between projections.
3. A map in the center shows the projections and the earthquake data plotted on top.

An example using the `Robinson` projection looks like this:

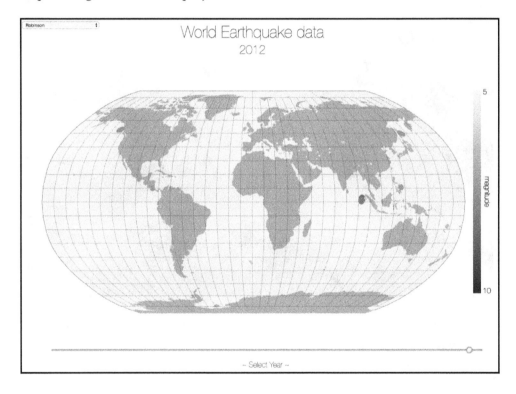

This is a fairly standard projection, but D3 also comes with a number of more interesting projections. For instance, the `InterruptedSinuMollweide` projection renders the same information like this:

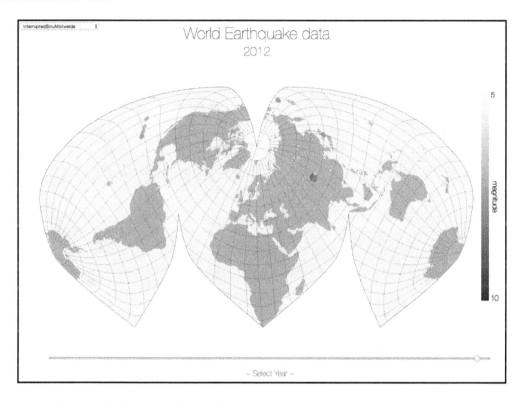

First, as we do for all the examples, we'll show you how to get the data.

Getting the data

For this example, we use two different data sources. First we use a TopoJSON map of the world, which we use to draw the map. This time we'll use information from the TopoJSON world atlas project (`https://github.com/topojson/world-atlas`), which provides pre-built TopoJSON files. For our example we use the `world-110m.v1.json` file (which you can download from here: `https://d3js.org/world-110m.v1.json`). This file contains country data:

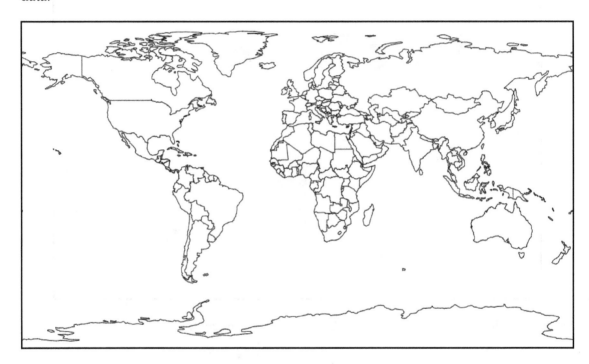

This file contains land data:

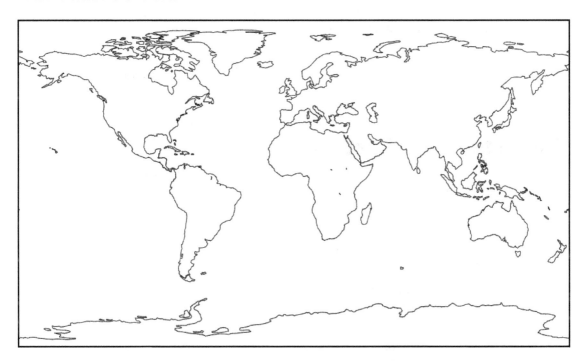

For our example, we'll use the land data to draw the map.

Besides the land data, we also need data that shows when a specific earthquake took place. We can get that information from the NOAA:

`https://www.ngdc.noaa.gov/nndc/struts/form?t=101650&s=1&d=1.`

On that page, select earthquakes with a magnitude larger than five, from the time period 1850 to now. At the bottom of the form, check the option to download the file as TSV. The result is a tab-delimited file which looks like this:

```
I_D FLAG_TSUNAMI   YEAR  MONTH DAY   ... EQ_PRIMARY ... LATITUDE  LONGITUDE
1905               1850  9     12    ...    7.5     ...  27.800    102.300
1903               1850              ...    5.0     ...  34.700    104.900
```

The `earthquakes.tsv` file (which you can find in the `data` directory for this chapter), contains a lot of information. The most important fields are listed in the preceding code. What this means is that, in 1850 an earthquake with a force of 7.5 took place at that specific location.

The data for both sources is already in an easy to use format, so there is no need to sanitize it.

Create the visualization

To draw the map and the circles, we first set up a couple of global scales and variables, as we do for most examples:

```
// contains data when loaded
var quakes = [];
var topo = {};
var currentYear = 1850;

// containers for the map and the circles on top
var map = svg.append("g").attr("class","map");
var circles = svg.append("g");

// setup the projection, and the path generator
var projection = d3.geoAiry();
var path = d3.geoPath().projection(projection);

// setup the title
var text = svg.append("g").attr("transform",
  "translate(" + (width/2) + " -60)") text.append("text").attr("class",
"title")
  .attr("text-anchor", "middle")
    .text("World Earthquake data");
text.append("text").attr("class", "year")
  .attr("transform", "translate(" + 0 + " 40)")
    .attr("text-anchor", "middle");

// setup scales
var radiusScale = d3.scaleLinear().domain([5, 10]).range([0.2, 4]);
var colScale = d3.scaleLinear().domain([5, 10]).range([0,1]);
var color = function(m) { return
  d3.interpolateBlues((colScale(m)));};
```

In the setup, we create two g groups. One will contain the map (`map`), and the other one the earthquake circles (`circles`). Next, we create the `projection` and the `path` variable, just as we did in the previous example.

We start with the `Airy` projection (just because that's the first one alphabetically), but if you open the example, you can see that we use a select dropdown to select other projections (more on that later). With the projection defined, we also add the output `text` elements, which we use to render the title and the year. Finally, we set up a number of scales: the `radiusScale` is used to map the earthquake's magnitude to the size of the circle; and the `colScale` maps the magnitude to a range of 0 to 1, which we then use in the color function to determine the color of each circle.

Loading the data

Next, we load the data:

```
// load the data, and pass it on to the updateYear function.
d3.queue()
    .defer(d3.json, "./data/world-110m.v1.json")
    .defer(d3.tsv, "./data/earthquakes.tsv")
    .await(function (error, topoData, quakesData) {
        topo = topoData;
        quakes = quakesData;
        quakes.forEach(function (d) {
            d.LATITUDE = +d.LATITUDE;
            d.LONGITUDE = +d.LONGITUDE;
            d.EQ_PRIMARY = +d.EQ_PRIMARY;
            d.YEAR = +d.YEAR;
        })

        process(topo);
        updateYear(1850, quakes)
    });
```

Since we have two sources, we use the `d3.queue` function to load the data. We use `d3.json` to load our map data, and `d3.tsv` to load and parse the downloaded TSV file. When it is done, we assign the values to the global `topo` and `quakes` properties. We clean up the `quakes` data a bit, by converting some values to numbers for easier processing and then call the `process` function to render the map, and the `updateYear` function to render the circles.

Rendering the map

First let's look at how we can render the map:

```
function process (topo) {

    // first remove everything, cause we might have
        switched projection
    map.selectAll("path").remove();

    // define a custom feature, which creates the outline of the map
    var f = {type: "Sphere"}
    // first remove everything, cause we might have switched projection
    projection.fitSize([width, height], f)

    // create a path and draw it.
    var outline = path(f);
    map.append("path").attr("class", "sphere").attr("d", outline);

    // first display all the counties.
    map.selectAll(".country")
        .data(topojson.feature(topo, topo.objects.countries).features)
        .enter()
        .append("path")
        .attr("class","country")
        .attr("d", path)

    // add lines
    map.append("path").datum(d3.geoGraticule()())
        .attr("class","graticule").attr("d", path);
```

As you can see, you only need a couple of D3 calls to render the map. The first thing we do in the code fragment, is to remove any `path` elements already present by calling `remove()` on a D3 selection. We could also have used the standard `enter()`, `exit()`, `merge()` approach here instead. Next we're going to scale our map and draw the circumference of our map. D3 projections have a special way of doing this. First you define a new GeoJSON feature: `{type: "Sphere"}`. This feature, when processed by D3, renders the circumference of the map. When passed into the `fitSize` function of the `projection`, we tell D3 to scale the map in such a way that it matches the provided feature (you could also use this to zoom into a specific country). Now our map will have the correct scale settings to show our complete map. To render the circumference, we just use the `path` function to convert the feature to a string which we can assign to the `d` attribute of a `path` element. The result of just this call looks like this:

Now let's add the countries. Here, we use the same approach we used in the previous example. Use `topojson` to convert the TopoJSON data to GeoJSON, and render the countries with the `path` function:

Finally we use the d3.geoGraticule function to draw lines for latitudes and longitudes. By default when you call the d3.geoGraticule it will draw lines every ten degrees:

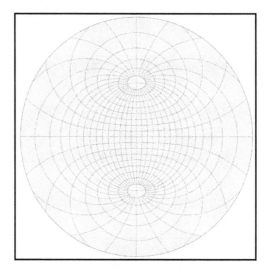

You can easily customize this through the following functions:

Function	Description
d3.geoGraticule()	Creates a feature generator, which you can use to create graticules. The following functions can be called on this feature generator.
()	Generates a single GeoJSON object, which contains all the lines.
lines()	Generates an array of GeoJSON objects, where each represents a single line.
outline()	Returns a GeoJSON object, showing the outline of all the graticules.
extent()	Sets the area for which graticules should be created.
extentMajor() / extentMinor()	Sets the minor and major extents of this generators.
step() / stepMinor() / stepMajor()	Sets the interval at which to generate lines.
precision()	Sets the precision of the generated lines.

At this point, we have drawn the circumference, the countries and the graticules. We now have a map which looks like this:

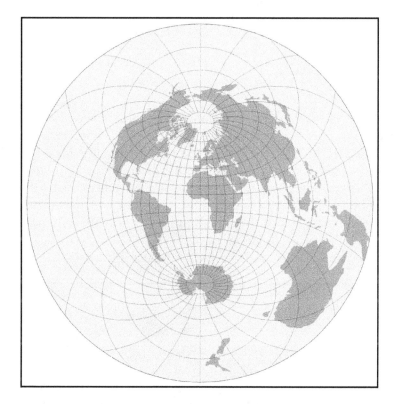

Now all that is left to do is to render the earthquake circles on top of this map.

Rendering the earthquake circles

We render the circles in the updateYear function, which looks like this:

```
// update the earthquake circles
function updateYear(year, quakes) {
    d3.select("text.year").text(year);
    var toShow = quakes.filter(function(d) {return d.YEAR === year});
    var circle = d3.geoCircle()
    var paths = circles.selectAll("path")
        .data(toShow);

    var bpaths = paths.enter()
        .append("path")
```

```
        .merge(paths);

    bpaths.attr("d", function(d) {
        return path(circle.center([d.LONGITUDE,
  d.LATITUDE]).radius(radiusScale(d.EQ_PRIMARY))())
        }).attr("style", function(d) {return "fill: " +  color(d.EQ_PRIMARY)});

    paths.exit().remove();
  }
```

We first filter the quakes array by only selecting earthquakes where d.YEAR === year. Next we create a d3.geoCircle feature generator. With this generator we can generate circles which we can pass into a projection so that they are rendered just like other geometry features. To add the circles we use the standard enter(), merge(), exit() pattern. To draw the circles, we pass the longitude and latitude of the earthquake to the center function of the d3.geoCircle generator. The size of the circle is based on the magnitude of the earthquake which we pass through the radiusScale scale, and finally we set the color using the color function we defined earlier. Now we've got the final map, where we can render circles based on the provided year:

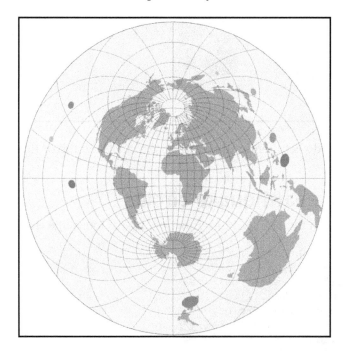

Not that we've got the code to render the map and the earthquake circles, all we need to do is t0 create the HTML elements to select the year, and select the projection to use.

Connect the html elements

First we need to define the input elements in our HTML. We do that like this:

```
<div id="geo" style="position: absolute">
    <select id="geoSelection">
        <option value="geoAiry">Airy</option>
        <option value="geoAitoff">Aitoff</option>
        <option value="geoAlbers">Albers</option>
        <option value="geoBaker">Baker</option>
        ...
    </select>
</div>

<div class="year-select" style="text-align: center">
    <input id="slider" style="width: 1100px;" type="range"
          min="1850" max="2016" step="1" value="1850" />
    <p><span class="year-text">~ Select Year ~</span></p>
</div>
```

These are just standard HTML elements. Connecting these to our visualization is very easy, and can be done by just calling the d3.select function.

```
// setup and connect the slider
d3.select(".year-select")
    .attr("width", width + margin.left + margin.right);
d3.select("#slider").on("change", function() {
    currentYear = +this.value;
    updateYear(currentYear, quakes)
});
// select and connect the dropdown
d3.select("#geoSelection").on("change", function() {
    projection = d3[this.value]();
    path = d3.geoPath().projection(projection);

    updateYear(currentYear, quakes);
    process(topo);
});
```

We add an on("change", ..) handler to these elements. So, when the year is changed we, just re-render the earthquake circles, and when we select a different projection with the dropdown, we redraw both the map and the earthquake circles.

We're not completely done, however. When you browse through the different projections, you'll notice that for some of these there are some unwanted artifacts (Polyhedral Waterman projection in 2012):

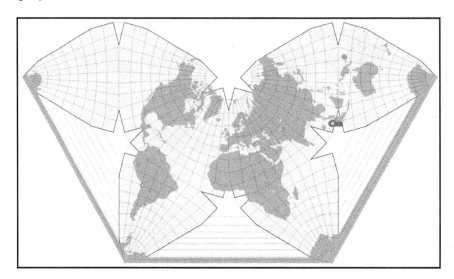

Here you can see that some of our earthquake circles are stretched out (in the area of Indonesia), and that in multiple places, the countries are stretched out over the empty map area, and the graticules as well. What we need to do is add a clipping mask to make sure that only the area within the map boundaries is rendered.

Fix clipping

Luckily, though, this is very simple to do. Remember that we created a feature, `var f = {type: "Sphere"}`, which was rendered as the outline/circumference of our map. This is also the exact area that we could use for clipping. For this we add a `clipPath` element to our chart:

```
d3.selectAll("defs").remove();
circles.attr("clip-path","url(#clip-1)");
d3.select(".chart").append("defs").append("clipPath")
        .attr("id","clip-1")
        .append("path").attr("d", outline);
```

We created the `outline` earlier by calling `var outline = path(f);`. We assign this outline to `clipPath` with the name `clip-1`. Now we just add this clip path to the circles and the map:

```
circles.attr("clip-path","url(#clip-1)");
map.attr("clip-path","url(#clip-1)");
```

If you now look at the same map, it limits the area that is shown to the outline of the map:

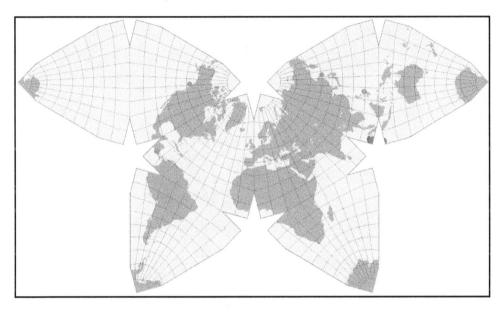

In the final visualization, we've also added a simple legend at the right to show which color corresponds to which magnitude. If you're interested in how this is done look at the code here: `DVD3/src/chapter-05/js/D05-03.js`.

So far, we've only shown a static map. In the next example, we're going to create a 3D map, which rotates, and can be dragged around based on the user input.

Rotating the world globe

For this example, we're going to create the following visualization (see
`DVD3/src/chapter05/D05-03.html`):

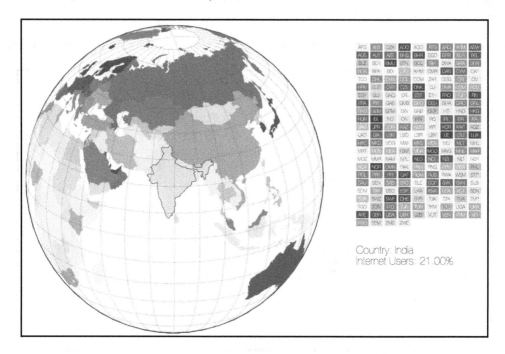

In this visualization, we show the percentage of adults who are using the iUnternet. You
can rotate the globe with your mouse, and when you click one of the countries on the right
side, the map will automatically rotate to that specific country. Let's start by looking at the
data that we'll use for this sample.

Getting and sanitize the data

For the topography world data, we're going to use the same source as we did in the
previous visualization. Before we look at the other sources, let's look a bit closer at this one
(`https://d3js.org/world-110m.v1.json`):

```
{"type":"Topology","objects":{"countries":{"type":"GeometryCollection","geo
metries":[{"type":"Polygon","id":"004","arc ...
```

This is part of the first line of this geometry file. As we've seen in the previous example, we can use this to draw countries using a specific projection. Besides just the shape of the country, each entry also contains an `id`. In this case `004`. This is the ID of the country following the ISO-3166-1 numeric standard (`https://en.wikipedia.org/wiki/ISO_3166-1_numeric`). So, for our example, when we find data, we need to be able to map it to that number to correctly color the country on the globe.

The data we want to use is based on data from `http://worldbank.org`. From there you can download information from the *World Development Indicators* database. One of those reports contains the percentage of Internet users. We've already downloaded those, and you can find them in the `data` directory for this chapter. That data looks like this:

```
Internet users (per 100 people),IT.NET.USER.P2,Afghanistan,AFG,7
Internet users (per 100 people),IT.NET.USER.P2,Albania,ALB,60.1
Internet users (per 100 people),IT.NET.USER.P2,Algeria,DZA,25
```

This data looks very straightforward. It shows the country, and it shows the percentage. However, in this data, the country is mapped by three letters, instead of by three numbers, that we've got available in our topography data. So before we can use the data, we need to map these two values somehow. We can buy the official mapping from ISO, but luckily someone has also made a free one, which you can download from here: `https://gist.github.com/ihough/2044416`. This mapping contains the following data:

```
FIPS 10-4, ISO 3166-1 A2, ISO 3166-1 A3, ISO 3166-1 N3, Country Inclusive
AF,AF,AFG,004,
AX,,,,GB
AL,AL,ALB,008,
AG,DZ,DZA,012,
AQ,AS,ASM,016,
AN,AD,AND,020,
AO,AO,AGO,024,
AV,AI,AIA,660,
AY,AQ,ATA,010,
```

As you can see, we got the `ISO-3361-1 A3` column, which we need to map to the `ISO-3361-1 N3` column. Note that the file you can download from that website isn't 100 percent correct. When creating this visualization, a couple of mappings were found to be incorrect. They are fixed in the version `iso-mappings.csv`, which you can find in the sources for this chapter. Now that we've got all the pieces of our data, we're going to preprocess them, so that we've got a simple data file to work with in the visualization code. What we're going to do, is add some additional data directly to the TopoJSON (stored in the `properties` attribute), so that we can work with a single file:

```
{"type":"Topology","objects":{"countries":{"type":
  "GeometryCollection","geometries":[{"type":"Polygon",
  "id":"004","properties":{"value":"7","countryA":
  "AFG","name":"Afghanistan"}, "arc ...
```

As we do for the other data wrangling examples in this book, we use a simple Node.js script:

```
const d3 = require('d3');
const fs = require('fs');

d3.queue()
    .defer(d3.json, "file:world-110m.v1.json")
    .defer(d3.csv, "file:worldbank_popular_2014.csv")
    .defer(d3.csv, "file:iso-mapping.csv")
    .await(function (error, topoData, worldbank, mapping) {

        // get the mapping between the numeric and alpha one.
        var isoKV = mapping.reduce(function (res, el) {
            res[el[' ISO 3166-1 A3']] = el[' ISO 3166-1 N3'];
            return res;
        }, {});

        // convert to array with country and the correct code
        var inetData = worldbank
            .filter(function (d) {
                return d["Series Code"] === 'IT.NET.USER.P2'
            })
            .map(function (d) {
                return {
                    countryA: d['Country Code'],
                    countryN: isoKV[d['Country Code']],
                    value: d['2014 [YR2014]'],
                    name: d['Country Name']
                }
            });

        // create a kv map so we can lookup the
           value when processing
        // the topojson.
        var inetDataKV = inetData.reduce(function (res, el) {
            res[el.countryN] = el;
            return res;
        }, {});

        // add to topoJSON, is undefined if not found.
        topoData.objects.countries.geometries
            .forEach(function (d) {
```

```
              var data = inetDataKV[d.id]
              if (data) {
                  d.properties = {
                      value: data.value,
                      countryA: data.countryA,
                      name: data.name
                  }
              }
         });

         fs.writeFile('./world-110m-inet.json',
             JSON.stringify(topoData))
    });
```

This is a very simple script, where we combine information from the various source files, and enrich the countries TopoJSON. Now that we've got an easy set of data to work with, we can create the visualization.

Render the visualization

We render the visualization in two steps. First, we set up the globe with the countries, and then we render a legend, which can be used to navigate to a specific country. As you'll see in the code, the steps we use are much the same as we did in the previous example.

Render the globe on a HTML canvas

In all the examples so far, we've used SVG to render all the visualizations. While this works well when we're not working with too many elements, it can become slow, when adding and updating many elements. In this example, we want to create a globe which rotates. If we used SVG we'd have to recreate or update hundreds of SVG elements during the rotation. So, for this example, we'll use the HTML canvas instead. D3 allows you to very easily draw to a canvas, and manipulate the canvas using pretty much the same code as you'd use for working with SVG. We'll create the legend itself using SVG, since that won't be animated, and will just consist of some simple `rect` and `text` elements.

Setting up the HTML page and the output elements

Let's start with the HTML page. This page will now contain the following two main `div` elements.

```
<div id="output" style="display: inline-block;">
    <canvas class="chart"></canvas>
```

```
    </div>
    <div id="legend" style="display: inline-block;">
        <svg class="legend"></svg>
    </div>
```

We'll render the globe to the `canvas` element, and the legend to the `svg` element. Setting up these two elements is done like this:

```
var margin = {top: 40, bottom: 10, right: 40, left: 10},
    width = 900 - margin.left - margin.right,
    height = 900 - margin.top - margin.bottom;

var canvas = d3.select(".chart")
    .attr("width", width + margin.left + margin.right)
    .attr("height", height + margin.top + margin.bottom)

d3.select("#output")
    .attr("style", "padding-left: " + margin.left + "px; "
        + "padding-right: " + margin.right + "px; "
        + "padding-top: " + margin.top + "px; "
        + "paddin-bottom: " + margin.bottom + "px; "
        + "display: inline-block; ");

var svg = d3.select(".legend")
    .attr("width", (width/2-100) + margin.left + margin.right)
    .attr("height", height + margin.top + margin.bottom)

var c = canvas.node().getContext("2d");
canvas.call(d3.drag().on("drag", dragged));
```

In this fragment you can see that we create the `canvas` just like we'd normally do for the `svg` element. This time, however, we use CSS to position the canvas using the specified margins. For the legend, we limit the `width`, since we won't need that much space. Next, we create a 2D canvas context `c`, which we'll use later on from the `path` functions. Finally, we attach a `d3.drag` listener on the canvas, so that we can re-render the globe when the user drags the globe around.

Next, we set up the scales, projections and colors we'll be using:

```
var colorScale = d3.scaleLinear().domain([0, 100]).range([0, 1]);
var color = function (i) { return d3.interpolateOranges(colorScale(i)) };

var projection = d3.geoOrthographic();
var path = d3.geoPath().projection(projection).context(c);

// make the complete map fit into the designated width and height
var f = {type: "Sphere"};
```

```
projection.fitSize([width, height], f)
```

As you can see we use the `d3.interpolateOranges` function together with a
`d3.linearScale` function which we'll use to determine the color of a country. We'll render
the globe using the `d3.geoOrthographic()` projection, which renders the map as a globe.
Finally, we again use the `Sphere` feature to determine the circumference of our map, and
set the scale of the projection to nicely fit that sphere.

Loading the data and drawing the map

Now we can load the data, and render the globe:

```
var countries;
var countryKV;

d3.json("./data/world-110m-inet.json", function(loadedTopo) {
    // make the data available to the callbacks
    countries  = topojson.feature(loadedTopo,
        loadedTopo.objects.countries).features;    countryKV =
countries.reduce(function (res, el)
        { res[el.id] = el; return res; }, {});

    // draw the map and the legend
    redrawWorld(countries);
    ...
});

function redrawWorld(countryToShow) {
    c.clearRect(0, 0, width, height);
    drawOutline();
    countries.forEach(drawCountry);
    if (countryToShow) {
        highlightCountry(countryToShow);
    }
    drawGraticules();
}

function drawGraticules() {
    c.strokeStyle = "#666", c.lineWidth = 0.5, c.beginPath(),
        path(d3.geoGraticule()()), c.stroke();
}

function drawOutline() {
    c.strokeStyle = "#000", c.lineWidth = 2, c.beginPath(),
        path(f), c.stroke();
}
```

```
function drawCountry(toDraw) {
    if (toDraw.properties.value) {
        c.fillStyle = color(toDraw.properties.value),
            c.beginPath(), path(toDraw), c.fill();
    } else {
        c.fillStyle = '#ccc', c.beginPath(), path(toDraw),
            c.fill();
    }
}

function highlightCountry(toDraw) {
    c.strokeStyle = "#000", c.lineWidth = 1, c.beginPath(),
        path(toDraw), c.stroke();
}
```

The interesting part of this code is the `redrawWorld` function. From that function we directly render to the 2D context (`c`) we created earlier. With SVG we just updated and removed elements. However, with a canvas, we can't change data once we've written it. So the first thing we do is to clear our complete canvas by calling `clearRect` with the dimensions we've set up. Next we'll draw the circumference of our globe with the `drawOuline` function. When drawing to the context, we first set the color (`strokeStyle`), the fill (`fillStyle`), and the line width (`lineWidth`) we want to use. Then we tell the context we want to start drawing `beginPath()`, draw our path (`path(...)`), and finally call `stroke()` to draw an outline, or `fill()` to fill the path. After we've drawn the outline, we apply the same principle for the countries and the graticules. The result is a drawn globe on the canvas:

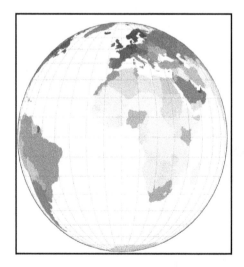

Now that we've got the globe drawn, let's look at the drag event.

Handle the drag event

We've already connected the d3.drag to the canvas, and connected the drag event to the dragged function. The implementation of this function looks like this:

```
function dragged(e) {
    var oldRotate = projection.rotate();

    var change = [d3.event.dx / 8, d3.event.dy / 8];
    projection.rotate([oldRotate[0] + change[0],
        oldRotate[1] - change[1]]);
    redrawWorld();
}
```

Whenever we drag the globe the dragged function is called. In this function, we first use the projection.rotate() function to determine the current location. This returns the *yaw*, *pitch*, and *roll* of the current rotation. Based on the distance that was dragged (d3.event.dx and d3.event.dy), we update this rotation, and redraw the world. That is all that is needed to rotate our globe:

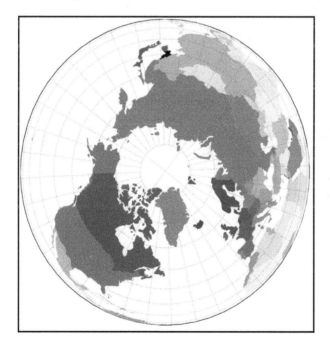

Next let's add the legend which you can see at the right-hand side of the screen.

Render the legend

We call the draw legend as soon as the data is loaded:

```
d3.json("./data/world-110m-inet.json", function(loadedTopo) {
    ...
    drawLegend(countries);
});
```

To draw the legend, we use techniques we've seen in the previous chapters:

```
function drawLegend(countries) {
    // filter out the countries, for which we don't have data
    var infos = svg.selectAll(".country-info")
        .data(countries.filter(function(d) {return d.properties.value &&
+d.properties.value > 0}));

    // create new ones
    var newInfos = infos.enter().append("g")
        .on("click", function(d) {
            d3.select(".country-text").text("Country: " +
d.properties.name);
            d3.select(".country-value").text("Internet Users: " +
(+d.properties.value).toFixed(2) + "%");
            moveTo(d.id)
        })
        .attr("class", "country-info")
        .attr("transform", function(d, i) {return "translate(" + ((i%9) *
40) + " " + (Math.floor(i/9) * 22 + 50) + " )"})
    newInfos.append("rect").attr("width", 35).attr("height", 20)
    newInfos.append("text").attr("dy", "15px").attr("dx", "17px")

    // set values for all
    var allInfos = newInfos.merge(infos);
    allInfos.select("rect")
        .attr("fill", function(d) { return color(d.properties.value); })

    allInfos.select("text")
        .attr("class", function(d) {
            return colorScale(+d.properties.value) > 0.4 ? "legend-text-
white" : "legend-text-black"
        })
        .text(function(d) {return d.properties.countryA})

    svg.append("text").attr("class","country-text").attr("x",0).attr("y",
630)
    svg.append("text").attr("class","country-value").attr("x",0).attr("y",
660)
```

```
}
```

For the legend, we use a very simple approach where we create g elements which will
contain the colored rect elements and the text elements with the shortened name of the
country. We determine the position of the g elements ourselves (we could have also used a
d3.bandScale for this). We also add some user interaction to the g elements. Whenever
such an element is clicked we set the name of the country (on .country-text) and its
current value (on .country-value), and then call the moveTo function to rotate the globe
to the specific country:

```
function moveTo(country) {
    var countryToShow = (countryKV[country]);
    if (countryToShow) {
        var transition = d3.transition()
            .duration(2000)
            .tween("rotate", function () {
                var target = d3.geoCentroid(countryToShow);
                var interpolator = d3.interpolate(projection.rotate(), [-
target[0], -target[1]]);
                return function (t) {
                    projection.rotate(interpolator(t))
                    redrawWorld(countryToShow);
                }
            });
    }
}
```

In this function we convert the passed in country code to a TopoJSON country object
(countryToShow), and use a d3.transition function to handle the animation. This
transition will run for 2000 milliseconds, and use the custom returned function to redraw
the world. Our function uses the d3.interpolate function to create an interpolator from
the rotation at the moment we click (projection.rotate) to the center of the country we
want to move to d3.geoCentroid(countryToShow). Now our globe will move
automatically to the country we click on in the legend.

For example, the following screenshot shows the globe moved to the center of Japan:

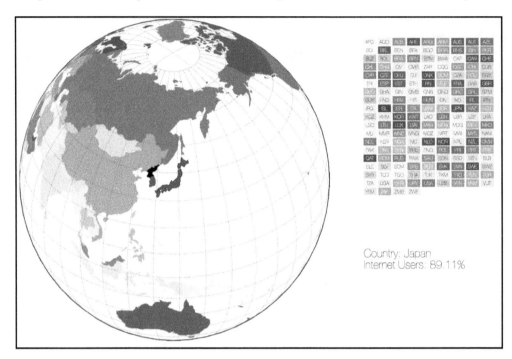

If you've already explored the previous example (which allowed you to experiment with the different projections), you've seen that there are a large number of projections you can use with D3. The nice thing about using these projections is that your code doesn't need to know anything about how they are implemented. In this example, we used the d3.geoOrthographic projection, but any of the others work just as well, without requiring any change to your code (although you might need to add a clip path, as we did in the previous example).

For instance, with the `d3.geoGringortenQuincuncial()` the map, centered on Japan, looks like this:

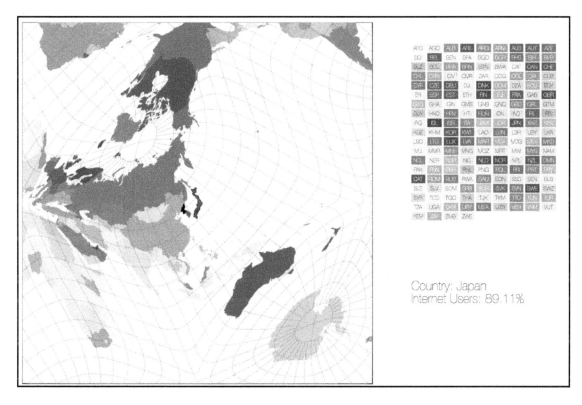

And that's all there is to it.

Summary

In this chapter we've explored the support D3 has for geo-related visualizations. We started with explaining the different ways geo data can be represented and projected. We've seen that D3 supports many different kinds of projections, from the standard Mercator projection to very specific projections like the Albers US projection. For the first visualization in this chapter we showed how easy it is to combine different data sources and quickly create an election map using the same principles we've used in previous chapters. After that, we showed how can add custom shapes, circles in this case, to the map to enhance the standard projections. In that example, we also provided a simple dropdown which can be used to explore the different supported projections. Finally, we showed that it is also very straightforward to animate the projections by creating a rotating globe. In this final example, we once again combined various data sources together to create our final visualization.

Within this chapter on geo-based visualization we've discussed the most important parts of the D3 API. In the next chapter, we'll look at an alternative way we can apply the patterns we've seen in the previous chapters by creating a visualization which visualizes data which is streamed directly to the browser using WebSockets.

6
Visualizing Streaming Data

In the previous chapters, we've discussed most of the standard visualizations and components provided by D3. In this chapter, we're going to look at a specific implementation where we visualize streaming data, using a number of the building blocks we've seen in the previous chapters.

In this chapter, we're going to create the following visualizations:

- We're going to start very simply by just creating a line graph which is fed by mouse data. This data represents the streaming data that we want to visualize. We'll use transitions to animate the line, drawn through the randomly created values, from right to left.
- In the second example, we're going to connect to a **WebSocket** which provides us with ECG and respiratory data. Whenever the WebSocket pushes an element to our visualization, we'll update the drawn lines.
- In the previous chapters, we've already seen how you can use D3 to draw area charts. An alternative area visualization that is provided by D3 is called a streamgraph. In this example, we'll create a streamgraph that visualizes data received by a WebSocket.
- There's a website called **Meetup.com**, which you can use to easily organize meetups in your region. When a meeting is created, participants can send an RSVP to indicate whether they will attend or not. For public meetings, Meetup.com provides an open WebSocket API which sends out updates whenever an RSVP is received. We'll use this information to show real-time information on top of a map rendered with D3.

Let's quickly get started with our first streaming example.

Simple streaming line

For our first example, we're going to create two simple streaming lines. The result we'll be aiming for is the following (which you can see by opening up the `DVD3/src/chapter-06/D06-01.html` example):

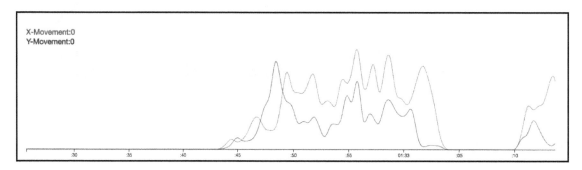

In this image, we have got two horizontal lines which move from the right of the screen to the left. Whenever you move your mouse, the distance traveled is stored and rendered as two lines. Each point in the graph represents the total distance traveled along the x-axis or the y-axis. The bottom of this graph is a simple axis which shows the current time, and which moves together with the line graph.

To accomplish this graph, we need to take the following steps:

1. The first thing we need to do is define the various scales which we can use for rendering the scale at the bottom, and which we use to determine the x and y positions of each graph element.
2. When we've got the scales, we can start collecting the mouse information which we'll use to draw the line graph.
3. Once we've got the mouse data, we'll set up the animations for the line graph and the bottom axis.
4. Finally, we'll clean up the visualization a bit by adding the text in the upper-left corner and use a clip path to hide the new points entering at the right side of the graph.

Setting up scales

To render this graph, we'll be using a couple of scales:

```
// set up some control points
```

```
var duration = 500;
var nPoints = 120;

// the array that will keep our data
var data = d3.range(0, nPoints-1).map(function()
   {return  {x:0, y:0}}); // setup the scales. The domain is the x-axis,
   containing 400 points
// the y axis is based on the min and max values of the data
var x = d3.scaleLinear().domain([0, nPoints -
   2]).range([0, width]);
var y = d3.scaleLinear().domain([0, 500]).range([height, 0]);

// scale to use for rendering the time axis
var now = new Date(Date.now() - duration);
var xTime = d3.scaleTime()
   .domain([now - ((nPoints - 2) * duration), now])
   .range([0, width]);
```

In the beginning of this code fragment, we first define some properties which we use throughout this visualization. The duration property determines the period we collect mouse data for. With nPoints, we define how many points make up the graphs we draw. In this case, we use 120 points, with a duration of 500 ms, so the complete line graph represents a time period of 1 minute. Finally, we create an array, which we fill with empty data (called data), that we'll use to draw the line.

Next we set up the scales. We use three scales:

- x: Used to determine the x position of the points in the line graph. This is a simple linear graph, which divides the width based on the total number of points (nPoints). Note that we don't use a domain from 0 to nPoints, but to nPoints − 2. The reason we do this is that we don't want to render the newest two points; more on that later in this section.
- y: This linear scale is used to determine the y position of each point of the graph. This is a simple scale where we just set the max to an arbitrary value (500 in this case).
- xTime: For the time, we use a scale which we haven't seen before. The d3.scaleTime, this scale works in the same way as a normal linear scale, but uses dates to define its domain. In this case, we create a domain which mirrors the domain for the x-axis. We first define now with an offset of 1 duration (since we want to show the information we collected during that period). Next we define a timescale that represents the total duration of our graph (once again, ignoring two points).

Collecting mouse data

With the scales defined, we need some data to show. For this example, we'll use the mouse as our input. When you move the mouse, `mousemove` events are generated. We'll use information from this event, specifically the `screenX` and `screenY` values, to determine the mouse distance traveled. To collect this, we add a `mousemove` listener on the `body` element using the `d3.select(...).on()` function:

```
var previousEvent;
var totalX = 0;
var totalY = 0;
d3.select("body").on("mousemove", function() {
    if (previousEvent) {
        totalX += Math.abs(previousEvent.x - d3.event.screenX)
        totalY += Math.abs(previousEvent.y - d3.event.screenY)

        d3.select(".xText").transition().text("X-Movement:" + totalX)
        d3.select(".yText").transition().text("Y-Movement:" + totalY)
    }
    previousEvent = { x: d3.event.screenX, y: d3.event.screenY };
});
```

The total distance traveled is stored in the `totalX` and the `totalY` values, which we use later on, when rendering the individual data points. Now that we've got some input to show, let's render the graph.

Setting up the animations and the graphs

As we've seen in Chapter 2, *Basic Charts and Shapes*, we can draw lines in D3 using a `d3.line` function. To draw a line, you pass in a function which is used to determine the x coordinate based on the data, and a function used to determine the y coordinate. D3 also allows you to pass in what the line should look like. Should it be curved, closed, straight, or one of the other options (more options can be found here:). If you don't specify anything, you will get a linear curve, which is just a polyline through all the points:

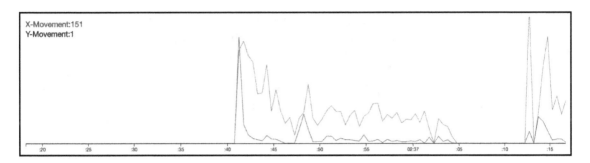

If we don't want direct lines between the points, we could also use the d3.curveStep function:

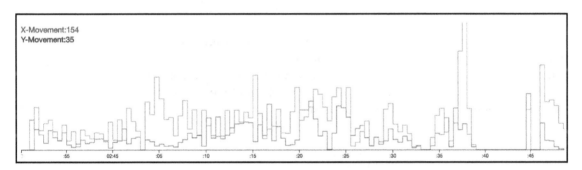

For our example, though, we'll use d3.curveBasis, which draws a nice fluent line through all the various data points, as we've seen in the beginning of this section:

```
// we use a line generator, based on the index and the data
var lineMx = d3.line()
    .curve(d3.curveBasis)
    .x(function(d, i) { return x(i) })
    .y(function(d) { return y(d.x); });

var lineMy = d3.line()
    .curve(d3.curveBasis)
    .x(function(d, i) { return x(i) })
    .y(function(d) { return y(d.y); });
```

One remark here: when we talked about the scales in the beginning of this section, we mentioned that we defined the domain of the scales so that they ignored the last two data points (`domain([0, nPoints - 2])`). The reason is that if we draw a curve, the `y` position of the last two points jumps around because D3 wants to draw the curve nicely through these points. By defining the scale like this, the last two points of the line are drawn outside the specified `width`. We still see them at this point, but by adding a clip path (as we'll do in the final section), we can hide these two fluctuating points, and the result is a nice streaming graph.

We start by creating a group that contains the lines:

```
var group = svg.append("g").attr("class", "group")
group.append("path").datum(data).attr("class", "lineX line")
group.append("path").datum(data).attr("class", "lineY line")
```

We don't do anything with the bound data yet, we just assign the array to the two different paths and add some classes for CSS so that we can easily select them later on. Note that we use `datum` instead of `data` to assign the array. With `datum`, we don't use the `enter`, `exit` functions, but directly bind the data to the `path` element we just added. Just what we did for the lines, we do for the axis at the bottom:

```
var axis = d3.axisBottom(xTime)
var axisGroup = svg.append("g")
    .attr("class", "axis")
    .attr("transform", "translate(0 " + (height) + ")")
    .call(axis)
```

Just like we did in the previous chapters, we define a `d3.axisBottom` function; by passing in the `d3.scaleTime` we created earlier, we automatically get the correct ticks and labels in the axis. We attach the `axis` to a newly created `g` group, and position it at the bottom of the graph.

At this point, we've created the groups that'll hold our lines, and we've drawn the bottom axis. We haven't, however, drawn the lines yet. To create a nicely flowing line from right to left, we're going to take the following approach:

1. Push a new data point onto the array.
2. Draw the lines with this new point (which is drawn off screen).
3. Start a transition to move the groups to the left.
4. Also start a transition to move the axis at the same time.
5. Once the transition is done, remove the first element from the array and restart the process.

In code, these steps look like this:

```
group.transition().on("start", render)
    .ease(d3.easeLinear).duration(duration)

function render() {
    // add new point to the array and reset the data
    data.push({x: totalX, y: totalY})
    totalX = 0; totalY = 0;

    // select current element
    d3.select(this).attr("transform", "")

    // redraw the lines
    d3.select(".lineX").attr("d", lineMy)
    d3.select(".lineY").attr("d", lineMx)

    // redefine the timescale, so we can move the axis
    var now = new Date(Date.now() - duration);
    xTime.domain([now - (nPoints - 2) * duration, now]);

    // for the duration, move the axis
    axisGroup.transition().duration(duration)
        .ease(d3.easeLinear).call(axis);

    // Move the lines
    d3.active(this).transition().on("start", renderX)
        .attr("transform", "translate(" +  x(-1) + ",0)")

    // remove element from the array
    data.shift();
}
```

We kick off the steps by first calling `group.transition()`; this will start a transition (which in itself doesn't interpolate anything). When the transition is started, we use the on event to trigger a call to the `render` function. In the `render` function, we execute the steps as discussed previously. We add a new element to the `data` array, Clean up any `transform` parameter previously set and draw the lines using the `lineMy` and `lineMx` path generators. Next we redefine the `domain` for our timescale, and start a transition to redraw the bottom axis. After drawing the lines, we start a transition to move the lines one step to the left. If the current transition is still running, this new one will be queued. Once this new one is being executed, it will queue another one and the process is repeated. At this point, we've got a fluently running graph that can be configured through the `duration` and `nPoints` properties we saw at the beginning.

For example, if we have a `duration` of 5000 and `nPoints` as 200, we get a line like this:

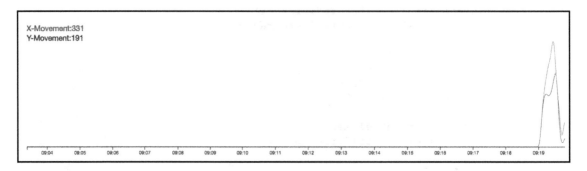

Clip path and extra information

If you run the example now, you'll see that the two rightmost points of the line graph fluctuate a bit. This is caused because we add new points at that location that suddenly pop into view, and the `curve` function we used uses multiple data values to determine its correct position. In the beginning of this section, we created the x scale like this:

```
var x = d3.scaleLinear().domain([0, nPoints - 2])
    .range([0, width]);
```

Basically, this means that the data points `data[nPoints]` and `data[nPoints-1]` are rendered outside the provided `width`. Since we always set up our chart to have margins, these two points will be drawn there, and still be visible. To hide these, we'll use a clip path again, so we can exactly determine what the visible area of the chart is. The clip path itself is defined as a simple `rect` element like this:

```
svg.append("defs").append("clipPath")
    .attr("id", "clip")
    .append("rect")
    .attr("width", "width")
    .attr("height", height + margin.bottom + margin.top);
```

The only thing left to do is assign this clip path to our main `svg` element:

```
svg.attr("clip-path", "url(#clip)")
```

Now, when we run the example, the graph smoothly transitions into view. The final items we add to our graph are two simple counters at the upper-left corner. These are just simple `text` elements:

```
svg.append("text").attr("class", "xText").attr("transform", "translate(0
20)")
    .attr("stroke", "steelblue").text("X-Movement: ")

svg.append("text").attr("class", "yText").attr("transform", "translate(0
40)")
    .attr("stroke", "red").text("Y-Movement: ")
```

The value of these elements is set whenever we receive an event in the `onmousemove` listener:

```
// in the mouse listener
d3.select(".xText").transition().text("X-Movement:" + totalX)
d3.select(".yText").transition().text("Y-Movement:" + totalY)
```

In the render function, we reset the value of those elements back to 0:

```
. . .
// in the render function
d3.select(".xText").text("X-Movement:" + 0)
d3.select(".yText").text("Y-Movement:" + 0)
. . .
```

In the approach we've seen in this chapter, we defined the update interval as a duration in our JavaScript. If you've got a high-frequency data source which pushes information at regular short intervals, we could also redraw the chart on each push. This is an approach we'll use for the upcoming example.

Heart rate and respiratory monitoring

For this example, we're going to show data pushed from a backend server. Specifically, we're going to visualize heart rate and respiratory data which is pushed over a WebSocket to our D3 frontend.

We're going to recreate the following visualization (the
`DVD3/src/chapter-06/D06-02.html` example):

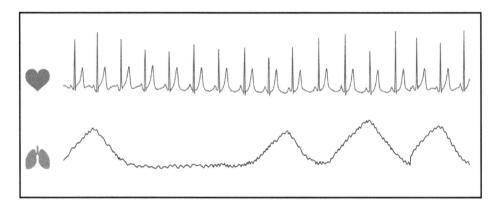

To get this example up and running, we're going to take the following steps:

1. Get sample respiratory data which we can push to the frontend.
2. Create a simple WebSocket server, which pushes the information.
3. Make the D3 visualization which responds to information pushed from the
   server.

We start with the sample data.

Getting the sample data

PhysioNet is an online research platform which provides free access to a large number of
recorded physiological signals. One of the datasets is called the **Fantasia Database**. The
description online best describes this data source:

*"Twenty young (21 - 34 years old) and twenty elderly (68 - 85 years old) rigorously-screened healthy
subjects underwent 120 minutes of continuous supine resting while continuous electrocardiographic
(ECG), and respiration signals were collected; in half of each group, the recordings also include an
uncalibrated continuous non-invasive blood pressure signal. Each subgroup of subjects includes
equal numbers of men and women."*

The name of the data source is derived from the movie *Fantasia*, which the test subjects
watched to avoid falling asleep. This gives us 2 hours of respiratory and ECG information
for a large number of people.

When you look through the Fantasia database
(`https://physionet.org/physiobank/database/fantasia/`), you can see that each
recording consists of three files:

f1o03.dat	26-Jul-1994 11:26	6.9M	digitized signal(s)
f1o03.ecg	15-Aug-1994 15:02	14K	corrected annotations
f1o03.hea	14-Mar-2009 08:48	125	header file
f1o04.dat	25-Nov-1994 17:51	6.9M	digitized signal(s)
f1o04.ecg	25-Nov-1994 18:40	12K	corrected annotations
f1o04.hea	14-Mar-2009 08:48	122	header file

We need to download all three files and convert them to a format more easily readable by
our WebSocket server. The original files are stored in the MIT Signal file format, so we need
something to convert that binary format to a simple text format. Luckily, PhysioNet also
provides the software we can use for conversion:
`https://physionet.org/physiotools/binaries/`.

After installing the binaries for your platform, we can use the provided `rdsamp` tool to
convert this binary format to a text format:

```
rdsamp -r f1y01 | head -n 15000 > yng.csv
```

Here we convert the `f1y01.dat` files using the `rdsamp` tool, and only store the first 15,000
records. The sample rate used in these files is 250 Hz, so with 15,000 records, we get 1
minute of raw ECG and respiratory data. The output looks like this:

```
0    16000    15904
1    16088    15872
2    16000    16008
3    16104    16128
4    16024    15960
5    16128    15912
6    16056    15968
7    16120    16144
8    16056    15992
9    16168    15856
```

Here the first column is a sequence number, the second one contains respiratory
information, and the third column is the ECG. Now let's look at how we can create a
WebSocket server which can push this information to our script.

Setting up the WebSocket server

For the WebSocket server, we've used a simple Node.js script. First move to the `<DVD3>/chapter-06/bin` directory, and run the `npm install` command from there. This will install the WebSocket library which we're going to use.

In this directory, you can find a script called `server-hr.js`, which we can use to start up a WebSocket server. This simple server takes a few arguments:

1. `fileName`: The first argument refers to the file we created with the `rdsamp` command.
2. `sendInterval`: We can specify the frequency to send data with. If we want to have real-time representation, a `sendInterval` of 4 ms should be used (which is 250 Hz).
3. `toSkip`: Finally, we can set the number of records we'd like to skip. If for instance, we set a `setInverval` of 8 ms, we should skip every other record so the data received by our frontend has the correct timescale.

The code for this server is shown here:

```
var fs = require('fs')
var ws = require('ws')

if (process.argv.length != 5) {
  console.log("Please specify the data to stream ," +
    " the send interval and the records to skip as arguments")
  process.exit(1)
}

var sendInterval = +process.argv[3]
var toSkip = +process.argv[4]

fs.readFile(process.argv[2], 'utf8', function (err,data) {
  if (err) {
    console.log("Error loading file", err); process.exit(1)
  }
  startupServer(data.split('\n'))
});

function startupServer(data) {

  // convert the data into a simple json structure
  var processed = data.map(function(el) {
    var splitted = el.trim().split(/\s+/);
    return {
```

```
      "id" : splitted[0], "resp" : +splitted[1], "ecg" : +splitted[2]
   }
})

var WebSocketServer = ws.Server;
var wss = new WebSocketServer({ port: 8081 });

function broadcast() {
   var skipped = processed.splice(0, toSkip);
   var toSend = processed.shift();
   wss.clients.forEach(function each(client) {
      client.send(JSON.stringify(toSend), {}, function(cb) {});
   });

   skipped.forEach(function(el) {processed.push(el)})
   processed.push(toSend)
};

   setInterval(function() { broadcast(); }, sendInterval);
}
```

This script, as you can see, reads in the data file (fs.readFile) which we provide as a command-line argument. Once loaded, we split the data into its segments and store that in the processed array. Next, we start up a WebSocketServer listening on port 8081. We also define a function called broadcast which sends one data element, as a JSON string (JSON.stringify(toSend)), to all connected listeners based on the sendInterval, and after sending, pushes the data to the back of the array. So even with only this 1 minute of data we have, we can run this server indefinitely.

Let's start the server, and see what the data sent by this server looks like:

```
node server-hr.js ../data/yng.csv 16 3
```

This time we send out a message every 16 ms, and so we should skip three records, for each one we sent. When we now connect to this WebSocket, we'll receive data which looks like this:

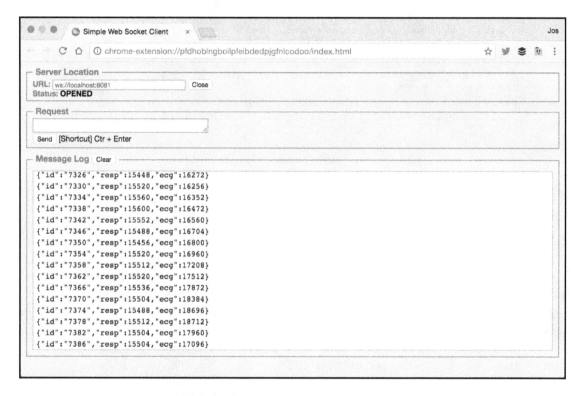

As you can see, each record contains an **id**, a **resp** field, and a **ecg** field. At this point, we've got a nice-looking data stream; in the next section, we'll connect D3 to it.

Creating the visualization

This visualization will have the following features:

- We're going to draw a line showing the ECG and respiratory information
- We load two external SVG images, a heart and a set of lungs, and animate those based on the data we receive

We once again start with setting up the data structures and the scales.

Scales, lines, and array initialization

The first thing we need to do is define some variables:

```
var ecgAvg  =  16800;
var respAvg = 16000;
var n = 800;

var data = d3.range(n).map(function(d) {return {
    "ecg": ecgAvg,
    "resp": respAvg
}});
```

We use the `ecgAvg` and `respAvg` to prefill an array with our initial data. This will allow us to start our visualization with an empty line, while new data comes in. The n variable in this fragment determines how many points we're going to render for each line. The lower this number, the less compact our line will be. Like many other visualizations, playing around with these values allows us to fine-tune the final result.

We're also going to need some scales:

```
var x = d3.scaleLinear().domain([0, n - 1]).range([100, width]);
var yEcg = d3.scaleLinear().domain([15800, 26000]).range([height/2, 0]);
var yResp = d3.scaleLinear().domain([14800, 24000]).range([height/2 +
height/2, 0]);
var sEcg = d3.scaleLog().domain([15800, 26000]).range([1, 0]);
var sResp = d3.scaleLinear().domain([14800, 24000]).range([1, 0]);
```

These are fairly standard scales; we use the x scale to determine the x position of the points in the lines, and the `yEcg` and `yResp` will determine the y position of the points. We're also going to use two additional scales: `sEcg` and `sResp`. These two scales will respectively control the opacity of the heart SVG image, and the lungs SVG image.

Since we're going to draw lines, we need a couple of `d3.line` generators:

```
var lineEcg = d3.line()
    .x(function(d, i) { return x(i); })
    .y(function(d) { return yEcg(+d.ecg); });

var lineResp = d3.line()
    .x(function(d, i) { return x(i); })
    .y(function(d) { return yResp(+d.resp); });
```

You might notice that we don't specify a dedicated `curve` function on these elements. The reason is that we draw so many small points (n = 800), that we don't need additional interpolation, since the line will be smooth anyhow. If we zoom into the line, you can see that we're drawing normal straight line segments:

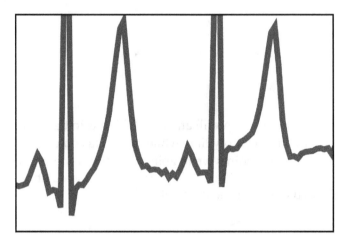

Now we can draw the lines:

```
svg.append("g").append("path").datum(data)
    .attr("class", "ecg")
    .attr("d", lineEcg);

svg.append("g").append("path").datum(data)
    .attr("class", "resp")
    .attr("d", lineResp);
```

At this stage, this is just a simple line, since we've initialized all the elements of the data array with the same value. Next, we're going to load the heart and lungs images and set up the connection to the WebSocket.

Loading the images and setting up the WebSocket connection

For loading the images, we use `d3.queue` to call `d3.xml` with the locations of the images:

```
d3.queue()
    .defer(d3.xml, 'data/heart.svg')
    .defer(d3.xml, 'data/lungs.svg')
    .await(start)
```

Once loaded, we can add the images to the SVG element, and do some scaling, to make them the same size:

```
function start(err, heart, lungs) {

    var addedHeart =
svg.append("g").attr("class","heartContainer").node()
            .appendChild(heart.documentElement.querySelector("g"))
        d3.select(addedHeart).attr("class","heart")
            .attr("transform", "translate(0 " + (yEcg(ecgAvg)-30) + " )
scale(0.1 0.1)")

    var addedLungs = svg.append("g").attr("class",
"lungContainer").node()
            .appendChild(lungs.documentElement.querySelector("g"))
        d3.select(addedLungs).attr("class","lungs")
            .attr("transform", "translate( 0 " + (yResp(respAvg)-30) + " )
scale(2 2)");

    ...
}
```

Adding external SVG images is always kind of a hassle. Usually, they are embedded themselves in an `svg` root element, which makes transforming them a lot more difficult. For example, the `heart.svg` file looks like this:

```
<?xml version="1.0" encoding="UTF-8" standalone="no"?>
<!-- Created with Inkscape (http://www.inkscape.org/) -->
<svg
    xmlns:svg="http://www.w3.org/2000/svg"
    xmlns="http://www.w3.org/2000/svg"
    version="1.0"
    width="645"
    height="585"
    id="svg2">
  <defs
      id="defs4" />
  <g
      id="layer1">
    <path
      d="M 297.29747,550.86823 C 283.52243,535.43191
249.1268,505.33855 220.86277,483.99412 C 137.11867,420.75228
125.72108,411.5999 91.719238,380.29088 C 29.03471,322.57071
2.413622,264.58086 2.5048478,185.95124 C 2.5493594,147.56739
5.1656152,132.77929 15.914734,110.15398 C 34.151433,71.768267
61.014996,43.244667 95.360052,25.799457 C 119.68545,13.443675
131.6827,7.9542046 172.30448,7.7296236 C 214.79777,7.4947896
223.74311,12.449347 248.73919,26.181459 C 279.1637,42.895777
```

```
310.47909,78.617167 316.95242,103.99205 L 320.95052,119.66445 L
330.81015,98.079942 C 386.52632,-23.892986 564.40851,-22.06811
626.31244,101.11153 C 645.95011,140.18758 648.10608,223.6247
630.69256,270.6244 C 607.97729,331.93377 565.31255,378.67493
466.68622,450.30098 C 402.0054,497.27462 328.80148,568.34684
323.70555,578.32901 C 317.79007,589.91654 323.42339,580.14491
297.29747,550.86823 z"
        id="path2417"
         />
    <g
       transform="translate(129.28571,-64.285714)"
       id="g2221" />
  </g>
</svg>
```

As you can see, a fixed `width` and `height` are defined for this image, and it already has a `transform` attribute defined. Since we're only interested in the path, we just select the first `g` element from the file (`querySelector("g")`) and add that one to our own group. The result from adding the external SVG images like this is that we can easily define our own `transform` attributes to it, and control it just like any other element. Once added and experimenting with the `scaletransform` attribute, we have the following:

Now that we've loaded our external images, we can start listening for WebSocket events. Connecting to a WebSocket from JavaScript is very straightforward:

```
function start(err, heart, lungs) {
    ...

    var connection = new WebSocket('ws://localhost:8081');
```

```
connection.onerror = function (error) {
    console.log('WebSocket Error ' + error);
};

connection.onmessage = function (e) {
    process(JSON.parse(e.data));
};
}
```

We make a connection (new WebSocket) and pass in the URL of the server that is listening (ws:e//localhost:8081). Now when the server pushes a message, the connection.onmessage function is called, with the string message. This message is converted to a JavaScript object (JSON.parse(e.data)) and passed into the process function, where we display it.

Handling the update from the server

In the previous example, we only had a limited number of points, so we needed to make sure ourselves that the line transitioned at a specified interval. For this example, we let the backend server control the speed of the line graph. Each time an event is received, we just put it at the end of the array and redraw everything:

```
// display the data
function process(received) {
    // Push a new data point onto the back.
    data.push(received);

    d3.select(".ecg").attr("d", lineEcg);
    d3.select(".resp").attr("d", lineResp);
    d3.select(".heartContainer").attr("opacity", sEcg(+received.ecg))
    d3.select(".lungContainer").attr("opacity", sResp(+received.resp))

    data.shift();
}
```

Because we've specified that we want 800 data points in the beginning of this section ($n = 800$), this results in a smoothly flowing graph. Note that we set the opacity of the two loaded SVG images as well. After redrawing the image, we remove the first element from the data array, effectively pushing it a single step to the left. The result is an animating line graph, which slowly moves from right to left, whose speed and detail level can be controlled by the server.

For instance, when we run the server like this: `node server-hr.js ../data/yng.csv 80 19`, we draw the lines approximately 12 times a second:

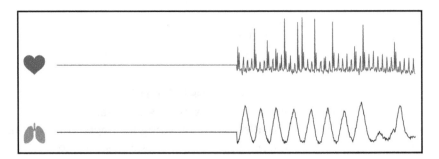

As you can see, the detail level of the lines, especially the ECG one, isn't that great. The reason is that we skip every 19 elements, and we don't do any averaging in our server. The advantage of using a lower update interval, however, is that we only need to redraw the image a couple of times per second instead of 250 times.

For our next example, we're going to show how you can create a streamgraph, which is an alternative way of rendering an area chart.

Random data-driven streamgraph

When you draw a streamgraph, the data of the different series are put one on top of another, just like for an area chart. Instead of an area chart, though, the bottom of the chart isn't fixed to a single position, but fluctuates, providing a visually appealing way of showing different series:

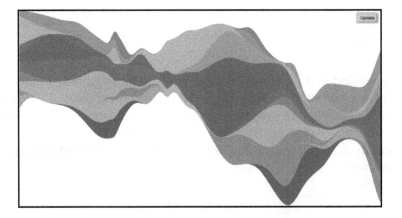

For our example, we're going to create a streaming variant of this streamgraph. We're going to use a server which pushes random data over a WebSocket to the browser and, based on that data, updates the streamgraph and moves it to the left. The final result we're aiming for is the `DVD3/src/chapter-06/D06-03.html` example.

When you open this example, and you have the random WebSocket server running (more on that in the next section), you'll see the following streamgraph moving from right to left:

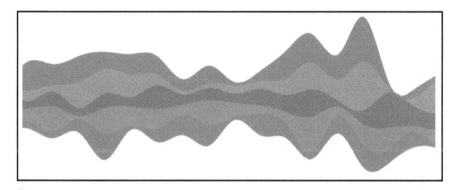

We start again by looking at the server side where we've created a simple node server which can generate the random data.

Random data WebSocket server

The WebSocket server isn't really that much different than the one we saw in the previous section. This time, however, instead of passing information from an external ECG file, we just generate a set of random data at a specific interval:

```
var fs = require('fs')
var ws = require('ws')

if (process.argv.length != 4) {
  console.log("Please specify the number of streams and the interval as
arguments.")
  process.exit(1)
}

var n = +process.argv[2];
var sendInterval = +process.argv[3]

startupServer(n)

function startupServer(n) {
```

```
// start a server
var WebSocketServer = ws.Server;
var wss = new WebSocketServer({ port: 8081 });
var count = 1;

wss.on('connection', function connection(ws) {
  console.log('received connection');
});

// called at the specified interval
function broadcast() {

  var data = { n: n };
  for (var i = 0 ; i < n ; i++) {
    data[i] = Math.random()*Math.random()*Math.random();
  }

  wss.clients.forEach(function each(client) {
    client.send(JSON.stringify(data), {}, function(cb) {});
  });

  count++;

};

  setInterval(function() { broadcast(); }, sendInterval);
}
```

This script takes two arguments: the first argument is the number of data elements to generate, and the second argument specifies the interval at which to push data to the client. To start the server, run the following command from the `DVD3/src/chaptert06-/bin` directory:

```
$ node server-random.js 7 100
```

Now when we connect a WebSocket client, we see the following data coming in:

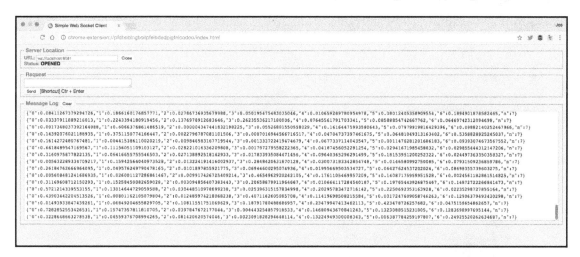

The result is a JSON object which contains seven values, from 0 to 6, each containing a random value. We'll read and visualize this data through the streamgraph.

Creating a streamgraph

For the streamgraph, we take a similar approach to the one used in the first example of this chapter. To get this working, we need to take the following steps:

1. Set up the scales and the generators.
2. Define the data and the transition.
3. Set up a clip path to hide the elements going into view and going out of view.

Let's look at the first step.

Setting up the scales and the generators

Just as for most examples, let's start by setting up the scales and the generators:

```
var totalDatapoints = 20;  // number of points used to draw the streamgraph
var numberSeries = 5;      // number of series to show
var interval = 1000;       // interval at which to rerender

var x = d3.scaleLinear()
    .domain([0, totalDatapoints-3])
    .range([0, width]);

var y = d3.scaleLinear().domain([-2, 5]).range([height, 0]);
var color = d3.scaleLinear().domain([0, numberOfSeries-1]).range(["red",
    "orange"]);

var area = d3.area().curve(d3.curveNatural)
    .x(function(d,i) { return x(i-1); })
    .y0(function(d)  { return y(d[1]); })
    .y1(function(d)  { return y(d[0]); });
```

We use a couple of variables to configure our streamgraph. `totalDatapoints` determines how many control points make up a single line of the streamgraph. So in this case, we draw the streamgraph based on 20 data points per series. `numberOfSeries` defines how many areas we're going to show. In this case, we show five areas. The `interval` determines how often we add a new point to the streamgraph and redraw the graph. For the position on the x-axis, we've defined the x scale. This is a simple `d3.scaleLinear` scale, which runs the complete width of the chart. As you can see, we limit the domain, by excluding the last three elements (`totalDatapoints-4`; if we wanted all the elements, we'd use `totalDatapoints-1`). We do this since the position of the points of the streamgraph is based on not just the data itself, but also the two previous elements. This way, we avoid jumps in data that is already rendered on screen. For the y-axis, we define a simple scale (`y`), whose domain (which is determined by some experimenting and is dependent on the number of series, and the values coming back from the server) is fixed and which uses the full height. For the last scale, we simply map the series to a color in the range from `red` to `orange`. Finally, we define the generator we're going to use to draw the areas, which is a standard `d3.area()`.

Interesting to note here is that we render the x with an offset of 1; we do this to make sure that when a data point leaves the visible area on the left side, we avoid jumps in the data. In this d3.area() generator, we can also determine how the generated area elements are curved by specifying the curve function. In this case, a d3.curveNatural results in smooth areas, whereas a d3.curveStep results in this:

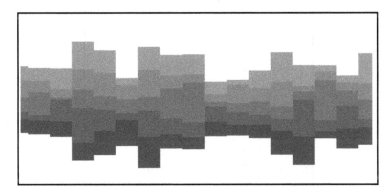

At this point, we haven't done anything which is specific to rendering a streamgraph. In the following section, we'll show how to render data, using the specified area generator as a streamgraph.

Defining the data and the transition

Let's start by looking at the data:

```
var data = initEmpty(totalDatapoints, numberSeries);
var stack = d3.stack().offset(d3.stackOffsetWiggle)
    .keys(d3.range(numberSeries).map(function(d) {return d}));

function initEmpty(totalDatapoints, numberSeries) {
   return d3.range(totalDatapoints).map(function(nc) {
       return d3.range(numberSeries).reduce(function(res, mc) {
           res[mc] = 0.7; return res;
       }, {id: nc});
   })
}
```

We initialize the `data` array with empty data, and then pass this data to the `d3.stack()` function, which prepares the data, so that we can use it with the `d3.area` generator. If you look at the `initEmpty` function, you can see that we create a structure which looks like this:

```
▼ Array[20]
  ▼ 0: Object
      0: 0.7
      1: 0.7
      2: 0.7
      3: 0.7
      4: 0.7
      id: 2
    ▶ __proto__: Object
  ▼ 1: Object
      0: 0.7
      1: 0.7
      2: 0.7
      3: 0.7
      4: 0.7
      id: 3
    ▶ __proto__: Object
```

We create an array which has a size of `numberSeries` (20 in our case), and for each array element, we define a value for each series. If you look back at the information provided by the WebSocket server, you can see that these match. Each message received from the WebSocket server already has the correct structure. In the `d3.stack()` function we defined in the previous code fragment, we set an `offset`; with this offset, we can configure the `d3.stack` to return data in a format which is rendered as a streamgraph instead of a normal area chart. For the streamgraph, we have two different options:

- `d3.stackOffsetSilhouette`: This offset sets the baseline of the streamgraph, so that the center of the streamgraph is zero. This remains the same, even when we add new data. So if you want a streamgraph that stays at the same position, this is a good option.
- `d3.stackOffsetWiggle`: With this setup, the baseline is set based on the weighted *wiggle* of the series. This means that the baseline can shift when data is added or removed. For our example, we use this one.

A streamgraph with the `d3.stackOffsetSilhouette` offset looks like this:

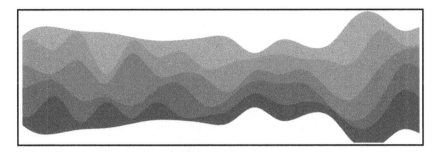

Now that we've got our initial set of data, and we've defined the `d3.stack` function, let's connect to the random data generating WebSocket server:

```
var receivedData = {};
var isRunning = false;
var connection = new WebSocket('ws://localhost:8081');
connection.onmessage = function (received) {
    var frame = JSON.parse(received.data);

    Object.keys(frame).forEach(function(key) {
        if (!receivedData[key]) {
            receivedData[key] = 0;
        }
        receivedData[key] += +frame[key];
    })

    // kick off processing.
    if (!isRunning) { isRunning = true; render(); }
};
```

We connect to the server just like we did in the previous example. Whenever we receive data from the WebSocket server, we add it to the `receivedData` object, so we can process it from the `render` function. We fire off the rendering of the graph the first time we receive some data. The `render` function looks like this:

```
function render() {
    data.push(receivedData);
    var stacked = stack(data)

    var existingEls = g.selectAll("path").data(stacked)
    var newEls = existingEls.enter().append("path")
        .style("fill", function(d,i) { return color(i); });
    receivedData = {}
```

```
        var all = existingEls.merge(newEls)
            .attr("transform", null)
            .transition().duration(interval).ease(d3.easeLinear)
            .attrTween("d", function(d, i) {
                var oldData = this._old
                    ? this._old
                    : d3.range(totalDatapoints + 1).map(function() {return
    {'0': 0, '1': 0}}));

                var currentData = d;
                var interpolator = d3.interpolate(oldData, currentData)
                return function(t) {
                    return area(interpolator(t))
                }

            })
            .attr("transform", "translate(" + x(-1) + ")")

        all.on("end", function(d, i) {
            d.shift();
            this._old = d;
            if (d.key === numberSeries-1) { render() }
        });

        data.shift();
    }
```

This is a large code fragment, but we use techniques we've already seen in previous examples. First we push the data we've received this interval onto the data array, then we use the standard select, enter, merge pattern to bind the data to our path elements. The interesting part happens after we merge the two selections. We define a transition, where we change two properties: the d attribute using a custom interpolator, and the transform attribute. The transform attribute works in the same way as we explained in the first example of this chapter. We use the x scale to move the path element one step to the left during the transition which takes interval milliseconds. In this same transition, we also create a custom interpolator for the d attribute. In this interpolator, we don't interpolate the final generated path, but interpolate the original data.

The reason is that the default `path` interpolator of D3 will create a *wiggle* effect when interpolating paths like this, instead of moving them along the y-axis. After the `transition` is done, we shift the data, assign the data to the `._old` variable so that we can use it next time in the interpolator, and kick off a new transition. Since the `end` function is called for each series, we make sure that we call the `render` function only once.

All that is left to do now is set up the mask to hide the fluctuating elements and we're done:

```
svg.append("defs").append("clipPath")
    .attr("id", "clip")
    .append("rect")
    .attr("width", x(totalDatapoints-4))
    .attr("height", height + margin.bottom + margin.top);
var g = svg.append("g").attr("clip-path", "url(#clip)");
```

By playing around with the number of series, the `color`, and the y scales, we can create very nice visualizations of streaming data:

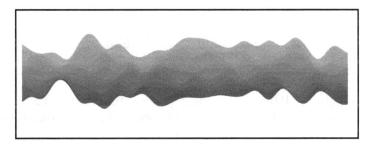

The previous image, for instance, shows a streamgraph with 12 streams and 30 data points.

For the final example in this chapter, we're going to visualize streaming data on top of a map. For this, we'll use the Meetup WebSocket API.

Visualizing Meetup.com RSVP data on a map

For our last streaming example, we're going to connect our web frontend to the public streaming API of Meetup. With Meetup, people can easily schedule meetups with people that share interests. An interesting aspect of Meetup is that it offers a publicly available WebSocket endpoint which provides RSVP information on public meetings.

When we connect to that endpoint, we get information back which looks like this:

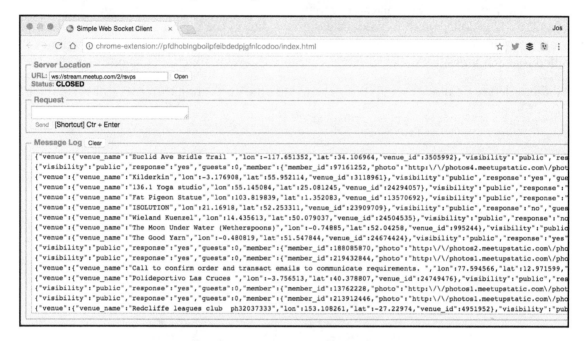

Each message is a single RSVP from someone either wanting to attend a meeting, or someone letting the organizers know they won't attend. When we look a bit closer at the JSON message, we see a lot of useful information:

```
{
    "venue": {
        "venue_name": "The Moon Under Water (Wetherspoons)",
        "lon": -0.74885,
        "lat": 52.04258,
        "venue_id": 995244
    },
    "member": {
        "member_id": 193383680,
        "photo":
"http://photos4.meetupstatic.com/photos/member/f/9/6/thumb_250263990.jpeg",
        "member_name": "Gareth"
    },
    "visibility": "public",
    "response": "yes",
    ...
    "group": {
        "group_topics": [
        ...
```

```
    ],
    "group_city": "Milton Keynes",
    "group_country": "gb",
    "group_id": 19760862,
    "group_name": "Tons Of Laughs and tequila!!!!",
    "group_lon": -0.75,
    "group_urlname": "Tons-Of-Laughs-and-Tequila",
    "group_lat": 52.02
  }
}
```

For this visualization, we're going to use the `lon` and `lat` coordinates to show a marker on the map whenever someone's response was either yes or no. The final result will look like this:

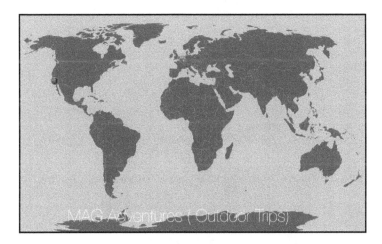

We have the following features in this visualization:

- Whenever a request is received on the WebSocket, we mark that location on the map. A response of `yes` is marked in green, and `no` is marked in red.
- The message from Meetup.com also contains a link to a member's photo. We'll quickly show this photo on the map as well.
- We keep track of the responses of the last minute, and show all these together on the map.
- Finally, we've added a simple text overlay, which shows the name of the last meeting someone RSVPed for.

The first thing we need to do is draw the map.

Drawing the map

We've already seen in the previous chapter how to draw a map with D3. In the following code fragment, we've done the same, but this time, we create a map which fits the complete screen by using `window.innerWidth` and `window.innerHeight` for the dimensions. This will make sure our map fills the complete browser window:

```
var margin = {top: 20, bottom: 50, right: 10, left: 10},
    width = window.innerWidth - margin.left - margin.right,
    height = window.innerHeight - margin.top - margin.bottom;

// create the standard chart
var svg = d3.select(".chart")
    .attr("width", width + margin.left + margin.right)
    .attr("height", height + margin.top + margin.bottom)
    .append("g")
    .attr("transform", "translate(" + margin.left + "," + margin.top +
")");

var mapGroup = svg.append("g");

// setup the projection, and the path generator
var projection = d3.geoNaturalEarth();
var path = d3.geoPath().projection(projection);

// load the data
d3.json("data/world-110m.v1.json", function(loadedTopo) {
    var countries  = topojson.feature(loadedTopo,
loadedTopo.objects.countries).features;
    var f = {type: "Sphere"};
    projection.fitSize([width, height], f)
    mapGroup.selectAll('.country').data(countries).enter()
        .append("path")
        .classed('country', true)
        .attr("d", path);

    mapGroup.append("text")
        .attr("x", (width/2))
        .attr("y", (height-50));
});
```

In this code fragment, we use the TopoJSON geometry we showed in the previous chapter, and show this geometry using the `d3.geoNaturalEarth` projection. We make sure our projection fits exactly by calling `projection.fitSize()` on the circumference of the projection (identified by the `{type: "Sphere"}` feature). We also add a `text` element, which we use to render the title of the meeting group, whenever we receive a message on the WebSocket.

Connecting to the Meetup WebSocket

To connect to the WebSocket, we just have to enter the URL in the constructor of the `WebSocket` class:

```
var connection = new WebSocket('ws://stream.meetup.com/2/rsvps');
connection.onmessage = function (received) {
    var frame = JSON.parse(received.data);
    // check if we've got venue coordinates, if not get the group
coordinates
    if (frame.venue && frame.venue.lon) {
        showSubscription(frame.venue.lat, frame.venue.lon, frame.response,
frame.member.photo, frame.group.group_name)
    } else if (frame.group && frame.group.group_lon) {
        showSubscription(frame.group.group_lat, frame.group.group_lon,
frame.response, frame.member.photo, frame.group.group_name)
    } else {
        // ignore this frame, since we can't show it
    }
};

function showSubscription(lat, lon, rsvp, image, name) {
  ...
}
```

When we receive data, we check whether the venue where the meeting is being held contains a `lon` attribute. If it does, we show that location on the map; if not, we get the location of the `group`. If that also fails, we ignore this message. When we can determine the location, we pass the location, the response (`yes` or `no`), the URL of the member's photo, and the name of the group to the `showSubscription` function.

Showing the information on the map

In the `showSubscription` function, we first add a circle on the location of the meetup:

```
function showSubscription(lat, lon, rsvp, image, name) {

    var position = projection([lon, lat]);
    mapGroup.append("g")
        .append("circle")
        .attr("cx",position[0])
        .attr("cy",position[1])
        .attr("class", "rsvp-" + rsvp)
        .transition().duration(1500).attr("r",circleSize*3)
        .transition().duration(1000).attr("r",circleSize)
        .transition().duration(1500).delay(60000)
            .attr("r",0)
            .on("end", function() {
                d3.select(this).remove()
            })
    ...
}
```

We first use the `projection` function to determine the x and y coordinates where to place the circle. Next, based on the `rsvp` value, we assign a different CSS class. The `rsvp-yes` class renders the circle green, and the `rsvp-no` class renders the circle red. Finally, we assign three transitions, which are executed one after another. The first transition grows the circle to `circleSize * 3`; next we shrink the circle to `circleSize` and finally, after waiting a minute, we shrink the circle to `0` and remove the element from the page using the `onend` event handler.

At the same time, we also set the `text` value:

```
function showSubscription(lat, lon, rsvp, image, name) {

    ...
    mapGroup.select("text")
        .text(name.length < 35 ? name :
            name.substring(0, 30) + "..." )
        .attr("text-anchor", "middle")
    ...

}
```

Here we just use the `text` function to set the value. If the name is too long, we replace the last part with . . . . Finally, we show the image, if present, of the member:

```
function showSubscription(lat, lon, rsvp, image, name) {

    ...

  if (image) {
      var imageContainer = mapGroup.append("g")
          .attr("transform", "translate(" + position[0]  + " " +
position[1] +") scale(0)")

      imageContainer.append("image")
          .attr('class','memberImage')
          .attr("x", -15)
          .attr("y", -15)
          .attr('width', 30)
          .attr('xlink:href', image)
          .attr("clip-path", "url(#clip)")

      imageContainer.append("circle")
          .attr("class", "image-" + rsvp)
          .attr("r", 15);

      imageContainer.transition().duration(1500).attr("opacity",1)
          .attr("transform", "translate(" + position[0]  + " " +
position[1] +") scale(1)")
          .transition().duration(1500)
          .attr("opacity",0)
          .attr("transform", "translate(" + position[0]  + " " +
position[1] +") scale(0)")
          .on("end", function() {
              d3.select(this).remove()
          })
  }
}
```

To show the image, we create a specific g to which we add an image element, which refers to the provided image URL. To create a nice rounded image, we use a clip path (see next code fragment), and we add a colored border using an additional circle element. When the group is added, we use a transition, to increase it in size and in opacity, and when that first transition is done, we hide the image again using another transition. When this last transition ends, we remove the element to nicely clean up everything.

For the clip path, we just define a simple circle like this:

```
svg.append("defs").append("clipPath")
       .attr("id","clip")
       .append("circle").attr("r", 15);
```

And that's it. Now we've got a map which responds to streaming data. One of the interesting parts of this approach is that we can use any projection, zoom factor, and translation of the map we want. We use the `projection()` function to determine where to show the images and circles, so this will work for all projections.

For example, here is the Albers projection:

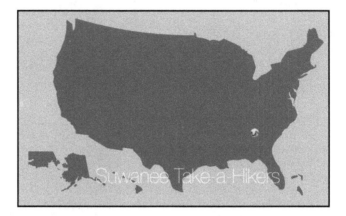

It also works for the exotic ones such as `d3.geoGringortenQuincuncial()`:

Summary

In this chapter, we've shown you different ways of working with streaming data. We started by showing the concepts of creating streaming graphs by creating a simple line graph that shows real-time information based on mouse movements. After that, we connected to a simple WebSocket server which provided us with ECG and respiratory information, and streamed the received data directly to two line graphs. We also provided a streaming alternative to area charts in the form of a streamgraph. With a streamgraph, we can create a visually pleasing visualization of multiple streams of streaming data. Finally, we connected to a publicly available WebSocket server and used the information from that server to update a map in real time. In the next chapter, we're going to look into two final visualization approaches using Voronoi diagrams and heatmaps.

7
Voronoi Diagrams and Heatmaps

In this chapter, we're going to look at two final diagrams. We're going to explore what is possible with the Voronoi support provided by D3, and we're going to create a heatmap diagram. To explore these two subjects, we'll create the following visualizations:

- We're going to start with a simple Voronoi diagram so we can better understand what a Voronoi is and what we can use it for.
- Next, we're going to create a Voronoi diagram of all the airport locations in the world to explore the aesthetic aspects of Voronois.
- We can also use Voronois to create very interesting-looking visualizations of random data. We'll use the approach we've seen in the previous two chapters to create a Voronoi fractal.
- Finally, we're going to create a heatmap that visualizes the usage of swearwords in movies.

We start by exploring Voronois. Before we start, though, I should mention that we'll only look at the visual aspects of Voronois in this book and not at the mathematics of the real-world usages Voronois can provide.

Simple Voronoi diagram

When we talk about Voronoi diagrams, it is good to start with understanding what a Voronoi diagram is. Wikipedia provides a nice short explanation of this:

In mathematics, a Voronoi diagram is a partitioning of a plane into regions based on distance to points in a specific subset of the plane. That set of points (called seeds, sites, or generators) is specified beforehand, and for each seed there is a corresponding region consisting of all points closer to that seed than to any other. These regions are called Voronoi cells.

In other words, we define a set of points on a 2D surface (for example, the screen), and the Voronoi diagram divides the surfaces into cells based on their distance to each of the points. It's easiest to understand by looking at an example. Say we've got the following set of random points:

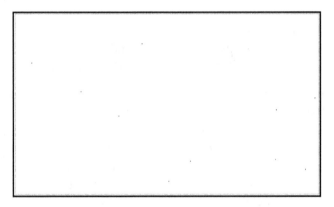

The resulting Voronoi diagram looks like this:

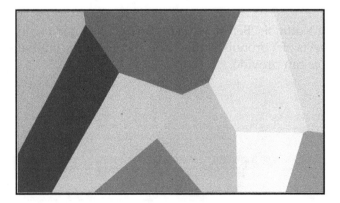

As you can see, the rectangle is divided into cells, based on the distance to each randomly positioned point. We can easily create the previous example using D3. The first thing we need to do is create the set of random points:

```
var nPoints = 10
var points = d3.range(nPoints).map(function(d) { return [Math.random() *
width, Math.random() * height]; });

    var points = d3.range(nPoints).map(function(d) { return [Math.random()
* width, Math.random() * height]; });

    svg.selectAll("circle").data(points).enter()
    .append("circle")
    .attr("cx", function(d) {return d[0]})
    .attr("cy", function(d) {return d[1]})
    .attr("r", 2)
```

Note that, while we explicitly draw them on the screen in this example, this isn't actually needed since D3 only needs to know the location of the points. Now that we've drawn the points, we can use the following D3 code to create the polygons for the Voronoi:

```
// use this to color the cells
var color = function() {return d3.interpolateOranges(Math.random())};

// set up the voronoi generator for the complete area
var voronoi = d3.voronoi().extent([[0, 0], [width, height ]]);

// create the polygons for the data points
var polygons = voronoi.polygons(points);
svg.append("g").selectAll("path").data(polygons).enter()
    .append("path")
    .attr("d", polyToPath)
    .attr("fill", color)

function polyToPath(polygon) {
   return polygon ? "M" + polygon.join("L") + "Z" : null;
}
```

Here we use the `d3.voronoi` function to convert the set of random points to a set of Voronoi cells we can draw. When creating a Voronoi, we also need to specify the area that is used to bound the Voronoi (the surrounding rectangle). For this example, we use the complete SVG area. When we call the `voronoi.polygons` function, we get a 2D array where each element contains an array of points that make up that specific Voronoi cell. The result of this function is what we saw at the beginning of this chapter. The interesting thing about Voronoi diagrams is that they become (subjectively) more beautiful when the number of points is increased. For example, the previous examples used 10 points. If we increase this to 1,000 points, we get some interesting-looking diagrams:

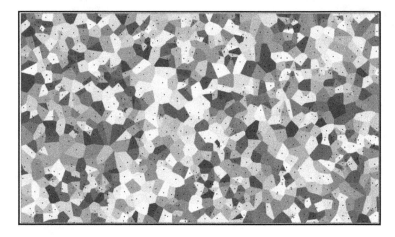

If you want to experiment with these simple Voronoi diagrams, you can find the code for this example in `DVD3/src/chapter-07/js/D07-01.js`.

Now that we've seen how we can create Voronoi diagrams in D3. In the next section, we create one from a list containing all the airports in the world.

Voronoi based on a list of airports

In this section, we're going to create a Voronoi diagram based on geographical data. We'll use a list of all the airports in the world, and use their locations to create a Voronoi diagram. We can create maps using this approach that look like this:

You can still see the general shape of the continents, even though we did not plot any geographic data. The first thing to do is get the data and sanitize it.

Prepare the data

We first download the list of airports from `http://ourairports.com/data/airports.csv`. This list contains information on all the airports and groups them by size. The data in this file looks like this:

```
"id","ident","type","name","latitude_deg","longitude_deg",...
6523,"00A","heliport","Total Rf Heliport",40.07080078125,-
    74.93360137939453,...6524,"00AK","small_airport","Lowell
Field",59.94919968,-
    151.695999146,...
```

We'll use a small script to filter out only the `name`, `latitude_deg`, and `longitude_deg` fields for the `medium_airport` and `large_airport` airports. You can find this script (named `filterAirports.js`) in the `data` directory for this chapter:

```
const d3 = require('d3');
const fs = require('fs');

d3.csv("file:airports.csv", process);

function process(data) {

    var filtered = data
        .filter(function(row) {return row.type === "medium_airport" ||
```

```
    row.type === "large_airport"})
        .map(function(row) {return {
            name: row.name,
            lon: row.longitude_deg,
            lat: row.latitude_deg,
        }})

    fs.writeFile('./ml_airports.csv',d3.csvFormat(filtered));
};
```

After we run this script, we get a small file with the following information:

```
name,lon,lat
Paraport Airstrip,-79.518586,41.788417
Aleknagik / New Airport,-158.617996216,59.2826004028
Honiara International Airport,160.05499267578,-9.4280004501343
Munda Airport,157.26300048828125,-8.327969551086426
Hongyuan Airport,102.35224,32.53154
. . .
```

In the next section, we'll load this information and use it to create the Voronoi map.

Show the points on the map

Let's first explore the data a bit more, and start rendering all the airports so we can see the data we're working with:

```
var projection = d3.geoNaturalEarth()
var path = d3.geoPath().projection(projection);
projection.fitSize([width, height], {type: "Sphere"})

d3.csv("data/ml_airports.csv",
    function(row) {return {
        name: row.name,
        lat: +row.lat,
        lon: +row.lon
    }},
    function (data) {

        var positions = data.map(function(row) {return [row.lon,
row.lat]})
        svg.selectAll("circle").data(positions).enter()
            .append("circle")
            .attr("cx", function (d) {
                return projection([d[0], d[1]])[0]
            })
```

```
        .attr("cy", function (d) {
            return projection([d[0], d[1]]) [1]
        })
        .attr("r", 2)
    })
```

In this code fragment, we create a `projection` using one of D3's provided projections, and use the projection to create a path generator (`path`). Next, we scale the projection to fit the available space using `projection.fitSize`. Now we can use `d3.csv` to load the data, change the `lat` and `lon` properties to numeric values, and pass the result to the second callback. To make the data easier to use when working with Voronoi diagrams, we convert the data to an array of coordinates and assign the resulting two-dimensional array to the `positions` variable. Finally, we render all the data points and determine their position by passing the coordinates into our `projection`. The result is a map showing just the airports:

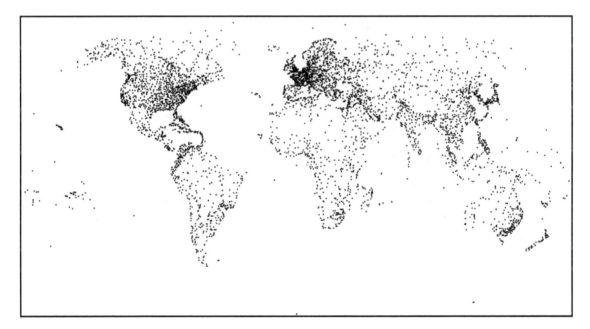

The next step is to use these points as input for a Voronoi generator.

Create the geo Voronoi

To create the Voronoi, we change the callback from the previous code fragment to this:

```
var color = function() {return d3.interpolateYlOrRd(Math.random())};

function (data) {
    var positions = data.map(function(row) {return [row.lon, row.lat]})
    var voronoi = d3.voronoi().extent([[-180, -90], [180, 90 ]]);
    var polygons = voronoi.polygons(positions);

    svg.append("g").selectAll("path").data(polygons).enter()
        .append("path")
        .attr("d", polygonToPath)
        .attr("fill", color)
})

function polygonToPath(polygon, i) {
  // strip the data attribute
  var points = d3.range(0, polygon.length).map(function(i) {return
polygon[i]});
  points.push(points[0])

  // ignore thie element, since it is rendered incorrectly
  if (i === 3835) { return ""; }
  return path({
      "type": "Feature",
      "geometry": {
          "type": "Polygon",
          "coordinates": [
              points
          ]
      }
  })
}
```

This time, we create a Voronoi generator and set the extent of the range that a longitude and a latitude can have. Next, we call `voronoi.polygons` to generate the polygons of the Voronoi cells we want to draw. The data returned from the `polygons` function looks like this:

```
▼ Array [5103]
  ▼ [0 … 99]
    ▼ 0: Array [5]
      ▼ 0: Array [2]
          0: -79.91890423440842
          1: 41.77417470611489
          length: 2
        ▶ __proto__: Array [0]
      ▼ 1: Array [2]
          0: -79.72296211992231
          1: 42.2098847553057855
          length: 2
        ▶ __proto__: Array [0]
      ▶ 2: Array [2]
      ▶ 3: Array [2]
      ▶ 4: Array [2]
      ▶ data: Array [2]
        length: 5
      ▶ __proto__: Array [0]
```

Each array element contains a set of coordinates that together form the polygon and the original data. We use the standard pattern of binding the data to SVG elements and use a simple `color` interpolator to set the fill of the polygon that is drawn. We determine the shape in the `polygonToPath` function. In that function, we convert the coordinates to a geoJSON feature object, which we can pass into the `path` function we defined earlier. For geoJSON, the polygons must be closed, which means that the last point in the array must be the same as the starting point, so we copy the first data point to the end of the array. While creating this example, the result didn't come out right. One of the cells overlapped most of the screen:

This was caused by the cell with index `3835`, so in the `polygonToPath` function we return an empty path to circumvent this. By playing around with the `color` interpolator and different projections, we can create different Voronoi maps of the airport data.

Let's look at the following configuration:

```
var projection = d3.geoEquirectangular();
var color = function() {return
    d3.interpolateBlues(Math.random())};
```

Using this configuration, we get the following result:

But we can also create a globe:

```
var projection = d3.geoOrthographic()
 var color = function() {return
  d3.interpolateYlGnBu(Math.random())};
```

Or we can use one of the more exotic projections:

```
var projection = d3.geoPolyhedralWaterman()
var color = function() {return d3.interpolateBrBG(Math.random())};
```

In the beginning of this chapter, we saw what a Voronoi looks like when created with random data. In the following example, we're going to dive somewhat deeper into generating Voronoi diagrams.

Generative art with nested Voronoi diagrams

Besides using Voronoi diagrams based on real data, we can also make a Voronoi of random data, like we did in the beginning of this chapter. Using this approach, we saw that you can quickly create nice-looking diagrams. In this section, we'll go one step further and create additional Voronoi diagrams inside the cells of an existing Voronoi diagram. If we do this a couple of times, we get a nice nested Voronoi diagram:

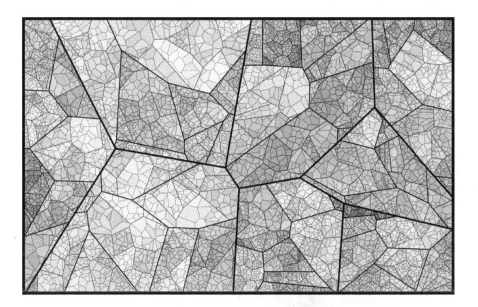

What you can see here is that each Voronoi cell itself is divided into more Voronoi cells, and these smaller cells themselves are divided once again. The result is a very nice-looking nested diagram.

In this section, we'll walk through the code to create this diagram.

Set up the Voronoi

The first thing we need to do is set up the area where we render the complete Voronoi diagram. This is a standard setup:

```
var pointSeed = 8;

// Generic setup
var margin = {top: 50, bottom: 20, right: 20, left: 20},
    width = 1200 - margin.left - margin.right,
    height = 600 - margin.top - margin.bottom;

// create the standard chart
var svg = d3.select(".chart")
    .attr("width", width + margin.left + margin.right)
    .attr("height", height+ margin.top + margin.bottom)
    .append("g")
    .attr("transform", "translate(" + margin.left +
        "," + margin.top + ")");
```

```
var defs = d3.select(".chart").append("defs");
var color = function() {return
    d3.interpolateRainbow(Math.random())};
```

There are a couple of things we do specifically for the recursive Voronoi. We define a `pointSeed`. This property defines how many random points we use to base the Voronoi on. So, with a `pointSeed` of 8, we generate eight random points in a specific area and create a Voronoi diagram based on that. We also add a `defs` sections to our chart, where we'll add our clip-paths, and define a simple random `color` generator that we'll use to fill the individual cells of our Voronoi. Here, we use the `d3.interpolatoRainbow`, but you can specify any interpolator you want here. For example, using the `d3.interpolateBrBG` interpolator results in the following diagram:

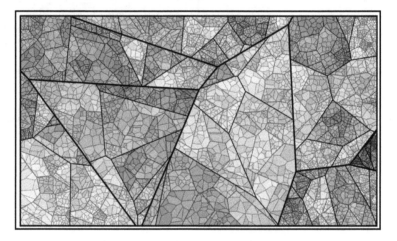

Now let's see the steps we need to take to render the first layer of the Voronoi.

Render the first layer

For the first layer, we're going to create a Voronoi for the complete area (we set the size a bit higher to avoid rendering artifacts). In this area, we generate a number of random points using the `generateRandomPoints` function:

```
var voronoi = d3.voronoi().extent([[-1, -1], [width + 1, height + 1]]);
var points = generateRandomPoints(pointSeed, 0, width, 0, height);
var polygons = voronoi.polygons(points);
drawVoronoi(svg, polygons, undefined, 0);

function generateRandomPoints(nPoints, minX, maxX, minY, maxY) {
    return d3.range(0, nPoints).map( function(i) {
```

```
                return [Math.floor(Math.random() * (maxX-minX)) + minX,
    Math.floor(Math.random() * (maxY-minY)) + minY]
        })
    }
```

With these randomly generated points, we determine the cells (the `polygons`) of our Voronoi and draw them using the `drawVoronoi` function:

```
function drawVoronoi(parent, polygons, clipArea, level) {
    parent.insert("g",":first-child")
            .attr("clip-path", function(d) { return clipArea ?
                "url(#" + clipArea+ ")" : ""})
            .attr("class", "polygons")
            .selectAll("path")
            .data(polygons)
            .enter().insert("path")
            .attr("data-level",level)
            .attr("stroke-width", function()
                {return 6 / ((level+1)*2) })          .attr("stroke", function()
{d3.hsl(
                "#000").brighter(level)})          .attr("fill", function()
{return level
                === 0 ? "" : color()})
            .attr("fill-opacity", "0.3")
            .attr("d", polyToPath)
}

function polyToPath(polygon) {
    return polygon ? "M" + polygon.join("L") + "Z" : null;
}
```

The `drawVoronoi` function takes a number of parameters, since we'll use it to draw the sublevels as well. The `parent` parameter determines the parent element the polygons belong to. The `polygons` parameter is the result from the `voronoi.polygons` call and contains the polygons we want to draw. The `clipArea` is the clip-path we'll apply to the drawn cells, and the `level` is the level we're drawing at. The first Voronoi elements are drawn at level 0, and the Voronoi diagrams that are drawn inside the cells of the first Voronoi elements are at level 1, and so on. We use this in this function to set the `stroke-width` and stroke `color` of the outline of each cell. So the outlines of the Voronoi diagrams get smaller when we go deeper.

We also set the `level` data property so we can easily reference the cells created for this specific level. Finally, we use the `polyToPath` function to determine the path to draw. If we just draw a single level, we see the following result:

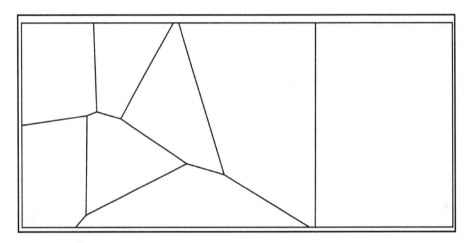

We've got our first level of Voronoi cells. Now we'll fill each of these cells with additional Voronoi cells.

Recursively creating Voronoi diagrams

To draw the nested polygons, we use the following code:

```
// draw the nested polygons
d3.range(1,4).forEach(drawSubPolygons);

function drawSubPolygons(level) {
    var parentLevel = level-1;

    // we process each of the parent polygons
    var selection = d3.selectAll('path[data-level="'
        + parentLevel +'"]');

    var totalPolygons = [];
    selection.each(function(d, i) {
        var box = this.getBBox();

        // generate some random points. The deeper we go,
            the more points we generate, based on the parent Voronoi
    var points20 = generateRandomPoints(pointSeed * level,
            box.x, box.x + box.width, box.y, box.y + box.height);         //
```

```
use the extent to define where the new
            Voronoi needs to be rendered.           var voronoi2 =
d3.voronoi().extent([[box.x, box.y],
            [box.x + box.width, box.y+box.height]]);
        var polygons2 = voronoi2.polygons(points20)

        // draw the new voronois
        if (polygons2.length > 0) {
            // the new voronois need to be added in the group with
                the parent clippath, to avoid them
            // spilling over to other cells
            drawVoronoi(d3.select(this.parentNode), polygons2,
                "cp-" + parentLevel + "-" + i, level);
            addClipPath(d, "cp-" + parentLevel + "-" + i);
        }
    });
}
```

Here we draw the levels 1, 2, and 3 (d3.range(1, 4)) by calling drawSubPolygons. In that function, we first select all the parent cells using the d3.selectAll function, and for each of the found cells, we create a new Voronoi diagram, just like we did on the first level. The only thing we change is that we also create a clip-path (by calling addClipPath), which we can use to limit the shown area of the child Voronoi elements. Now when we run this example, you can see the Voronoi being created in the following steps.

First, we render the highest level:

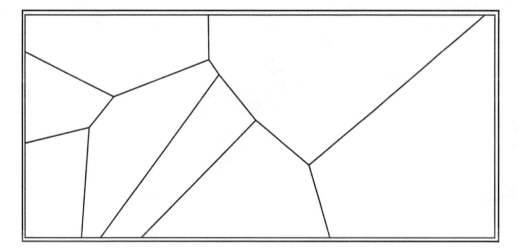

Then we fill in those Voronoi cells with newly created Voronoi diagrams:

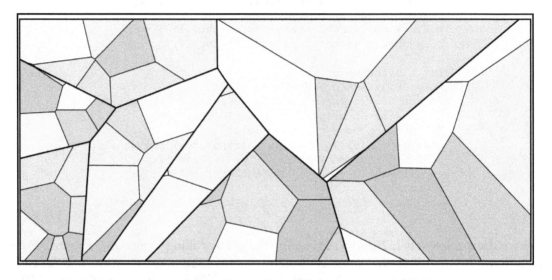

Then we repeat that process for the next set of created Voronoi cells:

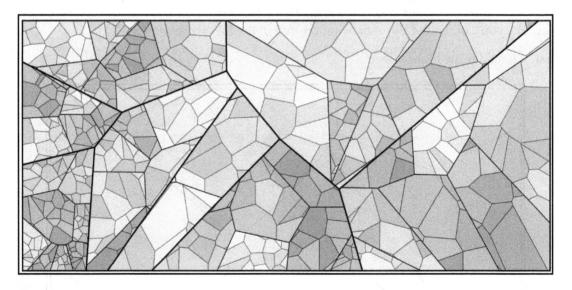

We do this until we get to our final result:

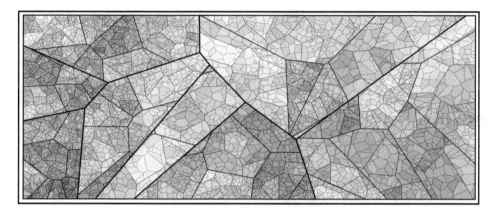

For our final example, we're going to create a simple heatmap.

Heatmap showing swearword usage in movies

For this last example, we're going to create a heatmap that shows how often swear words are used in movies. We're going to create a heatmap that looks like this:

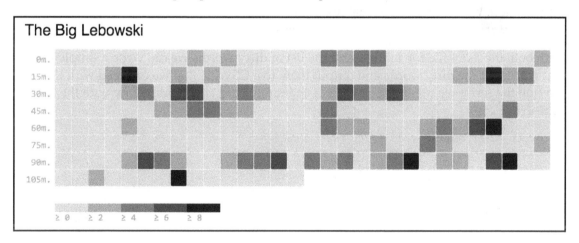

In this figure, the colors show how often someone swears in that specific part of the movie. For this example, the movie is divided into 30 second segments. The numbers at the left side show how far in the movie we are, and the legend at the bottom shows the color coding used.

The first thing we need, though, is some data to visualize.

Preparing the data

The easiest way to determine the amount of swearing in a movie is by analyzing the subtitles. For most popular movies, you can download a subtitle file (in .srt format), which shows the time of a specific sentence and all the words. For instance, the start of the subtitle file for *The Big Lebowski* looks like this:

```
1
00:00:41,500 --> 00:00:44,127
Way out West
there was this fella.

2
00:00:44,211 --> 00:00:46,546
Fella I wanna tell you about.
```

Besides the text of the movie, we, of course, also need some way to determine whether a word is a swearword. For this, we use a list that Google once created for an interactive visualization. We can download that list from https://gist.github.com/ryanlewis/a37739d710ccdb4b406d.

With both the .srt file for a movie and the list of dirty words, we can write a simple script that will count the dirty words and output them to a CSV file that we can read with D3. You can find the script we use in the <DVD3>/src/chapter-07/data directory with the name srtParser.js:

```
const d3 = require('d3');
const fs = require('fs');
const srt = require('srt');
const _ = require('lodash');

var timePeriod = 30;

d3.queue()
    .defer(d3.text, "file:dwList.txt")
    .defer(d3.text, "file:swearnet.srt")
    .await(function (error, dwList, subs) {
```

```
var dirties = dwList.split("\n");
// make sure the lineending are correct before parsing
var srts = srt.fromString(subs.replace(/\r\n/g, "\n"));

// get all the words, and approximate
   time they are spoken.
var timedWords = [];
var allKeys = Object.keys(srts);
allKeys.forEach(function(key) {
    var startTime = srts[key].startTime;
    var endTime = srts[key].endTime;

    // get the totalTime and the individual words
    var totalTime = endTime - startTime;
    var words = srts[key].text.match(/[a-zA-Z]+/g);

    if (words) {
        var timePerCharacter = totalTime / words.length;
        words.forEach(function(word, i) {
            timedWords.push({
                word: word,
                time: startTime + (timePerCharacter * i)
            });
        });
    }
});

// get the last element to determine the endtime
var lastElement = srts[allKeys.slice(-1)[0]];
var endTime = lastElement.endTime;

// filter out all the swearwords
var onlySW = timedWords.filter(function(timed) {
    return _.includes(dirties, timed.word)
})

// now group them in minutes
var grouped = _.groupBy(onlySW, function(timed) {
    return Math.floor((timed.time / (1000 * timePeriod)));
})


// And sum them for each minute.
// range + 1, since end is not inclusive
var groupedPerMinute = d3.range(0, Math.floor(endTime /
    (1000 * timePeriod)) + 1).map(function(i) {
    return grouped[i] ?
    { minute: i, count: grouped[i].length} :
```

```
            { minute: i, count: 0}
    });

    // and write to fs
    fs.writeFile('./sw-1.csv', d3.csvFormat(groupedPerMinute))
});
```

We won't go into too much detail about how this script works, since the steps are rather self-explanatory. From a high-level point of view, we take the following steps:

1. We read in the dirty words list and the subtitles file.
2. Next, we split the subtitles file into separate words and determine an approximate time when each word was spoken.
3. Then we start counting the swearwords by checking each word against the dirty words list.
4. Finally, we group the dirty words per time interval and write out the result to a CSV file.

The content of the final file looks like this:

```
minute,count
0,0
1,0
2,0
3,1
4,2
5,2
6,3
7,0
8,0
9,2
10,1
11,0
12,0
13,1
```

The first column contains the time interval we're working with and the second contains the amount of swearwords used in that time period. With this CSV, we can render a heatmap.

Rendering the heatmap

To render the heatmap, we take the following steps:

1. Write out the individual rectangles for each element in the input CSV.
2. Add extra information at the left side of the visualization showing the time in the movie.
3. Provide an additional legend at the bottom so we know what the scales represent.

Let's start with drawing the individual rectangles.

Create the heatmap

Before we look at how the heatmap is implemented, first let's look at how we configure the appearance of this chart:

```
// configuration for the heatmap
var elementsPerLine = 30,
    gridSize = Math.floor(width / elementsPerLine),
    legendElementWidth = gridSize * 2,
    buckets = 5,
    secondsPerElement = 30;
```

With these properties, we can configure how large each individual element is (gridSize) by setting the elementsPerLine. The buckets property is used to set the number of different colors we'll use for visualization, and secondsPerElement is used for the extra information to the left of the diagram, and should match timePeriod from our script, which we used to parse the subtitle file.

For instance, changing the `elementsPerLine` to `20`, results in the following diagram:

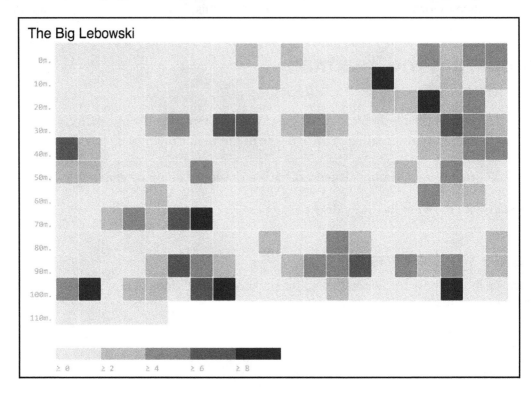

To render the data in a csv file, we've made a helper function, which looks like this:

```
function show() {
    addDiagram("data/TheBigLebowski.csv", "The Big Lebowski");
}
```

The implementation of the `addDiagram` is shown here:

```
var addDiagram = function (tsvFile, title) {

    // will contain the heatmap
    var chartGroup = svg.append("g")
        .attr("transform", "translate(" + margin.left + "," + margin.top +
")");

    // contains the title
    var textGroup = svg.append("g");

    d3.csv(tsvFile,
```

```
        function (d) {
            var minute = +d.minute;
            var column = minute % elementsPerLine;
            return {
                column: column,
                value: +d.count,
                row: Math.floor(minute / elementsPerLine)
            };
        },
        function (error, data) {

            // set the total height of the svg based on the number of rows
            var totalHeight = (Math.ceil(data.length / elementsPerLine)) *
(gridSize) + margin.top + margin.bottom;
            svg.attr('height', totalHeight);

            // calculate the maximum value, and create a colorscale
            var maxValue = d3.max(data, function(d) {return d.value});

            // create a set of buckets for the colors
            var colorScale = d3.scaleQuantize()
                .range(d3.range(0, buckets ).map(function(i) {
                    return d3.interpolateReds((i+1)/buckets);
                }))
                .domain([0, maxValue]);

            // draw all the individual rectangles
            chartGroup.selectAll("rect")
                .data(data)
                .enter().append("rect")
                .attr("x", function (d) { return (d.column) * gridSize; })
                .attr("y", function (d) { return (d.row - 1) * gridSize; })
                .attr("rx", 4)
                .attr("ry", 4)
                .attr("class", "column bordered")
                .attr("width", gridSize)
                .attr("height", gridSize)
                .style("fill", function(d) {return(colorScale(d.value))});

            ...
        }
    }
```

Most of the code is very straightforward, so let's look at a couple of interesting parts of the code. When we load the data, we have already set the `row` and `column` of each element. We use this later on to draw the rectangles at the correct position. The next one is the `colorScale`. We use a `d3.scaleQuantize` for this. With this type of scale, the domain is continuous (in our case, we set it from 0 to the maximum amount of swears per time period), but the range is set to a number of values, one for each `bucket`. So, basically, we divide the colors from the specified interpolator into a number of distinct groups. Drawing the rectangles themselves is just the standard D3 pattern where we bind the data and use the `enter` function to draw the newly added elements. In this case, we don't use scales to determine the x and y positions, but we set those based on the `column` and `row` values.

Add the minutes information

The minutes at the left are added like this:

```
function (error, data) {
  ...
  chartGroup.selectAll("text")
    .data(d3.range(0, Math.ceil(data.length / elementsPerLine)))
    .enter().append("text")
    .text(function(d, i) {
      return Math.round(i * elementsPerLine * secondsPerElement / 60) +
"m."
    })
    .attr("class", "mono")
    .attr("text-anchor", "end")
    .attr("y", function(d, i) {return i * gridSize})
    .attr("dx", -5)
    .attr("dy", -5)
  ...
}
```

For each line, we simply determine the text that we want to write, and position the text element at the correct position. Finally, we also add a legend.

Provide the legend

The legend is a set of five rectangles, which we create based on the number of buckets we want to show, as follows:

```
var legendPos = ((Math.floor(data.length / elementsPerLine) + 1) *
(gridSize));
```

```
var legend = chartGroup.selectAll(".legend")
    .data(d3.range(0, buckets))

var newLegends = legend.enter().append("g")
    .attr("class", "legend")

// append a rectangle for each element
newLegends.append("rect")
    .attr("x", function (d, i) { return legendElementWidth * i; })
    .attr("y", legendPos)
    .attr("width", legendElementWidth)
    .attr("height", gridSize / 2)
    .style("fill", function (d, i) { return colorScale.range()[i]; })

// add text to the legend
newLegends.append("text")
    .attr("class", "mono")
    .text(function (d, i) { return "≥ " + Math.round(maxValue / (buckets) *
i); })
    .attr("x", function (d, i) { return legendElementWidth * i; })
    .attr("y", legendPos + gridSize);
```

First, we determine the legend's position (legendPos) as one step below the final row. Next, we draw the legend by creating an array from 0 to 5 using the d3.range function. For each of the elements, we draw a simple rectangle and add a bit of text below it to show the value of that color.

And that's it. By playing around with the time periods, the bucket sizes, and the interpolators, we can easily create different visualizations of the same data:

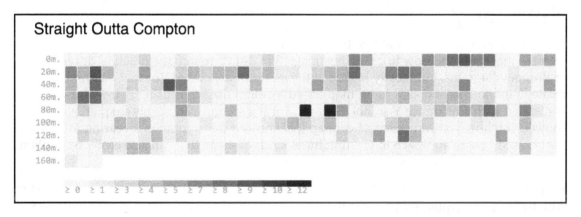

We can also use the `d3.interpolatorSpectral`:

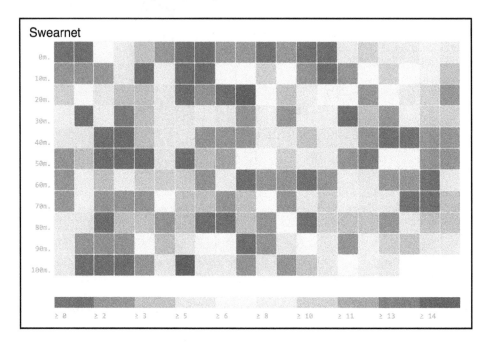

The approach used in this section can also be used to create calendars or other kinds of heatmaps.

Summary

In this chapter, we've looked at two final visualization forms. We've shown how to create Voronoi diagrams and how to create heatmaps. We didn't go into the practical applications of Voronoi diagrams, but mostly looked at the aesthetic aspects of Voronoi diagrams. We created random Voronoi diagrams, map-based Voronoi diagrams using real-world data, and ended with a recursive Voronoi diagram. For the second part of this chapter, we showed you how you can create a heatmap that showed the amount of swearing in a movie. We showed you an approach to creating these kinds of maps that can also easily be applied to different kinds of data sets.

With this chapter, we're finished with the most important visualizations and parts of the D3 API. In the next chapter, we're going to look at how you can use some of the D3 APIs and other external tools to create, load, and manipulate some basic shapes.

8
Custom Shapes and Paths and Using a Brush Selection

In this chapter, we're going to look at a couple of leftover subjects:

- **Symbols**: We start by looking at the different types of symbols that are supported by D3. A symbol is just a small SVG path, which looks like a cross, a diamond, and so on. You can use symbols to better annotate scatterplots or line graphs.
- **Paths**: We've already seen paths being used by the different path generators, but we can also construct paths directly. For this example, we'll look at how you can use the d3.path function to create paths from scratch and use them in SVG or on a 2D canvas.
- **Exporting SVG**: With D3, you can create beautiful-looking visualizations. However, they can usually only be accessed from a browser with JavaScript support. In this chapter, we'll also show you how you can export your D3 visualization as a PNG and as an SVG file.
- **Importing SVG**: In the previous chapters, we've already shown a couple of times how you can import SVG elements from external files. In this chapter, we'll look at that a bit closer and show you how you can use **Inkscape** (an open source SVG editor) to create or alter an SVG image, and import the resulting file into D3.
- **Brush selection**: Finally, we'll look at how you can select multiple D3 elements using a brush selection. For this, we'll randomly show a number of symbols, which we'll select using a brush.

The first subject we're going to look at in this chapter is the custom shapes provided by D3.

Symbols supported in D3

If you look at the d3.shape API (https://github.com/d3/d3-shape), you can see all the different standard shapes provided by D3, and you'll notice that we've already discussed most of them in the previous chapters. However, there is one part of this API that we haven't explored yet, and that is the symbols.

D3 provides a number of standard symbols that you can use in your visualizations. For instance, when drawing a line chart, instead of drawing circles for each point of the chart, you could use a cross or a star. D3 comes with the following list of standard symbols:

- d3.symbolCross: A cross symbol, or an addition (+) symbol
- d3.symbolCircle: A simple circle
- d3.symbolDiamond: A diamond symbol, as used on playing cards
- d3.symbolSquare: A simple square
- d3.symbolStar: A five pointed star
- d3.symbolTriangle: A simple triangle, point up
- d3.symbolWye: A Y symbol

Each of these symbols has a size function, which you can use to set the size of the symbol, which defaults to 64. In DVD3/src/chapter-08/D08-01.html, you can see what these symbols look like when rendered:

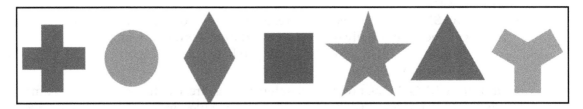

The required JavaScript to render these symbols is rather straightforward, and uses the same approach as all the other path generators:

```
var symbols = [
    {name: 'Cross', symbol: d3.symbolCross},
    {name: 'Circle', symbol: d3.symbolCircle},
    {name: 'Diamond', symbol: d3.symbolDiamond},
    {name: 'Square', symbol: d3.symbolSquare},
    {name: 'Star', symbol: d3.symbolStar},
    {name: 'Triangle', symbol: d3.symbolTriangle},
    {name: 'Wye', symbol: d3.symbolWye}
];
```

```
var color = d3.scaleOrdinal()
    .domain(symbols.map(function(s) {return s.name}))
    .range(d3.schemeCategory10);

var xBand = d3.scaleBand()
    .domain(symbols.map(function(s) {return s.name}))
    .range([0, width])
    .paddingInner(0.1);

var symbolGroups = svg.selectAll(".symbol").data(symbols)
    .enter()
        .append("g")
        .attr("class","symbol")
        .attr("transform", function(d) {
            return "translate(" + xBand(d.name)  + " 40)"
        });

symbolGroups.append("path")
    .attr("fill", function(d) {return color(d.name)})
    .attr("d", function(d) {
        return d3.symbol()
            .size(2500) // specifies area
            .type(d.symbol)();
    });
```

One thing to note in this code is that we set a rather large size. The reason for this is that the size for a symbol isn't in pixels; it is specified as the area the symbol occupies. So in this case, it is approximately a 50x50 size.

Since these are basic SVG shapes, we can also use transitions to animate them. For instance, in DVD3/src/chapter-08/D08-02.html we rotate the symbols:

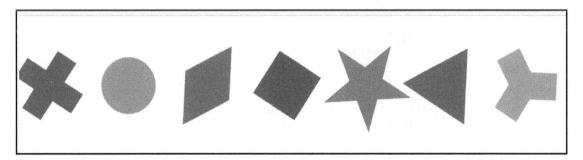

For this, we use a standard D3's `d3.transition`, as follows (we don't show the setup of the scales here):

```
...
redraw();
function redraw() {

    // select currently drawn symbols
    var symbolGroups = svg.selectAll(".symbol").data(symbols);

    // for newly added elements add the symbol and
    var newSymbols = symbolGroups.enter()
        .append("g")
        .attr("class","symbol")
        .attr("transform", function(d) {
            return "translate(" + xBand(d.name)
                + " 40) rotate(0)"
        });

    // add the symbol to the group
    newSymbols.append("path")
        .attr("fill", function(d) {return color(d.name)})
        .attr("d", function(d) {
            return d3.symbol()
                .size(2400) // specifies area
                .type(d.symbol)();
        })

    // merge with existing ones, and set up a transition.
    symbolGroups.merge(newSymbols)
        .transition()
        .on('end', function(d) {
            if (d.name === 'Wye' ) redraw(); // only redraw once
        })
        .duration(2000)
        .ease(d3.easeLinear)
        .attrTween("transform", function(d, i) {
            var interpolate = d3.interpolate(0, 360);
            return function(t) {
                return "translate(" + xBand(d.name)   + " 40)
                    rotate(" + interpolate(t) + ")";
            };
        })
}
```

That's it for the symbols in D3. In the next section, we'll look at exporting D3 visualizations.

Using d3.path to draw paths

In this section, we're going to explore the functions provided by the d3.path function to directly define a path that can be drawn with D3.

Drawing using the path API

Creating paths directly with SVG is rather complex, and it involves writing statements like this:

```
<path d="
  M 213.1,6.7
  c -32.4-14.4-73.7,0-88.1,30.6
  C 110.6,4.9,67.5-9.5,36.9,6.7
  C 2.8,22.9-13.4,62.4,13.5,110.9
  C 33.3,145.1,67.5,170.3,125,217
  c 59.3-46.7,93.5-71.9,111.5-106.1
  C 263.4,64.2,247.2,22.9,213.1,6.7
  z" />
```

As we've already seen in earlier chapters, D3 hides most of this complexity behind path generators. Sometimes, though, you might need to create a path generator yourself, or you might want to be able to draw a path yourself. Luckily, D3 provides an easier way to do this, so you don't have to write the SVG path definitions yourself. Through the d3.path function, you get a number of functions that you can use to define your path. The first thing you need to do is create a d3.path instance (var path = d3.path()). With this instance, you can start drawing a path using the following functions:

Function	Description
moveTo(x,y)	Move to a specific point specified by the x and y coordinates.
closePath()	Close the path by drawing a line to the first specified point.
lineTo(x,y)	Draw a line from the current position to the position specified by the x and y coordinates.

`quadraticCurveTo(cpx, cpy, x, y)`	Draw a quadratic curve to the specified x and y coordinates using the control point specified by `cpx` and `cpy`.
`bezierCurveTo(cpx1, cpy1, cxp2, cpx2, x, y)`	Draw a Bezier curve to the specified x and y coordinates using the control points specified by `cpx1`, `cpy1`, and `cpx1` and `cpx2` coordinates.
`arcTo(x1, y1, x2, y2, radius)`	Draw a circular arc segment following the HTML5 canvas specification `arcTo` function.
`arc(x, y, r start, end, anticlockwise)`	Draw a circular arc segment following the HTML5 canvas specification `arc` function.
`rect(x, y, w, h)`	Draw a rectangle using the x, y, w, and h variables.
`toString()`	Convert the current path to a string representation, which can be assigned to an SVG path's d attribute.

Let's create a simple D3 example that shows these functions in action. We're going to create a simple path, which looks like this (`<DVD3>/src/chapter-08/src/D08-07.html`):

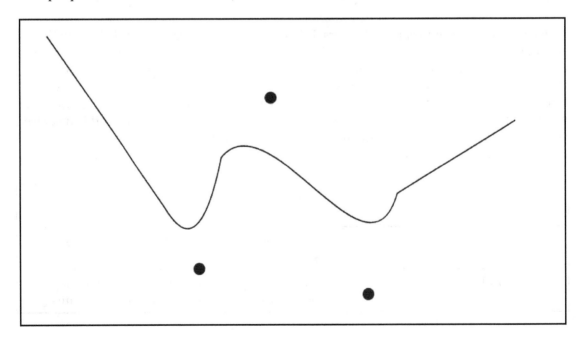

You can drag the blue circles around-which are the control points for the two curves-and see how it affects the path. To create this sample, we use the following code:

```
var cp1 = {x: 230, y: 200};
var cp2 = {x: 290, y: 10};
var cp3 = {x: 300, y: 200};
```

The first thing we do is define the control points for our curves. We're going to use the quadraticCurveTo and bezierCurveTo functions. For the first one, we need a single control point (cp1) and for the second one we need two control points (cp2 and cp3). With these control points defined, we can create our path. For this, we create a simple function that we can use as a path generator:

```
function getPath() {
    var path = d3.path();
    path.moveTo(100, 20);
    path.lineTo(200, 160);
    path.quadraticCurveTo(cp1.x, cp1.y, 250, 120);
    path.bezierCurveTo(cp2.x, cp2.y, cp3.x, cp3.y, 400, 150);
    path.lineTo(500, 90);

    return path.toString();
}
Now all we need to do is define the function which can draw everything:
function drawPath() {
    // draw the circles and add a drag listener
    var circles = svg.selectAll("circle").data([cp1, cp2, cp3])
    circles.enter().append("circle")
        .attr("r", 5)
        .attr("fill", "blue")
        .attr("class","cp1")
            .call(d3.drag().on("drag", dragcp))
        .merge(circles)
            .attr("cx", function(d) {return d.x})
            .attr("cy", function(d) {return d.y});

    var line = svg.selectAll(".line").data([0])
    line.enter().append("path")
        .attr("class","line").merge(line)
        .attr("d", getPath)
        .attr("stroke", "black")
        .attr("fill", "none");
};
```

Nothing special here. We first draw the blue circles based on the control points we defined, and next draw the line using our custom `getPath` path generator. To handle dragging the blue circles, we attach a `d3.drag` to those elements. When one of the circles is dragged, the `dragcp` function is called. In this function, we do the following:

```
function dragcp() {
    var ev = d3.event;
    ev.subject.x = ev.x;
    ev.subject.y = ev.y;
    drawPath();
}
```

Since we call `drawPath` again, whenever we drag one of the control points, our line is updated:

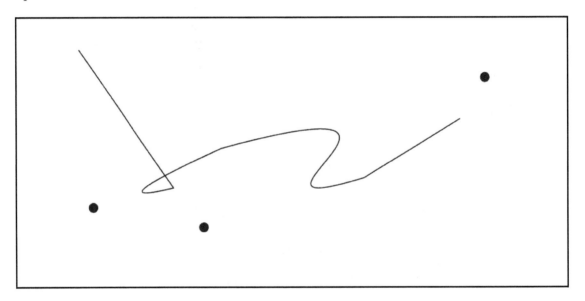

Animating along a line

One of the interesting parts of creating paths is that you can also use it for animation purposes. Once you have a path, it is very straightforward to animate an SVG object along that path. If you open example `<DVD3>/src/chapter-08/D08-08.html` in your browser, you'll see a blue circle moving along a path:

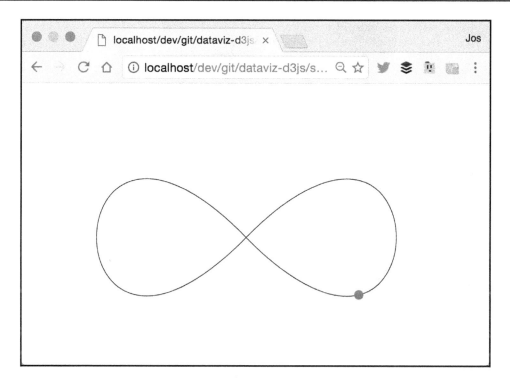

The following code fragments show how to create this animation:

```
// set the startingpoint
var startingPoint = {x: 300, y: 200};

// generate and draw the curve
var curve = generateCurve(startingPoint);
var drawnPath = drawPath(curve);

// draw a circle, which will be moved
var circle = svg.append("circle");
circle.attr("r", 7)
     .attr("fill", "steelblue")
     .attr("transform", "translate(" + startingPoint.x + " " +
startingPoint.y + ")");

   ...

   function generateCurve(startingPoint) {
     var path = d3.path();
     var center = startingPoint;
     var curve = {w: 300, h: 300}
```

```
        path.moveTo(center.x, center.y);
        path.bezierCurveTo(center.x + curve.w, center.y - curve.h, center.x +
curve.w, center.y + curve.h, center.x, center.y);
        path.bezierCurveTo(center.x - curve.w, center.y - curve.h, center.x -
curve.w, center.y + curve.h, center.x, center.y);
        path.closePath();

        return path.toString();
    }

    function drawPath(curve) {
        return svg.append("path")
            .attr("class","line")
            .attr("d", function(d) {return curve})
            .attr("stroke", "black")
            .attr("fill", "none");
    };
```

The first thing we do is define the path we want to traverse (generateCurve). Next, we draw this path and add a circle at the path's starting point.

Now that we've got the path and the element we want to move, we can create an interpolator (animateOnPath), which we can use from a transition, like this:

```
// kickoff the animation
move();

function move() {
    circle.transition()
        .duration(7500)
        .ease(d3.easeLinear)
        .attrTween("transform", animateOnPath(drawnPath.node()))
        .on("end", move);// infinite loop
}

function animateOnPath(path) {
    var l = path.getTotalLength();
    return function(i) {
        return function(t) {
            var p = path.getPointAtLength(t * l);
            return "translate(" + p.x + "," + p.y + ")";//Move marker
        }
    }
}
```

The interesting part happens in the `animateOnPath` interpolator, which uses the standard SVG function `getPointAtLength`. This function returns a point on the path that corresponds to a specific length. Using this approach, we can move our circle along the path, regardless of the complexity of the path. For instance, the following path (drawn using Inkscape), works in exactly the same manner (the path is commented out in the source code, if you want to try this):

In the next few sections, we'll look at how you can import and export SVG images.

Exporting visualizations

When we create a visualization and we want to export it, we can use two different approaches. We can export it as a bitmap image (for example, PNG) or we can export it as a vector image (SVG format). In this section, we'll look at both approaches.

Exporting visualizations as PNG

To export an SVG element as a PNG, we need to take a couple of steps. Let's first get one of our visualizations that we want to export. We'll work with one of the geographic examples from Chapter 5, *Working with Geo Data* (D05-01.html):

To export this map, we'll take the following steps:

1. Create a separate CSS for the styles we want to apply.
2. Convert the SVG element to a string.
3. Use the canvas to get a PNG file.
4. Save the content from the canvas to a file.

Let's start with defining a separate CSS file with the styles.

Custom export styles

The custom export CSS file is just a standard CSS file, and for this example it looks like this (called DVD3/src/chapter-08/css/D08-03-export.css):

```
.county { stroke-width: 0.1; stroke: rgb(204, 204, 204); }

text {
    font-family: "Helvetica Neue", Helvetica, Arial, sans-serif;
    font-weight: lighter;
}

.title {
    fill: black;
    font-size: 40px;

}
```

We changed the color of the title to black so it is more readable when we export the file. We'll use standard D3 functionality to load this CSS file:

```
function exportAsPng() {

    // first load the external css which will be
       applied to the image. For
    // instance we can set the color to black instead of white.
    d3.text('./css/D08-03-export.css', function(externalStyles) {
        // first convert the SVG node to a string.
        var svgString = nodeToSVGString(d3.select(
            'svg').node(), externalStyles);
// Clean up some inconsistencies in browser implementations
svgString = svgString.replace(/(\w+)?:?xlink=/g, 'xmlns:xlink=');
svgString = svgString.replace(/NS\d+:href/g, 'xlink:href');

        // next save
        svgString2Image(svgString, width * 2,
            height, function(datablob) {
saveAs(datablob,'elections.png');
            // FileSaver.js function
        });
    });
}
```

In the next few sections, we'll look at the other functions used by the exportAsPng function.

Converting the SVG element to a string

When we render data with D3, the elements are added to the DOM as nodes. To export this SVG, we need to first convert it to an SVG image, which is a big XML file. We do this in the `nodeToSVGString()` function:

```
function nodeToSVGString( svgNode, cssText ) {
    appendCSS( cssText, svgNode )
    return new XMLSerializer().serializeToString(svgNode);

    /**
     * Append the external css to the element, so it is correctly exported
     */
    function appendCSS( cssText, element ) {
        var styleElement = document.createElement("style");
        styleElement.setAttribute("type","text/css");
        styleElement.innerHTML = cssText;

        element.hasChildNodes()
            ? element.insertBefore( styleElement, element.children[0])
            : element.insertBefore( styleElement, null );
    }
}
```

What we do here is first use the standard browser functionality, `XMLSerializer().serializeToString`, to convert the `svgNode` to a string. We also add the externally loaded CSS styles to this string. Now we can use the HTML5 `canvas` to render this string as an image.

Using the canvas to get a PNG file

The following function takes our `svgString`, converts it to a data URL, and assigns it to an image:

```
function svgString2Image( svgString, width, height, callback ) {

    // create a dataURL object
    var blob = new Blob([svgString], { type: 'image/svg+xml;charset=utf-8'
});
    var imgsrc = window.URL.createObjectURL(blob);

    // create a canvas to load the image to.
    var canvas = document.createElement("canvas");
    var context = canvas.getContext("2d");
    canvas.width = width;
    canvas.height = height;
```

```
    // create the image, and define callback
    var image = new Image;
    image.onload = function() {

        // when loaded, draw the image, export it to a blob
        // and call the specified callback.
        context.clearRect ( 0, 0, width, height );
        context.drawImage(image, 0, 0, width, height);
        canvas.toBlob( function(blob) {
            var filesize = Math.round( blob.length/1024 ) + ' KB';
            if ( callback ) callback( blob, filesize );
        });
    };
    // set the dataurl as image source.
    image.src = imgsrc;
}
```

When the image is loaded, we draw it on the canvas, convert it to a blob, and call the specified callback to save the binary PNG data. One note on the use of the `canvas.toBlob` function: While this function is supported in most modern browsers, it is possible that a specific browser won't support this function. To make sure this will work across as many devices as possible, we could add the JavaScript-Canvas-to-Blob polyfill from `https://github.com/blueimp/JavaScript-Canvas-to-Blob`.

Saving the image

For saving the image, we use an external library called `FileSaver.js`, which allows us to simply call `saveAs`, and we're done. For this example, the SVG map only uses half the width of the screen, so we use `width*2` for the correct dimensions:

```
svgString2Image(svgString, width * 2, height, function(datablob) {
    saveAs(datablob, 'elections.png'); // FileSaver.js function
});
```

So now when we export our visualization using this script, the result looks like this:

You can do this for every SVG element you've created. The only thing you have to take into account is that, unless you specify an external stylesheet, like we did, no specific styles will be applied.

Exporting visualizations as SVG and importing them in an external program

In the previous section, we showed how to export our SVG visualization as an image, but we can, of course, also save the element as an SVG file so it can be imported into external programs, such as Adobe Illustrator, Boxy SVG, or Inkscape.

For exporting SVGs as `.svg` files, we can use two different approaches. If you use Chrome, there is a *Bookmarklet* that you can use, and which can be found at `http://nytimes.github.io/svg-crowbar/`. When you've installed this *Bookmarklet*, you can export SVG from any page you want. In this section, though, we'll provide an alternative approach that pretty much follows the same steps that we did for exporting SVG as a PNG file:

1. We'll once again start by defining the specific CSS style that should be included in the exported SVG file.
2. Then we combine the SVG and the CSS file into a single SVG string.
3. Finally, we'll save the SVG string as a file.

For this example, we'll export the radial tree shown in `Chapter 3`, *Working with Hierarchical Data*:

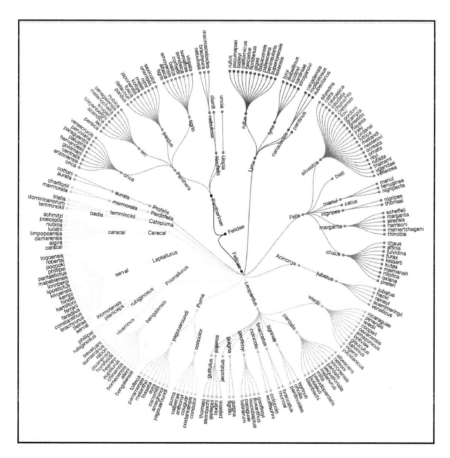

To be able to export this visualization, we use the same approach and define a function that handles the export:

```
function exportAsSVG() {
    d3.text('./css/D08-04.css', function(externalStyles) {
        // first convert the SVG node to a string.
        var svgString = nodeToSVGString(d3.select('svg')
            .node(), externalStyles);
        svgString2SVG(svgString);
    });
}
```

As you can see, we first load the CSS that we add to the exported SVG file and call the `nodeToSVGString` function we saw in the previous section. The only thing that has changed is that this time we call `svgString2SVG` to save the SVG string as a file:

```
function svgString2SVG( svgString, width, height, callback ) {
    // create a dataURL object
    var blob = new Blob([svgString], { type:
        'image/svg+xml;charset=utf-8' });
    saveAs(blob, "radial-tree.svg");
}
```

The result is a `radial-tree.svg` file, whose head looks like this:

```
<svg xmlns="http://www.w3.org/2000/svg" class="chart" width="800"
height="800">
...
 // the included css
...
</style><g transform="translate(390,380)"><path class="link"
 d="M30.579969329567756,68.48259250205628C15.289984664783878,34.241
 29625102814 -34.754050147910796,14.085666413645514 0,0"
 style="stroke: rgb(0, 0, 0);"/><path class="link" d="M-
 25.72837389542554,-70.44892317627847C-12.86418694771277,-
 35.224461588139235 -34.754050147910796,14.085666413645514 0,0"
 style="stroke: rgb(0, 0, 0);"/><
```

At this point, we've got an SVG file that we can edit using any of the programs mentioned. For instance, if we use Boxy SVG (which is a free editor that can be added to Chrome (see `https://boxy-svg.com/`)), we can load our exported SVG file and edit it:

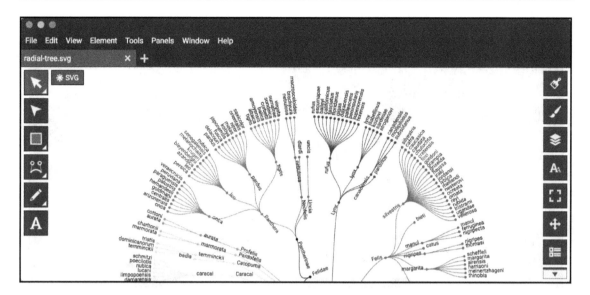

One other very well-known SVG editor is the open source Inkscape. Our SVG opened in Inkscape looks like this:

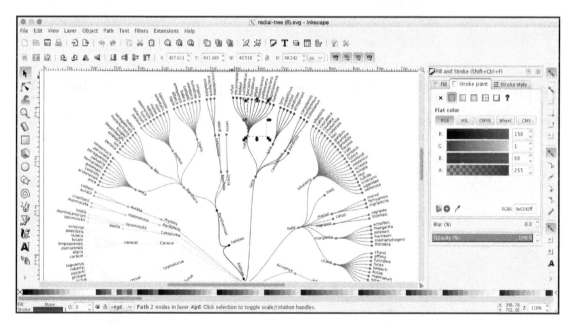

Note, though, that not all SVG programs work as well when editing these exported SVGs. For instance, when you open this file in Adobe Illustrator, it looks like this:

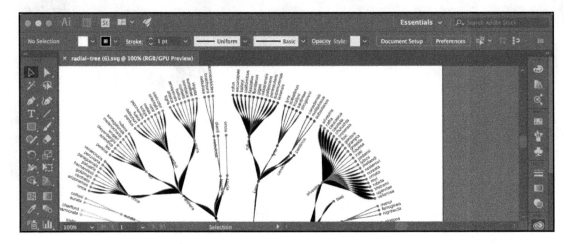

The reason is that while Adobe Illustrator supports the embedded styles that we add to our export, it only supports very specific class names. For example, if we changed all our classes from `.link` to those with a `cls-1` form, then we could use Illustrator to load our exported SVGs.

Importing SVG from Inkscape and use in D3

We've already shown you how to load external SVG files in a couple of the examples from the previous chapters. In this section, we'll give a quick overview of all the steps you need to load an SVG file that we modified ourselves in Inkscape and show it using D3.

For this, we've taken an SVG image of a tiger and used Inkscape to rotate it so that it looks like this:

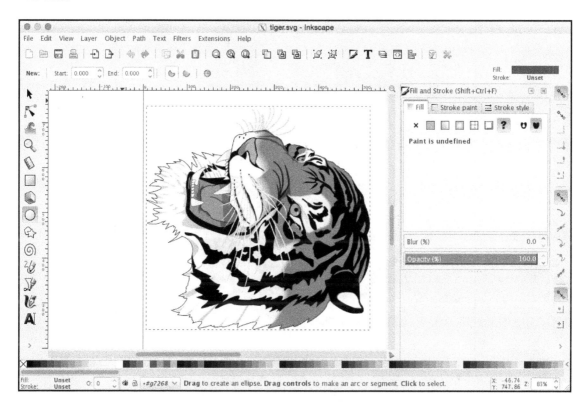

Now let's look at the minimal code required to import this tiger (DVD3/src/chapter-08/D08-05.html):

```
d3.xml('data/tiger.svg', loaded);

function loaded(err, tiger) {
    var tigerSVG =
d3.select(tiger.documentElement.querySelector("g")).attr("transform",
null).node();
    svg.append("g").node().appendChild(tigerSVG);
}
};
```

When we open this example in the browser, we can see our rotated tiger:

Now we can use D3 to modify the SVG.

Using brushes to select elements

For this last section in the chapter, we're going to look at how you can easily select an area on an SVG element using a d3.brush. The easiest way to understand what a brush does is by looking at an example. If you open up the example <DVD3>/src/chapter-08/src/D08-06.js in your browser, you're presented with 200 randomly placed symbols. When you use the mouse, you can left-click and select an area. The square you see is a d3.brush:

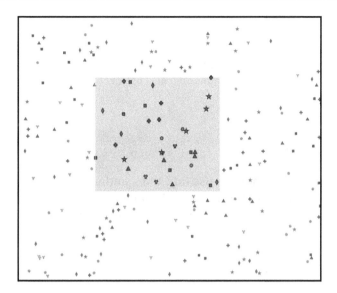

You can easily resize and move this d3.brush without any customizing using the mouse. For this example, we used d3.brush to select the symbols that fall within the area and highlight them. We'll explain the code to do this in the following sections. The first thing we do, for this example, is create the set of 200 symbols and color them just as we did in the beginning of this chapter:

```
var symbols = [
    {name: 'Cross', symbol: d3.symbolCross},
    {name: 'Circle', symbol: d3.symbolCircle},
    {name: 'Diamond', symbol: d3.symbolDiamond},
    {name: 'Square', symbol: d3.symbolSquare},
    {name: 'Star', symbol: d3.symbolStar},
    {name: 'Triangle', symbol: d3.symbolTriangle},
    {name: 'Wye', symbol: d3.symbolWye}
];

var data = d3.range(0, 200).map(function (d) {
    return {
        n: d,
        x: Math.random() * width,
        y: Math.random() * height,
        item: symbols[d%7]
    }
});

var color = d3.scaleOrdinal()
    .domain(symbols.map(function (s) {return s.name}))
    .range(d3.schemeCategory10);
```

```
// add 200 elements
svg.selectAll("symbol")
    .data(data).enter()
    .append("g")
        .attr("transform", function(d) {return "translate(
            " + d.x + " " + d.y + " )"})
        .attr("class", "symbol")
    .append("path")
        .attr("d", function(d) {return d3.symbol().type(d.item.symbol)()})
        .attr("fill", function(d) { return color(d.item.name)});
```

The main thing to note here is that we also add the x and y coordinates to our data. We do this so that we can more easily determine which element falls within the square we create with our brush. Now that we've added our data, we can create a brush and listen to events from this brush:

```
var brush = d3.brush()
    .on("brush", brushed)

svg.append("g")
    .attr("class", "brush")
    .call(brush);

function brushed() {
    var extent = d3.event.selection;
        var x0 = extent[0][0],
            y0 = extent[0][1],
            x1 = extent[1][0],
            y1 = extent[1][1];

        data.forEach(function (d, i) {
            if (x0 <= d.x && d.x <= x1 && y0 <= d.y && d.y <= y1) {
                d3.selectAll(".symbol:nth-child(" + (i+1) +")")
                    .select("path")
                    .attr("stroke", "black")
                    .attr("stroke-width", "2");
            } else {
                d3.selectAll(".symbol:nth-child(" + (i+1) +")")
                    .select("path")
                    .attr("stroke", null)
                    .attr("stroke-width", null);

            }
        });
}
```

In this code fragment, we first create a `d3.brush`, which we attach to our `svg` element. On this `brush`, we define a callback that is called whenever the brush is moved, resized, or closed. In this case, we call the `brushed` function. In the `brushed` function, we first get the x and y coordinates of the selection. Next, we walk through the various data elements to check whether they fall within the selection square. If they do, we highlight them by setting the `stroke` and the `stroke-width`. If not, we remove these values again. The result is that we can now very easily highlight (or do other things with) the elements that fall within our `brush` selection.

In the chapter on hierarchical data, we showed you how to use the `d3.zoom` function to pan and zoom around a graph. As you can imagine, using `d3.zoom` together with a `d3.brush` will lead to issues since both need to respond to a mouse click and drag event. If you want to use these two together, you can follow the approach shown in the example found at `https://bl.ocks.org/mbostock/34f08d5e11952a80609169b7917d4172`.

Summary

In this chapter, we've explored a couple of the D3 APIs that we skipped in the previous chapters. We first looked at the different symbols supported by D3 that you can easily use in line charts or scatterplots. Next, we looked at how you can use the `d3.path` API directly to draw lines and shapes. We also looked at an alternative use of paths, where we use them to define how an animated object moves across the screen. In the second part of this chapter, we focused on how to import and export SVG visualizations. We first showed how to export an SVG element as a PNG and as an SVG. After that, we showed how to load an external SVG file and use it in D3. Finally, we looked at the `d3.brush` API, which can be used to select multiple elements on the screen.

In the next chapter, which is the last one, we'll explore some of the third-party extensions of D3 and how you can use D3 in ES6 and TypeScript.

9
ES6, TypeScript, and External D3.js Libraries

In this final chapter, we're going to look into a couple of usages of D3 not directly related to the main D3 provided APIs. We're going to discuss the following subjects:

- **D3 and ES6**: ES6, also called ECMAScript 6 or ECMAScript 2015, is the latest version of the JavaScript language used in browsers and tools such as Node.js. ES6 has a number of features that can make working with D3 easier, but also a number of items you need to take into account, when working with D3 and ES6.

- **D3 and TypeScript**: Besides ES6, a very popular language for web development is TypeScript. The TypeScript language adds types to JavaScript, which makes development easier and prevents a number of common runtime errors. For instance, the popular Angular 2 framework uses TypeScript as its main programming language. Working with D3 and TypeScript provides a lot of features, but also a number of challenges.

- **External charting libraries**: There are a number of external D3-based charting libraries. In this section, we'll discuss several of these: **nvd3**, **C3**, **Dimple.js**, and **MetricsGraphics.js**.

- **D3 command-line tools**: D3 provides a number of command-line tools which you can use to access parts of the API directly from the command line. We'll look at a number of these tools, and use these to create a map using these command-line tools.

Using D3 with ES6 and TypeScript

In this section, we're going to explore D3 usage from ES6 and TypeScript. We'll start with how to use D3 from ES6.

D3 and ES6

When developing ES6, you have to take into account the browsers you're targeting. Most modern browsers have great support for the ES6 standard:

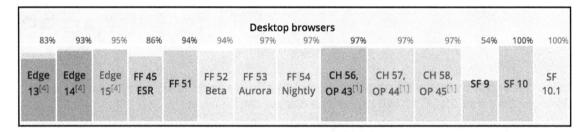

But pretty much the one subject that is barely supported is the module support. So for now we have to translate our ES6 code to ES5 so it can be loaded directly into any browser (this is often called *transpiling*).

We won't go through the complete ES6 specification, but look at a couple of the features which are especially interesting in combination with D3. For a complete overview of the features of ES6 you can look here: `http://es6-features.org/`.

Before we look at the interesting features, we first have to create a setup which can transpile ES6 code to normal JavaScript which can run in any browser. For this, we'll use a simple **webpack** (`https://webpack.github.io/`) setup. With webpack we can transpile our ES6 code, and package all the dependencies. We won't go into too much detail here, since it is out of scope for this book, but just show you how you can start the examples.

In the directory `<DVD3>/chapter-09/es6/` you can find all the configuration which is used to support the transpiling and bundling of our code. To work with it, you just have to run the following commands:

```
# First make sure that we've installed the correct dependencies
$ npm install
. . .
# Now we can start the webpack server
$ npm run start
```

```
   > d3.js-es6@1.0.0 start /Users/jos/dev/git/dataviz-
d3js/src/chapter-09/es6
   > webpack-dev-server --progress

   10% building modules 1/1 modules 0 active
   Project is running at http://localhost:8080/
   webpack output is served from /
   Version: webpack 2.2.1
   Time: 4043ms
               Asset      Size  Chunks                    Chunk Names
       main.bundle.js   1.04 MB      0  [emitted]  [big]  main
   main.bundle.js.map   2.08 MB      0  [emitted]         main
           index.html  185 bytes       [emitted]
              app.css    8 bytes       [emitted]
   chunk    {0} main.bundle.js, main.bundle.js.map (main) 1.01 MB [entry]
[rendered]
       [21] ./~/d3-scale/src/linear.js 1.59 kB {0} [built]
      [104] ./app/js/index.js 2.47 kB {0} [built]
      [105] (webpack)-dev-server/client?http://localhost:8080 5.03 kB {0}
[built]
      [149] ./~/d3-scale/index.js 5.01 kB {0} [built]
      [167] ./~/d3-selection/index.js 3.17 kB {0} [built]
      [169] ./~/d3-selection/src/local.js 660 bytes {0} [built]
      [200] ./~/d3-selection/src/touch.js 734 bytes {0} [built]
      [201] ./~/d3-selection/src/touches.js 650 bytes {0} [built]
      [217] ./~/d3/build/d3.js 488 kB {0} [built]
      [256] ./~/strip-ansi/index.js 161 bytes {0} [built]
      [258] ./~/url/url.js 23.1 kB {0} [built]
      [260] (webpack)-dev-server/client/overlay.js 3.6 kB {0} [built]
      [261] (webpack)-dev-server/client/socket.js 872 bytes {0} [built]
      [262] (webpack)/hot/emitter.js 89 bytes {0} [built]
      [263] multi (webpack)-dev-server/client?http://localhost:8080
./app/js/index.js 40 bytes {0} [built]
        + 249 hidden modules
   webpack: Compiled successfully.
```

This will transpile our code, and start a simple web server where we can directly see our ES6 application (which is the same as the first example from the previous chapter):

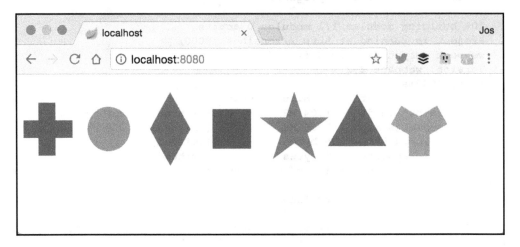

If you want to use ES6 in your own D3 projects, just look at the code for this example, which can be used as a quick starting point for your own D3 ES6 projects.

In the following section, we'll append the symbols example from the previous chapter and rewrite parts of it to ES6 to show you some of the features of D3 in combination with ES6.

Importing modules

The D3 distribution is divided into multiple modules. Without ES6 we could add the individual libraries as dependencies to the top of our HTML file like this:

```
<script src="../libs/d3-selection.v1.js"></script>
<script src="../libs/d3-scale-chromatic.v1.min.js"></script>
<script src="../libs/d3-geo-projection.v1.min.js"></script>
```

Then use it from our JavaScript file using the d3 namespace:

```
d3.select('.chart');
d3.geoGringortenQuincuncial();
```

With ES6 and modules, we don't have to add the individual D3 files to the index.html file, but can include them in our JavaScript file using an import:

```
import {scaleOrdinal} from "d3-scale";
import {select} from "d3-selection";
```

Now we can use the functions directly without using the d3. prefix we'd normally need to use. Our code will change like this:

```
# Standard
var svg = d3.select(".chart")
var color = d3.scaleOrdinal()...

# With ES6
var svg = select(".chart")
var color = scaleOrdinal()...
```

If you want to import the complete D3 library you can do this as well using imports:

```
import * as d3 from "d3";
```

An additional advantage of importing D3 (or parts thereof) is that it makes it easier for your editor to present you with the correct completions. For instance if we import d3-scale like this: import * as d3scale from "d3-scale", we can very easily see and access all the different scales:

With this approach, you can use D3 in the same way as is shown in this book, since all the functions are bound to the d3 name. When you're using imports, it is also much easier to divide your own application into multiple smaller files that each expose some functionality. More information on module support in ES6 can be found here:
https://github.com/lukehoban/es6features#modules.

Arrow functions and method shorthand

A very nice feature of ES6 is the way we can define functions using arrows. Normally, in JavaScript, and especially with D3, we define functions like this:

```
symbolGroups.append("path")
    .attr("fill", function (d) {
        return color(d.name)
    })
    .attr("d", function (d) {
        return d3.symbol()
            .size(2400)
            .type(d.symbol)();
    });
```

Here we define two functions to set the value of the `fill` and the `d` attribute. With arrow functions we can change this to the following:

```
symbolGroups.append("path")
    .attr("fill", d => color(d.name))
    .attr("d", d => {
        return d3.symbol()
            .size(2400)
            .type(d.symbol)()
    });
```

In this example, we show two examples of the arrow function. For the `fill` attribute we return the result of the `color(d.name)` function. This is a special case, where we only have a single expression. We could have done the same for the d attribute, but an alternative approach is writing out the body between parenthesis. You do have to add a `return` statement in that case. As you can imagine, this approach can really clean up your code a lot for all the various D3 callbacks, where you want to have the value of an attribute to be based on the passed-in data.

One thing to keep in mind when using arrow functions are references to `this`. When you use `this` inside arrow functions, they use the same scope as the surrounding code. In D3 that can cause issues, since sometimes `this` is used to pass around information; for example, accessing the current node which is being processed. For instance, we set an attribute using the following two calls:

```
symbolGroups.append("path")
    .attr("fill", d => color(d.name))
    .attr("attr1", d => { console.log(this); return "attr1"})
    .attr("attr2", function(d) { console.log(this); return "attr1" })
    .attr("d", d => {
        return d3.symbol()
```

```
            .size(2400)
            .type(d.symbol)()
    });
```

The first one is using the arrow notation, and the other one is using the standard notation. If you run this and look at the output, you see the following:

```
 undefined                                                                    index.js:48
```

As you can see, this is undefined for the arrow function, but defined for the normal function. In those scenarios you still need a function to access the passed in this context. For functions ES6 also provides a shorthand (at least for when you define these on an object):

```
var obj = {
    doSomething(name = 'd3') {
    },

    doSomethingElse(count = 100) {
    }
}
```

The preceding code defines two functions on the obj object with the names doSomething and doSomethingElse. We also see a feature of ES6, which allows us to define default parameters to functions.

Block-scoped binding constructs (let + const)

With ES6 you also get two new constructs for defining variables. In JavaScript we already had var to assign a variable. However, var is function scoped, instead of scoped to the current block. With function scope, it doesn't matter where in the function you define the variable, you can use it everywhere in that function, even before you declared that variable. So the following code is perfectly legal, since the var i declaration is pulled to the top of the function:

```
function varTest() {
    for (i = 10 ; i < 20 ; i++) {
        console.log(i)
    }

    if (i < 10) { var i; }
}
```

This is kind of non-traditional behavior and can lead to hard-to-find bugs. With ES6, we get the `let` and the `const` keyword. With `let` we make sure that the variable is only used in the code block it is defined in. And `const`, which is also block scoped, allows us to define values that can't be re-declared. So the code in our example would look something like this:

```
const margin = {top: 20, bottom: 20, right: 20, left: 30};
const width = 600 - margin.left - margin.right;
const height = 200 - margin.top - margin.bottom;

let svg = select(".chart")
```

Even though this doesn't make our code more concise to read, it does avoid a number of hard-to-catch bugs.

String interpolation

The final feature of ES6 which we'll look at in relation to D3 is string interpolation. In D3 we often use the `translate` property to move a `g` to a specific position. Code to do this usually looks something like this:

```
let svg = select(".chart")
        .attr("width", width + margin.left + margin.right)
        .attr("height", height + margin.top + margin.bottom)
        .append("g")
        .attr("transform", "translate(" + margin.left
            + "," + margin.top + ")");
```

Conversely, with the arrow functions we saw earlier:

```
var symbolGroups = svg.selectAll(".symbol").data(symbols)
    .enter()
    .append("g")
    .attr("class", "symbol")
    .attr("transform", d => "translate(" + xBand(d.name) + " 40)")
```

With string interpolation, we can avoid having to use + to concatenate the strings and variables. This code will now look like this:

```
. . .
.attr("transform", `translate(${margin.left}, ${margin.top})`);
. . .
.attr("transform", d => `translate(${xBand(d.name)} 40)`)
```

We add single backticks around the string we want to interpolate and reference the variable or expression by enclosing it like this: `${variable}`.

Besides the features described in this section, ES6 offers a lot more. The transition from ES5, the current JavaScript version, to ES6 is very small. It doesn't fundamentally change the language, but merely adds features and syntactic sugar to make working with JavaScript easier. The disadvantage, though, is that support still isn't 100 percent in modern browsers, so you'll need preprocessing to transpile your code to JavaScript which can be run in any browser.

An alternative to ES6 is TypeScript. TypeScript is a language which adds objects types to JavaScript, which allow you to catch more errors during compile time, and provides better code completion in your editors.

D3 and TypeScript

Just as we did for ES6, to work with TypeScript, we need to transpile our code to JavaScript which can run in any browser. While ES6 will eventually be supported by modern browsers without having to transpile code, TypeScript will always need to be transpiled to work in your browser. TypeScript closely follows the JavaScript specifications to make transitioning to TypeScript really easy. All the examples we gave with ES6 also apply to TypeScript. With TypeScript, however, we get the added advantage of having types and type checking.

To get up and running with TypeScript, we've created a simple sample project in the directory <DVD3>/chapter-09/ts/ which contains all the configuration you need to get started. Just as with the previous sample, we use https://webpack.github.io/ to handle all the compilation and transpiling.

All you have to do to get started is run the following from the <DVD3>/chapter-09/ts/ directory:

```
$ npm install
$ npm run start

> d3.js-ts@1.0.0 start /Users/jos/dev/git/dataviz-d3js/src/chapter-09/ts
> webpack-dev-server --progress

10% building modules 1/1 modules 0 active
Project is running at http://localhost:8080/
ts-loader: Using TypeScript@2.1.6 and /Users/jos/dev/git/dataviz-d3js
Time: 3223ms
            Asset        Size   Chunks                    Chunk Names
   main.bundle.js      766 kB        0   [emitted]  [big]  main
 main.bundle.js.map     927 kB        0   [emitted]         main
       index.html    185 bytes          [emitted]
          app.css      8 bytes          [emitted]
```

```
chunk    {0} main.bundle.js, main.bundle.js.map (main) 752 kB [entry]
[rendered]
  [35] ./app/js/index.ts 1.69 kB {0} [built]
...
```

Now we can open the browser once again and open `http://localhost:8080` to see the TypeScript version of this D3 visualization.

Using types in your editor

You can see the real strength of TypeScript when you open a project in an editor which supports TypeScript. For instance, when opening the `index.ts` file from this project, we get completion, including method signatures, whenever we want to use the functionality of `d3.js`:

This is really nice, especially because D3 offers a very large and sometimes complex API. With the TypeScript approach, exploring the API becomes much easier. For instance, if we want to know how to configure d3.scaleBand we can just use this dropdown, and hit F1 (in IntelliJ that is), to view the documentation:

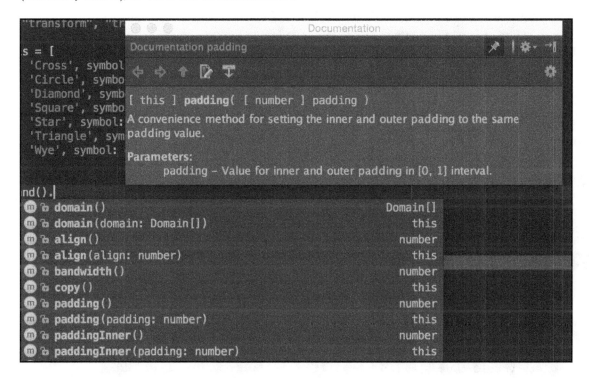

As you can see, TypeScript really works great when used together with an IDE which supports it. Besides helping during the writing of code, TypeScript can also do some checks while transpiling the code to JavaScript.

Preventing errors with compile-time checking of types

As you've seen in this book, the API of D3 is big. There are many different objects, each with their own function signatures, and while D3 is really consistent in the way you use the various objects, making mistakes is still easy to do. One of the mistakes often made is when you want to define a d3.scaleLinear. It is really easy to define the scale like this:

```
var yBand = d3.scaleLinear()
    .domain(0, 10)
    .range(0, height);
```

While this looks okay, and ES6 or standard JavaScript won't complain, when you want to use this you'll get unexpected NaN errors or strange values in the attributes where you use this scale. The reason this fails is that instead of taking two separate arguments the `domain` and `range` functions take an array as an argument. When you try to do that with TypeScript, the transpiler is smart enough to see that something is wrong:

```
ERROR in ./app/js/index.ts
(37,17): error TS2346: Supplied parameters do not match any signature of
call target.
webpack: Failed to compile.
```

Now you know that something is wrong with the code at the specific line, and you can look at the type signature to see how to fix it.

For most use cases, this approach works great, and you'll be able to capture a lot of potential bugs just by making sure your code transpiles correctly. Sometimes, though, the TypeScript compiler flags some code, which you know will work.

Handling complex type signatures

Take for instance the following piece of code (which looks the same in ES6 as in TypeScript):

```
let color = d3.scaleOrdinal()
    .domain(symbols.map(s => s.name))
    .range(d3.schemeCategory10);

let symbolGroups = svg.selectAll(".symbol").data(symbols)
    .enter()
    .append("g")
        .attr("class", d => "symbol")
        .attr("transform", d => `translate(${xBand(d.name)} 40)`);

symbolGroups
    .append("path")
        .attr("fill", d => color(d.name))
        .attr("d", d => d3.symbol().size(2400).type(d.symbol)());
```

Here we create a `d3.scaleOrdinal` which will map a name to a color from the `d3.schemeCategory10`. We use this `color` scale later on `symboleGroups` to set the `fill` attribute of a number of `path` elements. If you look at the code, nothing seems out of the ordinary. However, when you compile it you'll get a cryptic message like this:

```
ERROR in ./app/js/index.ts
(45,27): error TS2345: Argument of type '(this: BaseType, d: { name:
```

```
string; symbol: SymbolType; }) => {}' is not assignable to parameter of
type 'ValueFn<BaseType, { name: string; symbol: SymbolType; }, string |
number | boolean>'.
   Type '{}' is not assignable to type 'string | number | boolean'.
    Type '{}' is not assignable to type 'false'.
```

Lots of output, which doesn't really make it clear what is wrong. When you look at line 45 column 27, the code the transpiler is complaining about is this one: `.attr("fill", d => color(d.name))`. Somehow it can't correctly determine the result from the `color(d.name)` function, but it mentions that it should either be a `string`, a `number`, or a `boolean` type. Luckily, though, these kind of errors can be quickly fixed by adding this additional type information like this:

```
.attr("fill", d => <string>color(d.name))
```

Here we tell the transpiler that the result from the `color` scale is a `string`, which complies with what the compiler expects. This is enough information to correctly transpile and check the code.

Creating classes is easy

The final feature of TypeScript we want to highlight is how you create classes. Often in JavaScript when you need a structure to hold some data you create an object like this:

```
let symbols = [
    {name: 'Cross', symbol: d3.symbolCross},
    {name: 'Circle', symbol: d3.symbolCircle},
    {name: 'Diamond', symbol: d3.symbolDiamond},
    {name: 'Square', symbol: d3.symbolSquare},
    {name: 'Star', symbol: d3.symbolStar},
    {name: 'Triangle', symbol: d3.symbolTriangle},
    {name: 'Wye', symbol: d3.symbolWye}
];
```

This is an array of simple JavaScript objects, where we set the `name` and `symbol` properties. When we now want to use this object, we have to explicitly know why properties were used, and whether if any of these properties should change it would break other parts of the code without you knowing. With TypeScript creating classes is very simple and provides us with another layer of type checking. For the object we used previously, we can simply create a class like this:

```
class SymbolWrapper {
    constructor(public name: string, public symbol: SymbolType) {}
}
```

Now whenever we use this class, we have code completion and the types will be checked during transpilation. So the array definition now becomes something like this:

```
let symbols = [
  new SymbolWrapper('Cross', d3.symbolCross),
  new SymbolWrapper('Circle', d3.symbolCircle),
  new SymbolWrapper('Diamond', d3.symbolDiamond),
  new SymbolWrapper('Square', d3.symbolSquare),
  new SymbolWrapper('Star', d3.symbolStar),
  new SymbolWrapper('Triangle', d3.symbolTriangle),
  new SymbolWrapper('Wye', d3.symbolWye)
];
```

In this example, we've used the same names for the properties so we don't have to change the rest of the code for this to work. If we, however, decided to rename the `name` property to `id`, we would immediately see where we use this class, and what we need to change as well.

After changing the following errors are shown:

```
ERROR in ./app/js/index.ts
(37,32): error TS2339: Property 'name' does not exist on type
'SymbolWrapper'.

ERROR in ./app/js/index.ts
(41,32): error TS2339: Property 'name' does not exist on type
'SymbolWrapper'.

ERROR in ./app/js/index.ts
(49,50): error TS2339: Property 'name' does not exist on type
'SymbolWrapper'.

ERROR in ./app/js/index.ts
(53,40): error TS2339: Property 'name' does not exist on type
'SymbolWrapper'.
```

Identifying the exact problem, and location where we need to fix it.

Besides ES6 and TypeScript, there are a number of other popular languages which can be compiled to JavaScript, each with various support for D3. Regardless of the language though, the patterns to create visualizations with D3 stay the same.

If you don't want to create visualizations of charts from scratch, there are a number of libraries that can help you with this. In the following section we look at a couple of these.

External charting libraries

There are many extensions and additional charting libraries built on top of D3. In this section we'll discuss a couple of the best-known and popular ones. If you want a more extensive overview of what is available for D3 you can look here: `https://github.com/wbkd/awesome-d3`. Note though that you should always check whether the library is made for D3 version 3 or D3 version 4, the latter of which is the version used in this book.

In this section, we'll discuss the following four of these:

- **Dimple.js**: Dimple.js is a charting library that aims to make the basic usage of D3 easier. It aims to make D3 available to people not highly proficient with D3, and provides a simple-to-use API for creating axis-based visualization. Dimple.js is based on D3 v4.
- **MetricsGraphics.js**: This library provides additional tools and charts for creating time-series-based charts, such as line charts, histograms, and scatterplots. This library also makes use of D3 v4.
- **C3**: C3 is a library which provides a large set of different D3-based visualizations. Some of which we've also discussed in the first couple of chapters in this book. With C3, you only have to provide the data, and C3 will render the chart. This library isn't yet updated to D3 v4, so you can't use this together with the latest version of D3, discussed in this book.
- **nvd3**: This library also provides a large set of out-of-the-box chart types which can be used directly without having to understand too much about D3. This library also uses an older version of D3, and can't be used with the latest version of D3.

We'll look a bit closer at Dimple.js and MetricsGraphics.js, since they are based on the version of D3 discussed in this book, and only highlight some of the features of C3 and nvd3.

Dimple.js

Dimple is a library which provides a large set of charts out of the box (more information can be found here: `http://dimplejs.org/`). The goal of Dimple is to provide easy-to-use charts, and that is reflected in the way you define charts. We've provided a couple of example charts in `<DVD3>/src/chapter-09/dimple`. Let's start by looking at a simple bar chart:

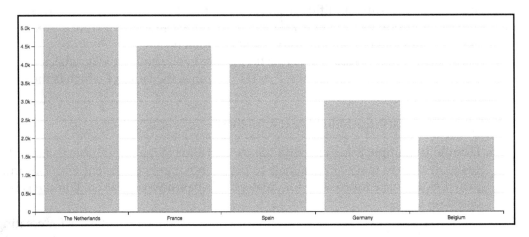

To create this chart you use the following code:

```
var data = [
    { "country":"The Netherlands", "value":5000 },
    { "country":"Germany", "value":3000 },
    { "country":"Spain", "value":4000 },
    { "country":"Belgium", "value":2000 },
    { "country":"France", "value":4500 }
];
var chart = new dimple.chart(svg1, data);
chart.setBounds(0, 0, width, height);
chart.addCategoryAxis("x", "country");
chart.addMeasureAxis("y", "value");
chart.addSeries(null, dimple.plot.bar);
chart.draw();
```

This example shows the basic setup of how Dimple works. First we define (or load) the data, and create a new `dimple.chart` where we add the `data` and the `svg` element, to which we want to render the chart (in this case, `svg1` is an SVG element like we use in our other examples). With `setBounds` we set the size of the chart, and then we define the two axes. The `addCategoryAxis` function means that on the x-axis we render the names of the countries (`country` property), and using the `addMeasureAxis` we tell Dimple to render the `value` property on the y-axis. Finally, we tell Dimple to render our data as a simple bar chart (`dimple.plot.bar`) and call the `draw` function. The interesting thing is that it is very easy to change this to a horizontally-oriented chart by just changing the `addCategoryAxis` and `addMeasureAxis` to this:

```
chart.addCategoryAxis("y", "country");
chart.addMeasureAxis("z", "value");
```

Which results in this:

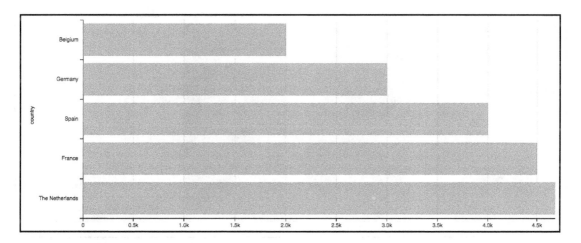

Dimple comes with a large number of different charts which all follow this principle. For instance if we wanted to draw a stacked chart, we'd do something like this:

```
var stackedData = [
    { "i" : 1, "country":"Netherlands", "value":2000, "Depth": 100 },
    { "i" : 1, "country":"Belgium", "value":3000, "Depth": 200 },
    { "i" : 1, "country":"Germany", "value":3000, "Depth": 200 },
    { "i" : 2, "country":"Netherlands", "value":3000, "Depth": 300 },
    { "i" : 2, "country":"Belgium", "value":3000, "Depth": 200 },
    { "i" : 2, "country":"Germany", "value":3000, "Depth": 200 },
    { "i" : 3, "country":"Netherlands", "value":1000, "Depth": 100 },
    { "i" : 3, "country":"Belgium", "value":4000, "Depth": 400 },
    { "i" : 3, "country":"Germany", "value":4000, "Depth": 400 },
```

```
        { "i" : 4, "country":"Netherlands", "value":2000, "Depth": 200 },
        { "i" : 4, "country":"Belgium", "value":100, "Depth": 700 },
        { "i" : 4, "country":"Germany", "value":100, "Depth": 700 },
];
var stackedChart = new dimple.chart(svg2, stackedData);
stackedChart.setBounds(0, 0, width, height);
stackedChart.addCategoryAxis("x", "i");
stackedChart.addMeasureAxis("y", "value");
stackedChart.addSeries("country", dimple.plot.bar);

stackedChart.addLegend(60, 10, width - 30, 20, "right");
stackedChart.draw();
```

Here we have data which is grouped by the i category, and we plot the country values in a stack. As you can see, the general structure of this piece of code is exactly the same.

Which results in this:

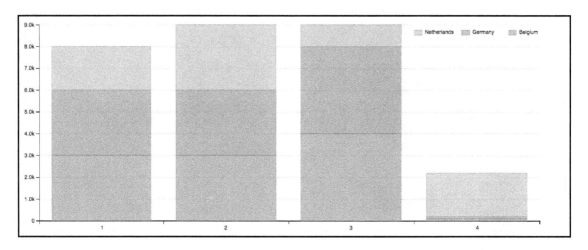

And by just making a couple of simple changes:

```
var stackedChart = new dimple.chart(svg2, stackedData);
stackedChart.setBounds(0, 50, width, height-50);
stackedChart.addCategoryAxis("x", "i");
stackedChart.addMeasureAxis("y", "value");
stackedChart.addMeasureAxis("z", "Depth");
stackedChart.addSeries("country", dimple.plot.bubble);
```

We now have a bubble chart (`dimple.plot.bubble`):

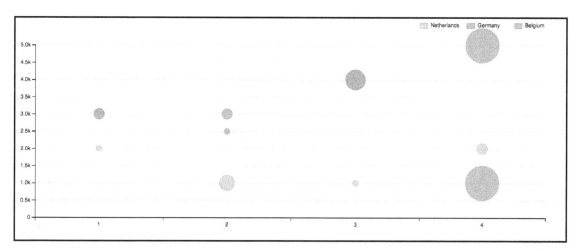

As you can see, very little code is needed to create these charts, and with Dimple.js you get a lot of functionality out of the box, which otherwise you would have to write by hand (as we did in `Chapter 2`, *Basic Charts and Shapes*).

Another library which supports version 4 of D3 is `MetricsGraphics.js`.

MetricsGraphics.js

While Dimple.js offers a large set of different chart types, `Metricsgraphics.js` focuses on providing time-based charts (although there are a number of experimental charts where they offer other types). Using MetricsGraphics.js is pretty much just as straightforward as Dimple.js is. You define your chart and feed it data, to create time-based charts:

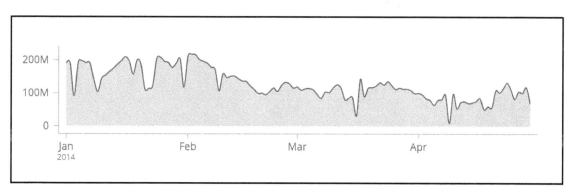

Besides time-series-based charts, it also supports other types, but these are still experimental. For example, a histogram:

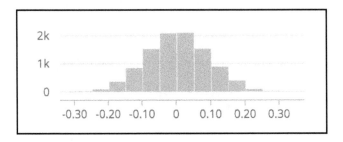

In the sources for this chapter, we've created a simple example where we plot the mean temperature deviation of the last 140 years (<DVD3>/src/chapter-09/metricgraphics). Let's look at the steps we need to take to generate such a graph. Let's first look at the data:

```
[{"Source":"GCAG","Year":"2016","Mean":"0.9363"},
 {"Source":"GISTEMP","Year":"2016","Mean":"0.99"},
 {"Source":"GCAG","Year":"2015","Mean":"0.8998"},
 {"Source":"GISTEMP","Year":"2015","Mean":"0.87"},
 {"Source":"GCAG","Year":"2014","Mean":"0.7408"},
 ...
]
```

This data provides values from two sources, GCAG and GISTEMP. To render this using MetricsGraphics.js, we need to use the following code:

```
d3.json("./data/annual.json", function (data) {

    MG.data_graphic({
        title: "Annual temperature mean",
        description: "Annual temperature mean",
        data: data.filter(function(el) {return el.Source === "GCAG"}),
        width: width,
        height: height,
        target: "#id-1",     // we've created a container with this id
        x_accessor: "Year",
        y_accessor: "Mean",
        area: false,
        min_y: -1,
        chart_type: 'line',
        baselines: [{value:0, label: 'mean'}],
        interpolate: d3.curveLinear,
    })
});
```

To create a line graph, we only need to call the `MG.data_graphic` function and configure the properties. If you look at the properties' names, they pretty much explain themselves. We use the data we've shown before and assign the `Year` to the x-axis, and the `Mean` to the y-axis. We use a `d3.cureLinear` interpolator to draw the line through the data points, and we add an additional line through the `0` value. The result is the following line graph:

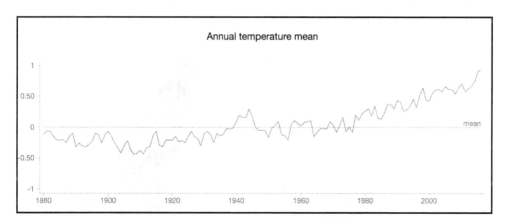

Both Dimple.js and MetricsGraphics.js support D3 v4, and can be easily used with the latest version of D3. In the next sections, we'll look at a couple of libraries, which are also built on top of D3, but use an older version.

C3

C3 is a very easy-to-use library for creating a large number of different types of charts. C3 doesn't support D3 v4 yet, so we won't go into too much detail on how to use it. If you do want to use this library, beware that you're bound to run into issues when you use D3 v3 and D3 v4 code in the same project.

To create charts with C3, the only thing you need to do is call the `c3.generate` function with a configuration object:

```
var chart = c3.generate({
    data: {
        columns: [
            ['data1', 30],
            ['data2', 120],
        ],
        type : 'donut',
    },
    donut: {
```

```
        title: "Iris Petal Width"
    }
});
```

This code speaks for itself, and nicely expresses the power behind C3. By just specifying the `type` of chart, and providing data in the correct format, C3 will handle the rest:

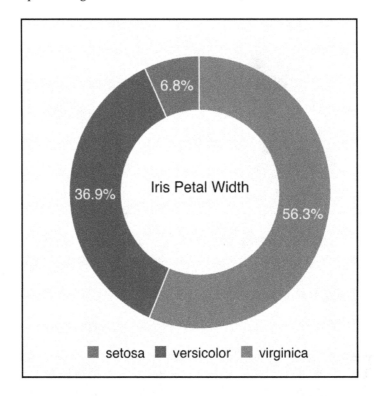

C3 has a wide range of charts (which you can use by specifying a different `type`), ranging from the standard line charts and bar charts (which you can also combine), to very specific chart types such as a gauge:

While the C3.js project provides a large number of good-looking charts, the project itself doesn't have much activity. The last release was May 2016, and the effort to port to D3 v4 unfortunately hasn't started yet.

nvd3

For **nvd3**, pretty much the same warnings apply as for C3. This project provides a number of different chart types which are easily customizable. However, nvd3 is also still based on an older version of D3. This means that using it together with the newest version, discussed in this book, won't work.

You can use nvd3 by creating an instance of a specific chart type and using the various functions to set their properties. You can find the following code on the `http://nvd3.org` site:

```
d3.json('multiBarHorizontalData.json', function(data) {
  nv.addGraph(function() {
    var chart = nv.models.multiBarHorizontalChart()
        .x(function(d) { return d.label })
        .y(function(d) { return d.value })
        .margin({top: 30, right: 20, bottom: 50, left: 175})
        .showValues(true)          //Show bar value next to each bar.
        .tooltips(true)            //Show tooltips on hover.
        .transitionDuration(350)
        .showControls(true);       //Allow user to switch between
"Grouped" and "Stacked" mode.

    chart.yAxis
```

```
        .tickFormat(d3.format(',.2f'));

    d3.select('#chart1 svg')
        .datum(data)
        .call(chart);

    nv.utils.windowResize(chart.update);

    return chart;
    });
});
```

As you can see from this code, what is happening is easy to understand from the code. We create a chart of the `multiBarHorizontalChart` type and configure the data and some additional properties by just calling functions on the created object. The result of this code fragment looks like this:

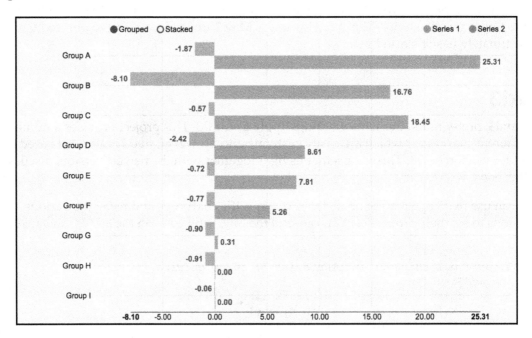

nvd3 provides a lot of different chart types. For instance, you can also very easily create nice-looking scatterplots:

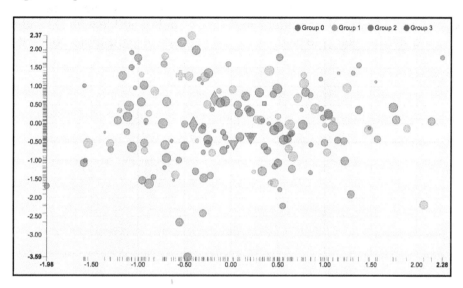

The nvd3 is still actively maintained, so if you're currently working with D3 v3 and need a charting library, this might be an interesting choice. Note though, that for this library the effort to migrate to the newest D3 version also hasn't started yet.

Summary

In this last chapter, we've looked at a number of different subjects. We started by looking at how you can integrate D3 into languages other than JavaScript. We showed how to use it together with ES6, and how you can use the features of ES6, to make the D3 code more concise. After that, we looked at integrating D3 with TypeScript. TypeScript offers all the features of ES6, and additionally allows you to work with a typed version of D3. Using TypeScript will allow us to make better use of IDEs for code completion, and can catch many errors during compile (transpile) time instead of when you open an example in your browser. We've also looked at a couple of libraries built on top of D3 that provide us with a number of different charts and visualizations out of the box. With Dimple.js and MetricsGraphics.js, we can create charts that work with the latest version of D3, and can thus be easily combined with the other examples in this book. C3 and nvd3 also provide a large set of chart and diagrams, but unfortunately haven't yet been updated to work with the latest version of D3.

And with that, we get to the end of this book on D3 v4. In this book, we've shown you many different types of visualizations you can create with D3-from simple line diagrams, to complex force diagrams, and interactive maps. With everything you've learned and seen in this book you should have a good understanding of what is possible with D3 and hopefully have some good starting points to begin using D3 to create visualizations yourself.

Index

W

www.ingramcontent.com/pod-product-compliance
Lightning Source LLC
Chambersburg PA
CBHW062037050326

40690CB00016B/2965